INTERPRETING SYNGE

INTERPRETING SYNGE

Essays from the Synge Summer School
1991–2000

Edited by Nicholas Grene

THE LILLIPUT PRESS
DUBLIN

First published 2000 by
THE LILLIPUT PRESS LTD
62-63 Sitric Road, Arbour Hill,
Dublin 7, Ireland
www.lilliputpress.ie

A CIP record for this title is available from
The British Library

ISBN 1 901866 47 5

The Lilliput Press receives financial assistance from
An Chomhairle Ealaíon / The Arts Council of Ireland

Set in 10.5 on 13.5 Galliard by Sheila Stephenson
Printed in Great Britain by MPG Books, Bodmin, Cornwall

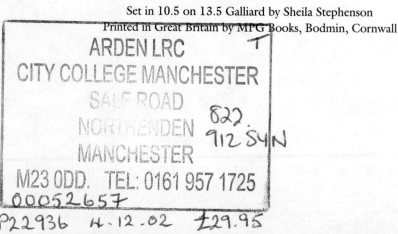

Contents

Acknowledgments

This book arose out of the Synge Summer School, and my first and fullest acknowledgments must go to all those who made the School possible. I wish to acknowledge the School's many generous donors including our major sponsors: Wicklow County Council, which originally proposed the idea for the School and has supported it unfailingly throughout, and Schering-Plough (Avondale). I want to thank my fellow committee members, who, I am sure, will not mind my picking out for special mention our irreplaceable Secretary, Irene Parsons. I have to pay tribute to the School's many speakers, who have set such high standards of expertise, enthusiasm and engagement. And finally I need to salute the hundreds of students whose warm and lively involvement has made the School such a pleasure to direct.

In planning the book I benefited from the shrewd and experienced advice of Jonathan Williams. Brian Cliff of Emory University acted not just as research assistant; with his detailed knowledge of the subject and his sensitivity to style, he has made a major contribution to the editing of the book. I have very much appreciated, also, the skilful and critically acute copy-editing of Brendan Barrington. I acknowledge most gratefully the financial support for the volume made available from the Patrick Kavanagh Bursary of the School of English, Trinity College, Dublin.

I owe most of all to the generosity and goodwill of my contributors, without whom *Interpreting Synge* would not exist.

Four of the essays in this book have been previously published in other versions as follows:

R.F. Foster, 'Good Behaviour: Yeats, Synge and Anglo-Irish Etiquette', in *Paddy and Mr Punch: Connections in Irish and English History* (London: Allen Lane, The Penguin Press, 1993).

Nicholas Grene, 'Synge and Wicklow', in *Wicklow: History and Society*, ed. Ken Hannigan and William Nolan (Dublin: Geography Publications, 1994).

Antoinette Quinn, 'Cathleen ni Houlihan Writes Back: Maud Gonne and Irish National Theater', in *Gender and Sexuality in Modern Ireland*, ed. Anthony Bradley and Maryann Gialanella Valiulis (Amherst Mass.: University of Massachusetts Press in association with the American Conference for Irish Studies, 1997).

Ann Saddlemyer, 'Synge's Soundscape', *Irish University Review*, 22.1 (1992).

Grateful acknowledgment is made to the editors and publishers with whose agreement these materials appear here.

Christopher Morash's essay is to form part of *A History of the Irish Theatre*, forthcoming from Cambridge University Press.

Abbreviations

The following abbreviations are used for the texts of Synge cited throughout the book:

CL I   *The Collected Letters of John Millington Synge*, Volume One: 1871–1907, ed. Ann Saddlemyer (Oxford: Clarendon Press, 1983)

CL II   *The Collected Letters of John Millington Synge*, Volume Two: 1907–1909, ed. Ann Saddlemyer (Oxford: Clarendon Press, 1984)

CW I   J.M. Synge, *Collected Works*, Volume I: *Poems*, ed. Robin Skelton (London: Oxford University Press, 1962; rept. Gerrards Cross: Colin Smythe, 1982)

CW II   J.M. Synge, *Collected Works*, Volume II: *Prose*, ed. Alan Price (London: Oxford University Press, 1966; rept. Gerrards Cross: Colin Smythe, 1982)

CW III   J.M. Synge, *Collected Works*, Volume III: *Plays* Book I, ed. Ann Saddlemyer (London: Oxford University Press, 1968; rept. Gerrards Cross: Colin Smythe, 1982)

CW IV   J.M. Synge, *Collected Works*, Volume IV: *Plays* Book II, ed. Ann Saddlemyer (London: Oxford University Press, 1968; rept. Gerrards Cross: Colin Smythe, 1982)

Introduction

'We will have a hard fight in Ireland before we get the right for every man to see the world in his own way admitted. Synge is invaluable to us because he has that kind of intense narrow personality which necessarily raises the whole issue.'[1] So wrote Yeats, in a letter to the American patron John Quinn in 1905. They had their hard fight, Synge's work did raise the whole issue, and the fight was won, in no small part due to the often belligerent and provocative championship of Yeats. Patrick Pearse, one of Synge's most vehement critics at the time of the *Playboy* controversy, who had claimed then that Synge 'railed obscenely against light, and sweetness, and knowledge, and charity',[2] by 1913 could praise him in Pearsian terms of admiration as 'a man in whose sad heart glowed a true love of Ireland, one of the two or three men who have in our time made Ireland considerable in the eyes of the world'.[3] Synge has long since been accepted as a major figure of Irish literature, of European theatre. His plays, particularly his masterpiece *The Playboy of the Western World*, continue to hold the stage around the world ninety years after his death. Yet his work has never attracted the exhaustive industry of interpretation devoted to his great contemporaries Yeats and Joyce, and his most important successor Beckett. Why?

There is a short and easy answer to the question. Synge was a late developer who died before his thirty-eighth birthday. He was granted hardly more than six years of mature writing life. For him there was to be none of that extraordinarily extended artistic development which is the distinguishing feature of Yeats, no time for growth like that of Joyce from *Dubliners* and *A Portrait of the Artist* to *Ulysses* and *Finnegans*

11

Wake, no opportunity for the creative genesis that took Beckett from *More Pricks than Kicks* to the *Trilogy*, *Waiting for Godot*, and beyond. Synge left only the limited and relatively homogeneous *oeuvre* of six achieved plays, *The Aran Islands*, a handful of essays, and a very slim volume of verse. No mean monument, but apparently limited as thesis-quarry.

Apart from his restricted output, in Ireland there has been another dimension to the relative neglect of Synge. In his own time, in his own country, Synge's work occasioned fierce contention. Since then, though his stature has been widely acknowledged, there remains a legacy of unease with his work, a residue of distrust of his language and his vision of Ireland. Accompanying such remaining resistance, perhaps indeed a mutated version of it, has been an increasing feeling that his imagined Ireland, if it ever existed, belongs to a past that we want to forget. Here in Ireland at the end of the century, the Irish modernists can be claimed with pride as an internationally accredited cultural property. Synge's drama, by contrast, is associated with a late romantic cult of the peas-ant, a pastoral kitsch particularly distasteful in a country bent on estab-lishing its credentials as a fully modernized urban society. The mist that does be on the bog can stay there. And so, though lip-service is paid to Synge's genius and the canonical status of his work is accepted, there has been no new critical monograph on Synge in fifteen years,[4] and books on his work published in Ireland have been particularly rare.[5]

It was against such a background and to challenge this kind of neglect that the Synge Summer School was established in 1991. It took from the beginning a much broader remit than the study of Synge's work alone; the mission of the School has been to explore the whole rich and living tradition of Irish theatre in which Synge played such a crucial role. It has, though, been one of the School's principal aims not to rehabilitate Synge, much less to set up an adulatory shrine to his memory, but to set going again a proper critical debate on the nature and significance of his achievement. That too has been the design of the present book, published on the occasion of the tenth Synge Summer School in 2000. The appendix to the book, setting out the full range of programmes over the ten years, will demonstrate that it would have been impossible to publish a fully comprehensive proceedings of the School. Even to collect just the lectures devoted to Synge would have made for an unviably bulky volume. I decided therefore to invite ten of our speakers to contribute essays derived from their School lectures as a way to illustrate the range of possibilities for interpreting Synge that the Synge Summer School has helped to open up over its first decade. Some of the contributors took this as an opportunity to develop their arguments into fully elaborated scholarly papers; some chose to retain the immediacy of the spoken style. I have deliberately kept that diversity, have not sought to impose an editorial consistency of tone, because I wanted this book, like the School, to be hospitable to the different languages of interpretation, to accommodate the various fields of vision from which Synge can be seen. Some, but by no means all, of the writers in this volume have a background of specialist interest in Synge; the book's success depends on the interplay established between the several interpreting voices and the particular vantage-points they represent.

The broad arrangement of the volume is into three groups of essays, the first situating Synge in a number of social, literary and theatrical contexts, the second focusing on individual works, the last concerned with patterns running through his writing as a whole. Given that the Synge Summer School is based in Rathdrum, close to where all the four Wicklow plays are based,[6] it seemed logical to begin with my own essay on Synge and Wicklow. My interest in it was turned towards local history, to the county specifics of family class and position from within which Synge wrote and the details of local life which he observed and shaped into his work. Roy Foster, as an Irish cultural and political historian at present writing the definitive biography of Yeats, was in a position to take another bearing on Synge and his family background. His essay calibrates the precise differences between the background and milieux of Yeats and Synge, and demonstrates just how this contributed to the figure Synge made in the Yeatsian imagination. Frank McGuinness comes to Synge as a leading Irish playwright who has created versions of several Ibsen plays for the contemporary stage. He is therefore attuned to the echoes of Ibsen in Synge, not only in the abandoned country house play *When the Moon Has Set*, but in the achieved drama of *The Playboy*. While this underacknowledged connection to a European dramatic inheritance is uncovered in McGuinness's 'John Millington Synge and the King of Norway', Angela Bourke, bringing to bear the specialist authority of an Irish-language scholar, illuminates the native communal 'theatre' on which Synge drew in his representations of the customs of the keen. Her careful analysis of Synge's own observations of keening on Aran and of the tradition of the mourning woman yields a new sense of the dramatic force of *Riders to the Sea* and *Deirdre of the Sorrows*.

Such are the contexts within which Synge's work is set in the first four essays of this book. But the distinction between text and context-related study is necessarily an artificial one, as Declan Kiberd's detailed study of *The Aran Islands* makes clear. Although he does indeed give to Synge's book the close critical attention which it deserves and has seldom had, this is in order to identify its diverse sources – from Wilde's 'The Soul of Man Under Socialism' to Frazer's *The Golden Bough* – and to bring out the precise nature of Synge's anthropologist-like relationship with Aran. Tom Paulin, reflecting on *Riders to the Sea* as a 'revisionist tragedy', re-reads the play in the light of the changes that contemporary politics have wrought on his understanding of it, and offers a juxtaposition of the play with *Cathleen ni Houlihan* and *The Playboy* in a three-way 'imaginary production'. Antoinette Quinn's 'Staging the Irish Peasant Woman: Maud Gonne versus Synge' places *Cathleen ni Houlihan* back in its original theatrical context in a sequence followed by *The Shadow of the Glen* and Gonne's play *Dawn*. The politics centring on the production of the *Shadow* are here reinterpreted as part of a continuing struggle over the representation of Irish women in which Maud Gonne played a leading role on and off the stage. Where Quinn approaches Synge's controversial drama from within women's studies, Christopher Morash writes about the riots over *The Playboy* as a historian of Irish theatre. His essay makes telling use of an earlier nineteenth-century theatre riot in Dublin to illustrate how the disturbances over *The Playboy* turned on changing attitudes towards audience behaviour, with their class and political implications. By contrast with this concentration on the first theatrical production of *The Playboy*, Martin Hilský is able to enlarge upon one aspect of its theatrical afterlife, its continuing popularity on the Czech stage. His commision to translate the play for the Czech National Theatre in 1995 prompted a search for an appropriate style in which to 're-imagine' Synge's language; his account of that search helps to illuminate both the texture of Synge's stage dialect and the meanings it supports in *The Playboy*.

The two remaining essays in the volume pursue patterns of feeling and imagination that go beyond any one work of Synge and represent the informing characteristics of his writing. Anthony Roche looks at the relationship between Synge and his fiancée Molly Allgood, not just for its biographical interest but for the performative roles of woman and tramp played out in Synge's letters to her, roles which answered to long-standing psychological preoccupations of the playwright. Roche's essay suggests the way in which these shaped the creation of his two greatest parts for women, Pegeen Mike and Deirdre, both written for and, in a sense, with Molly. Ann Saddlemyer's 'Synge's Soundscape' was the inaugural lecture of the first Synge Summer School, so there seemed a certain appropriateness in placing this essay by the doyenne of Synge scholarship at the end of this volume. Her intimate knowledge of all Synge's writing, his letters and notebooks as well as his finished work, has enabled her to bring out the special importance of his responsiveness to sound, the sounds of nature as of music, and how this rhythmical tuning of his ear to the world around him produces the special soundscape of his plays.

I have been writing so far as if this book were a collection of essays only. It isn't, and is distinctively different for not being so. The Synge Summer School has been a collaborative enterprise, bringing together scholars, writers, and theatre professionals in the conviction that the exposition of literature and drama is not the exclusive preserve of the academy, that interpretation and imagination are one – not two opposed activities. It was in such a spirit that I asked four poets, all of whom had spoken or read at the School, to contribute to the book poems that would in some way or other bear upon Synge. These poems are there for readers to read: they do not stand in need of glossing from me. What I will say is that this book would be immeasurably poorer without Seamus Heaney's 'Glanmore Eclogue', without Nuala Ní Dhomhnaill's 'Ar Oileán' (based on Synge's 'On an Island'), without Gerald Dawe's 'Distraction', without the *envoi* of Brendan Kennelly's 'Synge'. To set about interpreting Synge as this book does is also to imagine Synge again as these poets have.

Nicholas Grene
Ballinaclash, Co. Wicklow

SEAMUS HEANEY

Glanmore Eclogue

MYLES: A house and ground. And your own bay tree as well
And time to yourself. You've landed on your feet.
If you can't write now, when will you ever write?

POET: A woman changed my life. Call her Augusta
Because we arrived in August, and from now on
This month's baled hay and blackberries and combines
Will spell Augusta's bounty. I'll honour her
With a bouquet of ears and awns on the window-sill
And green nut clusters from under that hazel hedge.
It's thanks to her I'm here.

MYLES: Outsiders own
The country nowadays, but even so
I don't begrudge you. You're Augusta's tenant
And that's enough. She has every right,
Maybe more right than most, to her quarter acre.
She knows the big glen inside out, and everything
Meliboeus ever wrote about it,
All the tramps he met tramping the roads.
Talk about changed lives! Those were the days –
Caesar's Land Commission making tenants owners,
Rome taking notice finally too late …

17

But now with all this money coming in
And peace being talked up, the boot's on the other foot.
First it was Meliboeus' people
Went to the wall, now it will be us.
Small farmers here are priced out of the market.

POET: Backs to the wall and empty pockets: Meliboeus
Was never happier than when he was on the road
With people on their uppers. Loneliness
Was his passport through the world. Midge-angels
On the face of water, the first drop before thunder,
A stranger on a wild night, *out in the rain falling*.
His spirit lives for me in things like that.
Augusta understands that side of him.

MYLES: Our old language that Meliboeus learnt
Has lovely songs. What about putting words
On one of them, words that the rest of us
Can understand, and singing it for us here?

POET: I have this summer song for the glen and you:

Early summer, cuckoo cuckoos,
Welcome, summer is what he sings.
Heather breathes on soft bog-pillows.
Bog-cotton bows to moorland wind.

The deer's heart skips a beat; he startles.
The sea's tide fills, it rests, it runs.
Season of the drowsy ocean.
Tufts of yellow-blossoming whins.

Swallows swerve and flicker up.
Music starts behind the mountain.
There's moss, a lush growth underfoot.
Sedge and buttercups on marshland.

Bogbanks shine like ravens' wings.
The cuckoo keeps on calling *Welcome*.

The speckled fish jumps; and the strong
Warrior is up and running.

A little nippy chirpy fellow
Hits the highest note there is;
The lark sings out his clear tidings.
Summer, shimmer, perfect days.

NICHOLAS GRENE

On the Margins: Synge and Wicklow

I. THE SYNGES OF WICKLOW

The Synges of Glanmore Castle in County Wicklow, like so many landed Anglo-Irish families, had come down in the world by the time of the playwright at the end of the nineteenth century. Their Wicklow property had been established in the eighteenth century following marriages with the Hatch family and was at its heyday in the time of Francis Synge (1761–1831). He owned not only Glanmore, with its fifteen hundred acres of demesne including the Devil's Glen, but Roundwood Park as well, an estate in all of over four thousand acres. It was Francis who had the older house of Glenmouth enlarged and redesigned by Francis Johnson as what was then called Glenmore Castle, described in all its glory in Lewis's *Topographical Dictionary* (1837):

Glenmore, the splendid residence of J. Synge, Esq., is a handsome and spacious castellated mansion, with embattled parapets, above which rises a lofty round tower, flanking the principal parapet, in the centre of which is a square gateway tower forming the chief entrance; it was erected by the late F. Synge, Esq., and occupies an eminence, sloping gently towards the sea, near the opening of the Devil's Glen, and surrounded by a richly planted demesne, commanding a fine view of St George's Channel, and the castle, town, and lighthouses of Wicklow, with the intervening country thickly studded with gentlemen's seats.[1]

Unfortunately, this idyllic picture of natural beauty and civilized power was not to last. Francis's heir John (1788–1845), known in the family as 'Pestalozzi John' because of his enthusiastic advocacy of the Swiss educationalist Johann Heinrich Pestalozzi, became increasingly indebted and on his death the estates were bankrupt.[2] His son Francis Synge managed to buy back Glanmore but not Roundwood Park from the Commissioners of Encumbered Estates in 1850. Although in his lifetime the reduced estate of Glanmore was relatively prosperous, after his death in 1878 his widow, Editha, and her second husband Major Theodore Gardiner lived in the house only intermittently and the property suffered under erratic management. This was the state of the family fortunes which the adult John Millington Synge (1871–1909) would have known.[3]

He himself came from a younger branch of the Glanmore family. His father John Hatch Synge (1824–72), the seventh child of 'Pestalozzi John', was a barrister by profession who died when John Millington was only one, leaving his widow with five children to bring up. With an income of £400 a year derived from land investments, Mrs Synge did not live in poverty, but rather in what were known as 'reduced circumstances'. Her older children all became comfortably settled in middle-class professions. Edward was a land agent to (among others) Lord Gormanstown and, from 1884 on, to the Synge estates in Wicklow. He was, it seems, regarded by the tenants as a hard man, at least to judge by one incident reported by Mrs Synge: 'He heard them talking among themselves and one said "it would take a Synge to do that"' (Stephens MS f. 478). Robert trained as a civil engineer, then emigrated to Argentina, where for a number of years he ranched with cousins on his mother's side. Samuel, with qualifications in divinity and medicine, served as a medical missionary in China. Annie married a solicitor, Harry Stephens, and their family continued to live close to Mrs Synge. Only the youngest, 'Johnnie', proved a problem, horrifying the family with his aspiration, on graduating from Trinity College, of becoming a musician. 'Harry had a talk with him the other day,' Mrs Synge wrote Robert in January 1890, 'advising him very strongly not to think of making it a profession. Harry told him all the men who do take to drink!' (Stephens MS f. 586). Johnnie persisted, all the same, at first studying music in Germany, and then – equally unsatisfactorily from the family's point of view, and equally unrewardingly – living in Paris with some ill-defined aim of becoming a writer. In Mrs Synge's letters to her other sons, her youngest is a constant source of worry: 'My poor Johnnie is my failure' (April 1894); 'Johnnie is vegetating in Paris. He calls himself very busy, but it is a busy idleness, in my opinion' (November 1896) (Stephens MS f. 931, f. 1148).

John Synge's failure to find a respectable and respectably paid profession was not the only cause of worry for his family. There was also his loss of faith, deeply disturbing to his mother. On both sides of his family, his religious heritage was one of evangelical Protestantism. His grandfather John Synge and his uncle Francis had both been members of the Plymouth Brethren, which had its origins in Wicklow. His mother's father, Robert Traill, was a clergyman from Antrim who felt that he had been denied preferment in the Church because of his strongly evangelical views. Mrs Synge shared those views and it was a real grief to her when John, at the age of eighteen, declared that he no longer believed, and refused to attend church any more. Again and again over the years her letters record her prayers for him and her yearning for him to accept Jesus as his Redeemer.

Synge was at odds with his family politically as well. Although he canvassed for an Anti-Home Rule Petition in 1893,[4] and as late as 1895 was of the view that Home Rule would provoke sectarian conflict,[5] by 1897 he was prepared to join Maud Gonne's Association Irlandaise in Paris and, like most Irish nationalists, he took a strongly pro-Boer position in the Boer war (Stephens MS f. 1602). He was not only nationalist but socialist in principle. 'A radical', he told his young nephew Edward Stephens in an unusual outburst, 'is a person who wants change root and branch, and I'm proud to be a radical' (Stephens MS f. 1663). Such ideas were hardly likely to be acceptable to his family. 'He says', reported Mrs Synge indignantly to Samuel in 1896, 'he has gone back to Paris to study Socialism, and he wants to do good, and for that possibility he is giving up everything. He says he is not selfish or egotistical but quite the reverse. In fact he writes the most utter folly ...' (Greene and Stephens, 62).

There is nothing very unusual about a writer or artist from a conventional middle-class background diverging from his family's political, social and religious views. What is striking about Synge's case is that he maintained such close relations with the family in spite of his dissidence. From 1893 to 1902 he spent his winters on the Continent, but his home remained with his mother in Kingstown (Dun Laoghaire) and, with the exception of two brief periods when he took rooms in Dublin, he went on living with her until her death in 1908, not long before his own. He shared also the prolonged family holidays in Wicklow. Throughout Synge's youth and adolescence Mrs Synge had taken a holiday house each year in Greystones and lived there as part of the tightly knit Greystones Protestant community. From 1892 on, the houses she rented were in the Annamoe area, close to Glanmore, most frequently Castle Kevin. Most years the Wicklow stay lasted from June through September, providing a family base for Robert or Samuel Synge when they were home from abroad, for the Stephenses, and for cousins and missionary friends visiting Ireland. It was from these summer periods spent with his family around Annamoe that Synge formed the impressions of Wicklow which served as the basis for his essays and plays.

The Synges came to Annamoe as something between urban summer visitors and members of the local landowning family. They no longer stayed at Glanmore, as they had during the lifetime of Francis Synge; Francis's widow Editha and her second husband, Major Gardiner, when they were resident, lived on the hill farm of Tiglin for economy and rented out Glanmore Castle. The houses that the Synges rented were suggestive of their social position. Castle Kevin, a substantial early nineteenth-century house, home of the Frizell family, was vacant and could be rented cheaply because it was boycotted. The Synges spent in all seven summers there between 1892 and 1901. They did not seem to be troubled by the boycott, though Synge found on the doorpost of Castle Kevin (and later published) a triumphalist verse celebrating the departure of the Frizells.[6] When Castle Kevin was not available, Mrs Synge rented Avonmore, a big eighteenth-century house on the Castle Kevin property, lived in by Henry Harding, a local farmer and caretaker for the Frizells. For the month of August 1897 they stayed on the Parnell estate at Avondale, not in the big house, but in the steward's house, 'Casino', something which Harry Stephens felt was a social indignity. In other summers they had to be content with still less grand places to stay. In 1895 it was Duff House, a farmhouse with a beautiful situation on the southern side of Lough Dan. 'It was with some misgivings that Mrs Synge brought her future daughter-in-law [Robert's fiancée] there, for, as the house was owned by Roman Catholics, she feared that it would not be free from fleas' (Stephens MS f.1022). Tomriland House, where the Synges stayed in 1902, 1903 and 1904, was just as unpretentious, but the farmers who owned it were Protestant.

In her holiday homes, as in Dublin, Mrs Synge preferred to have to do with people of her own religion. There were the Hardings with whom the Synges stayed at Avonmore; there were the Colemans who owned Tomriland; there was Willie Belton who acted as carter for the Synges when they travelled down from Kingstown and who aroused

Mrs Synge's extreme anger by getting drunk on an outing to Glendalough with her maids. 'Is it not a dreadful thing', she wrote to Samuel, 'for one of our few protestants in this place to be going on in such a way?' (Stephens MS f. 2015). One exception was their close neighbour old Mrs Rochfort, known to the family by her favourite tag 'Avourneen', whose talk Synge incorporated into his essay 'The People of the Glens' (*CW* II 219–20). Still it must have been a significant part of Synge's Wicklow experience that so many of the people around him were of his family's religion. It adds a different dimension, for example, to the famous story of Synge listening in to the talk of the servant girls. In the preface to *The Playboy of the Western World* he wrote defending the authenticity of his language:

When I was writing *The Shadow of the Glen,* some years ago, I got more aid than any learning could have given me, from a chink in the floor of the old Wicklow house where I was staying, that let me hear what was being said by the servant girls in the kitchen. (*CW* IV 53)

The impression of the gentleman eavesdropper was unfortunate. But would the impression have been improved if he had added the detail that the girls whose talk so inspired him in Tomriland House in 1902 were Ellen the cook and Florence Massey the maid, both of whom had been brought up in a Protestant orphanage and did not necessarily come from Wicklow at all?[7]

If the range of Synge's social acquaintance in Wicklow was limited, his knowledge of the countryside was not. Within a radius of some fifteen miles from Annamoe, he walked and cycled every hill and valley, generally in company with his relations or with friends of the family. He spent most of July 1898, for example, on excursions with Robert, who was a passionate fisherman; in other summers he walked with Samuel. The guests at the Synges' holiday houses at different times included a number of younger women, Annie and Edie Harmar, sisters of Samuel's wife, and friends of theirs, Madeleine Kerr and Rosie Calthrop. These too were Synge's companions on long walks or cycle-rides and, interestingly, there never seems to have been any sense of impropriety at his going off unchaperoned for a day at a time with an unrelated woman of his own age. In the Wicklow essays Synge virtually always gives the impression of being alone on his journeys, but this was often not the case. Where, for example, in 'An Autumn Night in the Hills' he tells the story of going to fetch a pointer dog from the cottage where it had been recovering after a shooting accident, the essay ends most effectively with a description of his solitary walk back down Glenmalure (though it isn't named as such). What he does not reveal is that the dog in question belonged to his brother-in-law Harry Stephens, who had rented shooting rights in Glenmalure, and that Harry was with him on the mission to fetch the dog home.[8]

In his summers in Wicklow Synge lived a double life: the social life of the family in which he played a full part (attendance at church always excepted) and the life of the imagination slowly transmuted into writing. The Synges remained a close and united family, and John Synge never tried to escape from the closeness of those bonds. As Stephens commented on John's relations with Robert: 'The brothers differed about almost every subject, but they never quarrelled about their differences' (Stephens MS f. 1412). This is borne out also by Synge's own remark on Samuel, in a letter to his fiancée Molly Allgood: 'he is one of the best fellows in [the] world, I think, though he is so religious we have not much in common' (CL I 224). It was Synge's deliberate strategy to avoid subjects of dissension. Thus he adopted a 'rule against talking to us [his nephews Edward and Francis Stephens] about religious or political theory, with which our parents would not have agreed' (Stephens MS f. 1828). He remained deeply attached to his mother and she to him, for all their lack of understanding. So, for example, she was prepared to accept the prospect of Molly Allgood as daughter-in-law, though an ill-educated, nineteen-year-old Roman Catholic, a former shop-girl turned actress, must have offended nearly every prejudice she had. The rest of the family were less tolerant of the proposed marriage, but once again there was no outright quarrel.

Silence, repression, and instinctive family loyalty kept the Synges together. John Synge walked with Samuel, fished with Robert, shot with Harry Stephens, cycled with his in-laws and his in-laws' cousins. Yet he looked at Wicklow as they would never have done. He was an internal drop-out within a class which he, but not they, saw as defeated and obsolete. His most telling evocation of that state of affairs is the essay 'A Landlord's Garden in County Wicklow'. The essay was based on a real incident in the walled garden of Castle Kevin in the summer of 1901 when Synge set himself to guard some ripening cherries against the depredations of the local boys, ending up chasing one of them round and round the garden. 'John sent us into fits of laughter telling us the story,' Mrs Synge commented in her account of the matter in a letter to Samuel at the time (*My Uncle John,* 144). In writing the essay Synge turned the cherries into apples, more traditional fruit for orchard-robbing, and made the garden into an eloquent emblem of the decaying fortunes of the landowning class:

A stone's throw from an old house where I spent several summers in county Wicklow, there was a garden that had been left to itself for fifteen or twenty years. Just inside the gate, as one entered, two paths led up through a couple of strawberry beds, half choked with leaves, where a few white and narrow strawberries were still hidden away. Further on was nearly half an acre of tall raspberry canes and thistles five feet high, growing together in a dense mass, where one could still pick raspberries enough to last a household for the season. Then, in a waste of hemlock, there were some half-dozen apple trees covered with lichen and moss, and against the northern walls a few dying plum trees hanging from their nails. Beyond them there was a dead pear tree and just inside the gate, as one came back to it, a large fuchsia filled with empty nests. A few lines of box here and there showed where the flower-beds had been laid out, and when anyone who had the knowledge looked carefully among them many remnants could be found of beautiful and rare plants. (*CW* II 230)

This sounds a circumstantially precise description, but the substitution of the apples for the real-life cherries makes it clear that it is not literally accurate. Synge is in fact piling up the details to compound the sense of dereliction: the etiolated strawberries, the rank growth of the raspberries and thistles, the apple-trees neglected and mossed with age, the abandoned nests in the fuchsia, the 'waste of hemlock', the fine and exotic cultivated flowers only to be found by connoisseurs in the wilderness. It is no wonder that he entitled one draft of this essay 'The Garden of the Dead'.[9]

In this one essay, Synge allowed himself a measure of the class nostalgia traditionally associated with the image of the crumbling big house – in this essay only, and a measure of it only.

Everyone is used in Ireland to the tragedy that is bound up with the lives of farmers and fishing people; but in this garden one seemed to feel the tragedy of the landlord class also, and of the innumerable old families that are quickly dwindling away. These owners of the land are not much pitied at the present day, or much deserving of pity; and yet one cannot quite forget that they are the descendants of what was at one time, in the eighteenth century, a high-spirited and highly-cultivated aristocracy. The broken green-houses and mouse-eaten libraries, that were designed and collected by men who voted with Grattan, are perhaps as mournful in the end as the four mud walls that are so often left in Wicklow as the only remnants of a farmhouse. (*CW* II 230–1)

Synge is commenting here, and passing judgement, on his own class and his own family. 'Many of the descendants of these people have, of course, drifted into professional life in Dublin, or have gone abroad; yet, wherever they are, they do not equal their forefathers' (*CW* II 231). His most telling condemnation he omitted from the published essay: 'Still, this class, with its many genuine qualities, had little patriotism, in the right sense, few ideas, and no seed for future life, so it has gone to the wall' (*CW* II 231).

The essay makes it clear how deliberately Synge turned away from his own class and its situation as a subject for his writing:

The desolation of this life is often of a peculiarly local kind, and if a playwright chose to go through the Irish country houses he would find material, it is likely, for many gloomy plays that would turn on the dying away of these old families, and on the lives of the one or two delicate girls that are left so often to represent a dozen hearty men who were alive a generation or two ago. (*CW* II 231)

This was not the material from which Synge was to create his plays, though his first drama, *When the Moon Has Set*, is concerned with something very like the country-house subject he here rejects. Instead he turned to areas of local life outside the compass of his social background and brought to them attitudes very unlike those of his family. And yet we can see in the Wicklow essays and plays, refracted and transposed, the conditioned habits of mind of his own social situation. He is relatively little concerned with the rural community as a community, with its history and evolution. He remains someone from outside looking in, looking on, interested by those on the social margins or at the extreme peripheries of the region. He effaces, in so far as is possible, himself, his family, his class, and sees value and significance in what his own people would least regard. The wildness and primitiveness of local life represent a welcome contrast to the genteel repressions of middle-class Protestant late Victorianism. Still, the melancholy strain in his observation of Wicklow, and his tendency to focus on and treasure what is at social vanishing point, are in some sort of emotional correspondence with his position as alienated member of a declining class.

II. IN WICKLOW: THE ESSAYS

Synge made his first visit to Aran in 1898 and almost immediately conceived the idea of writing a book about his experiences there. With a draft of what was to become *The Aran Islands* largely completed in the winter of 1900–1, he turned to doing something similar for Wicklow. The paradox of Synge's creative development was that it took the visits to the unfamiliar landscape of Aran to enable him to see the Wicklow countryside with fresh eyes. The strangeness of Aran, and his strangeness in it, freed him from a social self-consciousness which would have been much stronger in Wicklow where he, or at least his family and family name, would have been well known and easily placed. From 1900 on he began to write up descriptive notes, interesting encounters of his Wicklow summers, and in 1901–2 he made a point of visiting fairs and races to collect material. By 1902 he seems to have had the idea of trying to gather together a book on Wicklow life.[10] He never completed this project and left only the eight essays which make up the 'In Wicklow' section of his posthumous *Works*.

'All wild sights appealed to Synge,' said Jack Yeats, 'and he did not care whether they were typical of anything or had any symbolical meaning at all'.[11] The wilder, the rougher the sights were, the better Synge liked them. Compare, for example, his account of an occasion such as the horse-races in Arklow in August 1901 with that of the *Wicklow News-Letter*. The *News-Letter* was the Unionist county paper, and its report on the races made them a very sedate affair. Headed 'Arklow Races', the article gave a full list of the organizing committee, before continuing:

Favoured with delightful weather, the above races came off on Thursday, on The Green, Arklow, in the presence of an enormous multitude of holiday-makers from all parts of the country, including many from North Wexford and Dublin. The meeting was held under the Irish Racing Association rules, and it was pleasing to find that both the executive and stewards discharged their duties so satisfactorily that not a hitch occurred in the arrangements, which were excellent, and a most enjoyable day's racing resulted. A few minor details were wanting, such as a telegraph board, refreshments saloon, &c., while a little more attention might have been paid to the levelling of a short piece of the course. However, everything passed off well, and the stewards are to be congratulated upon the grand success they achieved.[12]

The article concluded with a formal list of results, ending with the Farmers' Plate. Here is Synge on the same event:

The races in Arklow [...] are singularly unconventional, and no one can ... watch them on the sand-hills in suitable weather, when the hay and the wooded glens in the background are covered with sunshine and the shadows of clouds, without thrilling to the tumult of humour that rises from the people.

A long course is indicated among the sand-hills by a few scattered flag-posts, and at the portion nearest the town a rough paddock and grandstand – draped with green paper – are erected with about a hundred yards of the course roped off from the crowd.

This is Synge's version of the stewards discharging 'their duties so satisfactorily':

Some half dozen fishermen, with green ribbons fastened to their jerseys or behind their hats, act as stewards [...] and as they are usually drunk they reel about poking the public with a stick and repeating with endless and vain iteration, 'Keep outside the ropes'.

It is the crowd and the sideshows rather than the racing that takes Synge's eye:

At either side a varied crowd collects and straggles round among the faded roulette tables, little groups of young men dancing horn-pipes to the music of a flute, and the numerous stalls which supply fruit, biscuits and cheap drinks. These stalls consist merely of a long cart covered by a crescent awning which rises from one end only, and gives them at a distance a curious resemblance to the cars with sails which the Chinese employ. They are attended to by the semi-gypsy or tinker class, among [whom] women with curiously Mongolian features are not rare. All these are extraordinarily prolific, and at a few paces from each stall there is usually a pile of hay and sacking and harness that is literally crawling with half-naked children.

Finally, Synge gives us what are no doubt the contestants for the Farmers' Plate:

In the centre of the course there are a number of farmers from up the country riding about on heavy mares, sometimes bare-backed sometimes with an old saddle tied on with rope, and often with a certain dignity of costume that is heightened by the old-fashioned rustic tall hat. (*CW* II 197-8)[13]

The *News-Letter* description aims to regularize the event to its readers, turn the races into Fairyhouse in little; Synge's object is to make them strange and, in his account, Arklow races are well on their way to becoming the mule-race in *The Playboy*.

Again and again in the Wicklow essays Synge gives his admiring attention to those whom the community disregards or dislikes. He attends with special interest precisely to such people, who attract hostility for their difference from the social norm. The central essay here is 'The Vagrants of Wicklow'. The essay begins with a comment on the number of vagrants to be found in Wicklow, and takes issue with the standard tendency to deplore this:

Their abundance has often been regretted; yet in one sense it is an interesting sign, for wherever the labourer of a country has preserved his vitality, and begets an occasional temperament of distinction, a certain number of vagrants are to be looked for. In the middle classes the gifted son of a family is always the poorest – usually a writer or artist with no sense for speculation – and in a family of peasants, where the average comfort is just over penury, the gifted son sinks also, and is soon a tramp on the roadside. (*CW* II 202)

The nature of Synge's interest in the vagrants is here made clear. He is obviously thinking of himself when he speaks of 'the gifted son of a family' in the middle classes; with 'forty pounds a year and a new suit when I am too shabby',[14] he was much the poorest of the Synges. It is not a matter of naïve or sentimental identification with the vagrants but of a precise analogy. They are the outcasts of their class as he feels himself to be of his.

All through the essay the vagrants described evoke a variety of Synge's imaginative preoccupations. The centenarian tramp, whom E.M. Stephens says was well known around Castle Kevin as the 'Honest Tar' (Stephens MS f. 1442), supplied Synge with some of the features of Martin Doul in *The Well of the Saints,* particularly in the story of his quarrel with his wife (whom he married at the age of ninety) and his fierce complaints at having had his long white hair cut off in Kilmainham Gaol, where he had been committed for assaulting her:

All his pride and his half-conscious feeling for the dignity of his age seemed to have set themselves on this long hair, which marked him out from the other people of this district; and I have often heard him saying to himself, as he sat beside me under a ditch: 'What use is an old man without his hair? A man has only his bloom like the trees; and what use is an old man without his white hair?' (*CW* II 203)

The same grotesque yet irrepressible sense of self-dignity reappears in Martin Doul's imagination of himself with 'a beautiful, long, white, silken, streamy beard' and his fierce determination not to allow the Saint to take this illusion away from him.

Several of the other vagrants in the essay illustrate the antagonism between these figures and the settled community, the tramps and tinkers from the West with their 'curious reputation for witchery and unnatural powers', or the drunken flower-woman squaring up to the police: 'Let this be the barrack's yard, and come on now, the lot of you'

(*CW* II 207). While Synge is exhilarated by the flashpoints of defiance between the vagrants and the representatives of social order, he could find also the reflection of his own more melancholy strain:

In these hills the summer passes in a few weeks from a late spring, full of odour and colour, to an autumn that is premature and filled with the desolate splendour of decay; and it often happens that, in moments when one is most aware of this ceaseless fading of beauty, some incident of tramp life gives a local human intensity to the shadow of one's own mood. (*CW* II 204)

This has Synge's special plangent awareness of the pressure of mortality upon life, and he acknowledges that it is the 'shadow' of this mood of his that allows him to see the 'local human intensity' in the figure of the young tramp 'suffering from some terrible disease' that he goes on to describe. The vagrants of the essay come alive imaginatively as they correspond in their very independent being to the thoughts and feelings of the man who watches them.

Synge in Wicklow was preoccupied with the old, the odd and the mad. Many of the people who figure most prominently in the essays, in their extreme old age, represent a life that is past or passing. The vagrants, in their difference, stand for the 'variations which are a condition and effect of all vigorous life' (*CW* II 208). In 'The Oppression of the Hills' Synge sought to classify the several sorts of mental disturbance which he thought specific to the Wicklow mountains. The 'peculiar climate', with its alternation between prolonged periods of rain and an occasional 'morning of almost supernatural radiance', 'acting on a population that is already lonely and dwindling, has caused or increased a tendency to nervous depression among the people, and every degree of sadness, from that of the man who is merely mournful to that of the man who has spent half his life in the mad-house, is common among these hills' (*CW* II 209). With all his passionate feeling for the landscape of the hills and glens, Synge knew that life in these desolate places was not idyllic. He quotes 'one old man who may be cited as an example of sadness not yet definitely morbid':

'I suppose there are some places where they think that Ireland is a sort of garden,' he laughed bitterly, 'and I've heard them say that Wicklow is the garden of Ireland. I suppose there's fine scenery for those that likes [*sic*] it, but it's a poor place in the winter and there's no money moving in the country'.[15]

Such glum cynicism, however, is the least of the mental troubles that Synge saw besetting the people of the glens. He describes the hysterical fears of a young girl who is convinced her two sisters had been drowned in the bogs, based on an incident that took place at Castle Kevin in June 1899 (Stephens MS f. 1545), or the terrors of an older woman living alone: 'There's nothing I fear like the thunder. My heart isn't strong – I do feel it – and I have a lightness in my head, and often when I do be excited with the thunder I do be afeard I might die there alone in the cottage and no one know it' (*CW* II 210). 'The three shadowy countries that are never forgotten in Wicklow ', Synge tells us, are 'America (their El Dorado), the Union (the Poor House) and the Madhouse' (*CW* II 216). Madness is a threat to old and young alike. One victim is the woman Synge calls Mary Kinsella in 'An Autumn Night in the Hills':

'She was a fine young woman with two children' [Synge is told] 'and a year and a half ago she went wrong in her head, and they had to send her away. And then up there in the Richmond asylum maybe they thought the sooner they were shut of her the better, for she died two days ago this morning, and now they're bringing her up to have a wake.' (*CW* II 188)

The essay (originally entitled 'The Body of Mary Kinsella')[16] ends with the sight of her coffin after a walk through the wild desolation of the glen which suggests the causes precipitating the madness. For Synge, neurosis and dementia are associated with the mental exposure of those in lonely places to the oppressive emptiness of nature, its menacing power.

The essays contain some genre studies, such as 'At a Wicklow Fair', in which Synge describes a typical rural event, evoking the fair's sights, sounds and customs. His tone is sometimes that of the social commentator, drawing together observations into generalizing statements: 'The older people in county Wicklow, as in the rest of Ireland, still show a curious affection for the landed classes wherever they have lived for a generation of two upon their property [...] The younger people feel differently' (*CW* II 211–12). But his real interest is not in the representative or typical among people or social phenomena. He pays little attention to villages and towns, to the ordinary work of farming or marketing, to politics, money or religion. His imagination is held by individuals and incidents on certain margins: the tinkers, tramps and story-tellers at the rough edges of their community, the isolated shepherds of the remote hills, situations of mind and place close to alienation. These are the preoccupations of the essays fully dramatized in the plays.

III. PLAYS AND PLACES

One of the intriguing features of Synge's Wicklow plays is their combination of specificity and universality, of the locally realized and the purely imagined. The story of *The Shadow of the Glen*, for instance, originally had nothing to do with Wicklow at all. It was a folk-tale that Synge heard on Inis Meáin from a storyteller called Pat Dirane and that he recorded in *The Aran Islands* (*CW* II 70–2). In the earliest surviving draft of the play there is no sign that Synge had a Wicklow setting in mind. The story is dramatized very much in the spirit of the original, the tale of the cunning old man pretending to be dead to catch out his wife, the comedy of the obviously unfaithful wife and her vigorous young lover.[17] A number of quite distinct Wicklow experiences had to coalesce in Synge's mind to make *The Shadow of the Glen* the subtle and complex tragicomedy of mood it was to become.

The setting appears to have been suggested by memories of the visit to Glenmalure to collect Harry Stephens's pointer dog in August 1897, the episode described in 'An Autumn Night in the Hills'. Harry Stephens, along with a friend, Willie Ormsby, a judge retired from India, had rented grouse shooting from 'the two old Harney brothers who lived with their sister in the last cottage at the head of Glenmalure and grazed their sheep on the slopes of Baravore' (Stephens MS f. 1238). It was here that the dog was left when it was accidentally wounded out shooting, and here that Synge and his brother-in-law came to collect it. Pierce Harney's, a hundred years before, had figured in the 1798 Rebellion as a hold-out position for the rebels Dwyer and Holt.[18] The Harneys of Baravore in Synge's time, Michael (b. 1840), Esther (b. 1843), and James (b. 1846), lived in a house too large to be called a cottage and, with hill-grazing over twelve hundred acres, must have been comfortably off.[19] In the essay Synge describes the house as 'the cottage of an under-keeper or bailiff', though what he enters – 'a long low room with open rafters' – does not sound quite like a standard cottage kitchen.

What evidently struck Synge was less the actual details of the house and its people than the idea of its situation at the head of the glen. There was the 'old woman' (presumably Esther Harney) with her folk-lore of Lough Nahanagan and its evil spirit. There was the 'finely made girl', quite possibly a niece of the Harneys,[20] with her devotion to the pointer dog: 'it's herself will be lonesome when that dog is gone' (*CW* II 191). The men were absent on their mission to escort home the coffin of Mary Kinsella, whose death in the asylum for the insane was another suggestive element. The loneliness and need for companionship of women much left to themselves with the men out at work, the fears of haunting and enchantment associated with desolate places, the danger of madness – these are the imaginative impressions that carried over from 'An Autumn Night in the Hills' to *The Shadow of the Glen*. Nora Burke, in the original folk-tale a traditionally unfaithful wife, became in the setting of the glen a figure of melancholy and deprivation: 'It's in a lonesome place you do have to be talking with someone, and looking for someone, in the evening of the day' (*CW* III 49). The Tramp won't touch Dan's body for fear of the old man's curse – 'I wouldn't lay my hand on him for the Lough Nahanagan and it filled with gold' (*CW* III 35) – and when left alone with the 'corpse' asks for a needle as a talisman: 'there's great safety in a needle' (*CW* III 41). Even Dan Burke, the stock jealous husband, was turned into a creature of his situation: 'He was an old man, and an odd man [...] and it's always up on the hills he was, thinking thoughts in the dark mist' (*CW* III 35).

The most spectacular terror of *The Shadow of the Glen* is the madness and death of Patch Darcy. This too Synge took from a real event, though one quite unconnected with his visit to Glenmalure in 1897. It was in August 1901 on the road from Aughavannagh to Glenmalure that he was told the story which he later recounted in 'The Oppression of the Hills':

Not long ago in a desolate glen in the south of the county I met two policemen driving an ass-cart with a coffin on it, and a little further on I stopped an old man and asked him what had happened.

'This night three weeks,' he said, 'there was a poor fellow below reaping in the glen, and in the evening he had two glasses of whisky with some other lads. Then some excitement took him, and he threw off his clothes and ran away into the hills. There was great rain that night, and I suppose the poor creature lost his way, and was the whole night perishing in the rain and darkness. In the morning they found his naked foot-marks on some mud half a mile above the road, and again where you go up by a big stone. Then there was nothing known of him till last night, when they found his body on the mountain, and it near eaten by the crows.' (*CW* II 209–10)

The facts as recorded in the report of the inquest and the newspaper accounts of it (which Synge may well never have read) make for a more detailed but no less mysterious account.[21] The man was John

Winterbottom, a small farmer who lived with his wife and three young children in Sheeanamore above Aughrim.[22] He left his home early on the morning of Thursday 15 August 1901 to go to work at hay for a Mrs Byrne who lived two miles away. He seems to have drunk a good deal in the course of the day – the local tradition was that a barrel of porter was supplied at a hay-drawing – and by the evening he was 'the worse of drink'. His fellow-workers suggested to Mrs Byrne that 'she should get the car to send him home, but she said he would be able to walk'. The last one witness saw of him he was kneeling in the road outside Mrs Byrne's gate. This was where his clothes were discovered early the next morning, when Mrs Winterbottom went to look for her husband who had not returned home. His body was found a week later, on Thursday 22 August, five miles away from his clothes, on Slievemaan Mountain at Aughavannagh. The body was so disfigured that it could be identified only by a shirt button sewn with black thread on a small piece of shirt left on the body.[23]

The evidence of the inquest leaves much unclear. There was money missing from Winterbottom's clothes, eleven pence of the shilling's wages he had been given by Mrs Byrne, and apparently nowhere that he could have spent it. Different opinions were expressed about his mental state on the day. Mrs Byrne 'considered he was strange in his manner all day at the work, talking to himself'; Joseph Doyle, who worked with him, thought 'there was nothing peculiar about him'. Whether or not John Winterbottom suffered from any more chronic mental disability is equally uncertain in the reports. On the one hand it is said that 'he suffered from paralysis in his side, but there was nothing peculiar considered about him'; on the other, Dr O'Gorman of Aughrim, who 'knew the deceased well ... always thought he was a little peculiar in his mind'. Reports of inquest proceedings in a case like this may well not contain the whole truth and nothing but the truth. According to one family tradition, John Winterbottom was much bullied by his wife and, coming home drunk from the hay-drawing, was shut out of the house by her, and lost his way in the mountains.[24] This would not explain the abandoned clothes or the considerable distance to where the body was found, two of the strangest features of the case, but it suggests that there may have been aspects of the story that did not emerge at the inquest.

Whatever the truth about John Winterbottom and his sad end, Synge transforms him in *The Shadow of the Glen* into the crucial figure of Patch Darcy whom both Nora and the Tramp remember. 'If myself was easily afeard, I'm telling you,' says the Tramp,

it's long ago I'd have been locked into the Richmond Asylum, or maybe have run up into the back hills with nothing on me but an old shirt, and been eaten with crows the like of Patch Darcy – the Lord have mercy on him – in the year that's gone. (*CW* III 37)

Patch had been a close friend of Nora's (suspected by Dan as a lover): 'God spare Darcy, he'd always look in here and he passing up or passing down, and it's very lonesome I was after him a long while' (*CW* III 39). The Tramp praises him to the inadequate Mike Dara as the very type of the hill-shepherd:

That was a great man, young fellow, a great man, I'm telling you. There was never a lamb from his own ewes he wouldn't know before it was marked, and he'd run from this to the city of Dublin, and never catch for his breath. (*CW* III 47)

The terms of the eulogy here, which Synge puts into the mouth of a tinker in the essay 'At a Wicklow Fair' (*CW* II 228), he in fact heard from Willie Coleman, owner of Tomriland, in a conversation about mountain herds (Stephens MS f. 2022). By bringing in this admiring awe of the lowland or foothill farmer for the true 'mountainy man', Synge makes of Patch Darcy a heroic figure whose mad death is associated with his exceptional skills and his life of lonely isolation.

In this metamorphosis of the real-life John Winterbottom into the fictional Patch Darcy, there are a few details suggestive of a literalist strain in Synge's imagination. The Tramp remembers Darcy's death 'in the year that's gone' (*CW* III 37).[25] Winterbottom died in 1901, Synge was writing the play in 1902: he is thus imagining the Tramp in a contemporary present recollecting an event of the actual recent past. The Tramp claims to be the 'last one heard [Darcy's] living voice in the whole world'.

I was passing below on a dark night the like of this night, and the sheep were lying under the ditch and every one of them coughing, and choking, like an old man, with the great rain and the fog ... Then I heard a thing talking – queer talk, you wouldn't believe it at all, and you out of your dreams, – and 'Merciful God,' says I, 'if I begin hearing the like of that voice out of the thick mist, I'm destroyed surely.' Then I run, and I run, and I run, till I was below in Rathvanna. I got drunk that night, I got drunk in the morning, and drunk the day after, – I was coming from the races beyond – and the third day they found Darcy. (*CW* III 39)

'I was coming from the races beyond' – an odd detail that; why should it be included? Maybe as an explanation of why the Tramp had the money to get drunk? But look at the dating. Arklow races, which Synge attended, took place on Thursday 15 August; that was also the day that John Winterbottom went missing. The Tramp is conceived to have walked over from Arklow to Glenmalure (a long walk by most people's standards but not by Synge's), and in the rainy night on the road to Aughavannagh is imagined hearing the voice of the fictional Darcy close to where the real body of Winterbottom was finally found.

In an instance such as this, Synge seems to be re-creating in his play the exact circumstances, the precise location, of a real event. But he is equally prepared to change what is literally authentic if it suits his aesthetic or imaginative purposes. This is especially noticeable with place-names. In the passage just quoted, the Tramp describes how he ran from the voice in the mist 'till I was below in Rathvanna'. If this were Aughavannagh, it would make perfect geographical sense in terms of the actual events of John Winterbottom/Patch Darcy's death, and in an earlier draft of the play, 'Aughavanna' is what Synge originally wrote.[26] It was only at the stage of the final typescript that this was changed to 'Rathvanna', not only here but everywhere the name turned up in the play.[27] There is no such name as Rathvanna in Wicklow, and by the alteration Synge changes a real place into a fictional one. It is very unlikely that the motive here was the discreet disguising of the actual which we come across in the essays. Elsewhere in *The Shadow* he uses all real names – Glen Malure, Glen Imaal, the Seven Churches – which gives to the setting a definite locality. It seems rather that Rathvanna suited the rhythm of his language better, sounded better to his ear, than Aughavannagh, and this was why he made the substitution.[28]

Just as Synge's plays are set somewhere between a fictive and a real world, so they move in and out of real time. When he wrote the fable-like *The Well of the Saints*, set back 'one or more centuries ago', he did not differentiate the life in it from his nominally more modern pieces. In fact, one of the characters of *The Well*, Timmy the Smith, seems to have been suggested by a real blacksmith living in Ballinaclash (where the play is set) in Synge's time. George Smith had a forge in Ballinacarrig, just beside the mill on the Avonbeg river, about half a mile out of Ballinaclash on the road to the Meeting of the Waters. His situation did not correspond to Timmy's in the play insofar as he was an older man (sixty-seven in 1901), with a wife of his own age still alive, and several grown-up children.[29] But it appears likely that the identity of name and trade of George Smith gave Synge the cue for Timmy the Smith, who is so addressed throughout the play. Family surnames frequently derive thus from occupations; Synge imagines a stage in this evolution from 'the smith' to 'Smith'.

In one respect, the real-life George Smith had some affinity with his dramatic counterpart. The story is still told in Ballinaclash of the tinkers' fight in which the tinkers took over the village. The men, who were all away working in the mines, were summoned to defend their homes. It was George Smith, as the story is told, who heated red-hot bars in the forge, and helped to drive the tinkers from the village.[30] Timmy in *The Well* is equally the representative of the settled community in its strength, when he expels the beggar Martin Doul from his forge:

There's your old rubbish now, Martin Doul, and let you take it up, for it's all you have, and walk off through the world, and if ever I meet you coming again, if it's seeing or blind you are itself, I'll bring out the big hammer and hit you a welt with it will leave you easy till the judgement day. (*CW* III 121)

Violence is always potentially there in Synge's plays in the uneasy relationship between tramps, tinkers, beggars on the one hand, and the ordinary rural people on the other. The idea for *The Well* was taken from a fifteenth-century French *moralité* but it was fleshed out with Synge's observations of the Irish country people. It is easy to imagine the initial plot device of the play, the local conspiracy to make the two blind beggars think they are beautiful, as a rough village joke. There is a measure of tolerance and practical charity for the beggars with their disability, but no disguising the social stigma that attaches to them. Molly Byrne, Timmy the Smith's vacuous young fiancée, though she may flirt with Martin, is horrified that a mere beggar like him should seriously offer to make love to her:

Go off now after your wife, and if she beats you again, let you go after the tinker girls is above running the hills, or down among the sluts of the town, and you'll learn one day, maybe, the way a man should speak with a well-reared civil girl the like of me. (*CW* III 123)

When Martin chooses 'a wilful blindness' for himself and Mary, knocking the miraculous water out of the hands of the Saint, the people are appalled at his blasphemous challenge to the orthodoxy by which they live.

PEOPLE [*all together*]. Go on now, Martin Doul. Go on from this place. Let you not be bringing great storms or droughts on us maybe from the power of the Lord. [*Some of them throw things at him.*] (*CW* III 149)

Religion here supports a social status quo, and those who refuse to accept either or both are ultimately at risk of violent expulsion.

The Tinker's Wedding was never produced in Synge's lifetime because it was considered, as he wryly remarked, 'too immoral for Dublin' (*CL* I 148). It was feared that the incident of the priest being bound and gagged by the tinkers would have provoked outrage from the largely Catholic audience of the Abbey Theatre. The preface Synge wrote when the play was finally published in 1907 is defensive in tone:

In the greater part of Ireland [...] the whole people, from the tinkers to the clergy, have still a life, and view of life, that are rich and genial and humorous. I do not think that these country people, who have so much humour themselves, will mind being laughed at without malice, as the people in every country have been laughed at in their own comedies. (*CW* IV 3)

It is hard to imagine that this would have soothed many potentially ruffled feathers. Certainly Synge did well to emend his final sentence, which in an earlier draft read, 'I do not think these country clergy, who have so much humour [...] will mind being laughed at for half an hour without malice, as the clergy in every Roman Catholic country that had real religion were laughed at through the ages' (*CW* IV 3–4). Clearly for Synge the age he lived in, and the country, did not any longer have 'real religion'.

Yet Synge's plays are not truly anti-clerical or anti-Catholic, for all his satiric picture of the hardships of the Priest's life as he complains of them to Mary in *The Tinker's Wedding*:

What would you do if it was the like of myself you were, saying Mass with your mouth dry, and running east and west for a sick call maybe, and hearing the rural people again and they saying their sins? (*CW* IV 19)

Synge, in the Wicklow plays as in his other work, ignores rather than mocks or denigrates the Catholic belief of the people. The opposition between those who conform and those who do not, between the villagers and the vagrants, has its origins in his lapsed Protestantism rather than in any animus against the majority faith. The conflict is secularized insofar as, with the arguable exception of the Saint in *The Well*, there are no serious spokesmen of religious orthodoxy in the plays. What the

Tramp in *The Shadow*, Martin and Mary in *The Well*, and Mary Byrne in *The Tinker's Wedding* stand for is some sort of independent individuality of vision at odds with the social consensus that surrounds them. They are small-p protestants who protest, directly or indirectly, against seeing the world as their neighbours see it.

In this they are Synge's own representatives, for he saw the Wicklow which his imagination needed to see. Authenticity in this context has to be considered an irrelevant or discredited criterion. It obviously mattered to him that his imaginative works were based in the actual, and when criticized for inauthenticity he defended himself against the charge (unwisely as it turned out) in the preface to *The Playboy*. But in the end the imagination has to tell its own stories, however much or little they may correspond to verifiable facts. In the case of Synge and Wicklow, coming from where he did socially, there were areas of the local experience of the time that were not available to him as material for literature or drama: politics, religion, the social revolution of changing landownership. Instead he sought what could be represented as outside or on the edge of these historically conditioned circumstances. The natural world, particularly as it declared itself most essentially in the desolation of the glens, was the defining reality. Those who lived at the boundaries between it and the social community, marginal and alienated, offered figures for ultimate enduring patterns of human experience. The very specificity of the local underwrote the universal, and what Synge could imagine against the background of the desolate Wicklow mountains, inspired by the people he saw living among them, constituted its own form of compelling truth.

R.F. FOSTER

Good Behaviour: Yeats, Synge and Anglo-Irish Etiquette

I

William Butler Yeats and John Millington Synge were thrown together by circumstance, and remain welded by literary history; their relationship, as self and anti-self, has been the subject of intensive analysis.[1] Synge appears to have accepted philosophically Yeats's tendency to turn him into part of the Yeatsian myth, even while he was still alive; after Synge's premature death Yeats's hands (and his imagination) were comparatively untied. Thus, receiving the Nobel Prize in 1923 and talking about the Irish Dramatic Movement, he announced that a 'young man's ghost' should have stood on one side of him, and on the other 'an old woman sinking into the infirmity of age'. At a stroke, he cut out the Fay brothers from the foundation of the Abbey; he prematurely aged Lady Gregory, who still had a good few years ahead; and he claimed Synge. 'I no more foresaw her [Lady Gregory's] genius than I foresaw that of John Synge,' he remarks in *The Trembling of the Veil*; but, in fact, Synge was cast early on for a great role in Yeats's drama of his own life.

The great text of this remaking is, of course, Yeats's essay 'J.M. Synge and the Ireland of his Time'. It was dated September 1910 and appeared, elegiacally, in *The Cutting of an Agate* (1912) but had been begun as a kind of general introduction to Synge's work, and a reflection on the significance of the *Playboy* riots, probably in August 1908 (*CL* II 165n1). It could not appear as the introduction to Synge's posthumously collected works, because of Yeats's disagreement with

41

the family's decision to include work rejected by Synge himself. But publishing it in this form gave Yeats the opportunity to concentrate on the riots that had greeted the first run of *The Playboy of the Western World* in 1907. Thus his preoccupation was the reaction to Synge's work – rather than the work itself – as a vital emblem of the significance not only of Synge but of the Abbey and of Yeats. 'I stood there watching,' he wrote, 'knowing well that I saw the dissolution of a school of patriotism that held sway over my youth.'[2] Significantly it was in this essay too that he published in prose a sort of early draft of 'Easter 1916', in the passage about hearts enchanted to stone by a fixed idea. Thus Synge focused for Yeats all the ambiguity he felt about conventional Irish nationalism.

Yeats's response to the riots provides a key not only to his political and intellectual odyssey, but also to his relationship with Synge. Synge enabled Yeats, in certain ways, to adopt a stance which he had been nervous about beforehand. (Lady Gregory had something of the same effect, but with less bravura.) Both Synge and Yeats mixed hatred and love in their reactions to Ireland, and interrogated themselves about the relative proportions of the two emotions.[3] But there are other keys as well in unlocking the significance of what Synge meant to Yeats. Principally, one might consider what Synge's life, background and demeanour – and what he made of them – meant to Yeats's imaging of his own life. For Yeats's social and psychological insecurities were unconsciously thrown into relief by Synge, in a way that has great significance for Yeats's personal myth.

Certainly, after knowing Synge, Yeats's attitudes to class, family, background and (in a sense) race took a new turn. This can be monitored in the journal he kept in 1909, and later partially published in the long essay mentioned above; and, a few years before, while Synge was still alive, in his preface to *The Well of the Saints*. It is significant that Synge's effect on Yeats goes back to the early 1900s, because it must be read in terms of what Yeats was making of Nietzsche; clear clues lie in phrases Yeats applies to Synge, like 'astringent joy and hardness'.[4] Later on, Yeats's constantly refined image of Synge was put through yet another filter of philosophizing, when he was writing *A Vision*: here we find him trying to create a system of archetypes of human personality, through a sort of do-it-yourself transactional analysis. And here, too, Synge (or Yeats's idea of him) plays a vital part. So through his career Yeats memorialized Synge for his own purposes, building him into his philosophies, invoking him in his speeches, and finally, in the late 1930s, depicting him in the heroic frieze of 'The Municipal Gallery Revisited'. Perhaps the first thing to do is to scrape some of the varnish off that frieze and go back to how they were when they met, in Paris, probably on the 21st of December 1896.

II

Yeats recorded it in a famous passage – often recycled, but worth quoting in the version he published while Synge was still alive.

Six years ago I was staying in a students' hotel in the Latin Quarter, and somebody, whose name I cannot recollect, introduced me to an Irishman, who, even poorer than myself, had taken a room at the top of the house. It was J.M. Synge, and I, who thought I knew the name of every Irishman who was working at literature, had never heard of him. He was a graduate of Trinity College, Dublin, and Trinity College does not, as a rule, produce artistic minds. He told me that he had been living in France and Germany, reading French and German literature, and that he wished to become a writer. He had, however, nothing to show but one or two poems and impressionistic essays, full of that kind of morbidity that has its root in too much brooding over methods of expression, and ways of looking upon life, which come, not out of life, but out of literature, images reflected from mirror to mirror. He had wandered among people whose life is as picturesque as the Middle Ages, playing his fiddle to Italian sailors, and listening to stories in Bavarian woods, but life had cast no light upon his writings. He had learned Irish years ago, but had begun to forget it, for the only literature that interested him was that conventional language of modern poetry which had begun to make us all weary ... I said 'Give up Paris. You will never create anything by reading Racine, and Arthur Symons will always be a better critic of French literature. Go to the Aran Islands. Live there as if you were one of the people themselves; express a life that has never found expression.' (*CW* III 63)

The inaccuracies in this superb sketch have been relentlessly explored.[5] Yeats did not tell Synge to turn away from French things; in fact, he continued to advise him to go in for reviewing French literature. If he did give such advice to Synge when they first met, it was in 1896, not 1899, as this preface claims; though they *were* in Paris together in 1899, Synge by then had been to Aran. On the other hand, Yeats had just discovered Aran in 1896, so would probably (in his characteristic way) have been posing as an authority on it. On 21 June 1898 he wrote to Synge that at Coole they could 'talk about Aran and your work there ... Try if the people remember the names of Aengus &

Mannanan & the like; & if they know anything of the Dundonians as I have heard the De danaans called.'⁶ (He was also much more under Arthur Symons's sway in 1896 than in 1899.) In any case, it has been amply demonstrated that family connections with the island meant that Synge did not need Yeats to tell him about Aran. What should be noted is Yeats's determination to present himself as Synge's tutor; and also the significance of Paris as a meeting-place.

To Yeats, Paris meant a number of things. It signified cosmopolitanism; decadence; occultism as a general practice; and the intoxicating world of Maud Gonne, whose base it was. It also meant the theatre. Here his artistic life had been illuminated by seeing a performance of *Axël*; here too he was present at the first night of *Ubu Roi*. And in 1899 (in *Beltaine*) he had declared that the Irish theatre movement must 'do in Dublin something of what has been done in London and Paris'. France, in his mind, his fiction and his autobiographies, always symbolized various forms of liberation; but, unable to speak French, and deeply conscious of his own limitations, he experienced it through magus-figures like MacGregor Mathers and Maud Gonne. It was no accident that he dropped Symons's name when putting Synge in his place: Symons was his guide to the French Symbolists. For Synge, Paris would also remain important – especially in artistic terms.⁷ But he was far more at home there than Yeats. This was only one of the differences between them – and it was a difference of the sort which Yeats was not keen to emphasize, preferring to stress the quite untrue fact that Synge was 'even poorer' than he was. Let us look at them when they met in 1896.

They were both young, Yeats thirty-one to Synge's twenty-five. Both, obviously, were Irish; both middle-class Protestants, from clerical families. But Yeats's background was an important notch or two down that carefully defined ladder. Synge's ancestors were bishops, while Yeats's were rectors; Synge's had established huge estates and mock castles, while Yeats's drew the rent from small farms and lived in the Dublin suburbs. Yeats had no money, while Synge had a small private income. Yeats had no university education, whereas Synge had been to Trinity, as Yeats noted (in a feline way). Both retained powerful and emotive links to parts of Ireland; but Yeats's roots were with bourgeois business people in Sligo, whereas the Synges remained closely connected to Wicklow country houses and the memory of Glanmore Castle. Synge, in fact, was located in Wicklow and Dublin Protestant society in a way that Yeats, always marginalized by his bohemian background, was not. That Synge reacted against all this is irrelevant. The two shared the sense of growing up in a minority, against a background of lost social influence; but Yeats experienced this at a much more elemental level than Synge did.[8]

Another important difference between them, which reflects upon background and education, is that Synge, for all his unpretentiousness, was really cosmopolitan, whereas Yeats, when they met, was desperately trying to be. Synge was practically bilingual, wrote notebooks in French, translated Villon; Yeats rather bitterly later recalled, 'I have never heard him praise any writer, living or dead, but some old French farce-writer.'[9] That might have been one way in which Synge got a quiet revenge for Yeats's condescension: by invoking a writer whom Yeats could not read. Because for all his readiness to hand down advice, his lordly name-dropping of Symbolist critics, his relationship with Maud Gonne, his links in the romantic world of patriots in exile, his commitments to murky occult and drug-taking circles, Yeats was not quite at ease in Paris. It was the world he tried, clumsily, to evoke in his early unfinished novel, *The Speckled Bird*, which he was working on at this time. 'You wonder why I am in Paris,' he wrote to Robert Bridges on 10 January 1897, '& I can allege no better reason than a novel which I have undertaken to write and which brings its central personage from the Arran [*sic*] Islands to Paris.'[10] The novel delineates the same axis between cosmopolitanism and Gaelicism which he prescribed to Synge. The unsureness of that fragmentary fiction reflects his own unsureness in the world where Maud Gonne and Arthur Symons had swept him. The action swings from fishing-boats tossing off the Galway coast, to half-ruined castles in the west, to occult investigations in the British Museum and the Bibliothèque Nationale, to mysterious encounters with sages and gurus in Paris streets, while half-told loves change shape, renounce and flit by each other in a vague penumbra of signs and symbols. Most of all, it is full of people whom the author tries to make dignified and mysterious, but who rarely quite succeed in bringing it off. Embarrassing as it may be, it is an illuminating approach to Yeats when he was still remaking himself.

Synge, as presented in the famous Yeats quotation, fits into this world – a wandering music student with mystic interests.[11] And Yeats writes of him as if he were a draft character from *The Speckled Bird*, for whom Yeats himself was an all-knowing magus-figure. In fact, their connections in Paris were not so very close. Synge rejected Maud

Gonne's extreme circle round *Irlande Libre*, and his interest in mysticism and the supernatural was very different from the occult incantations of MacGregor Mathers. There were many ways in which mutual suspicion between the two young Irishmen was as likely as mutual sympathy. For one thing, at Trinity, Synge had been a student of Edward Dowden, to whom Yeats was at this time fiercely antipathetic. Again, the Trinity reference in that much-quoted description is relevant here. When they met in the 1890s, Yeats was still deeply sensitive on the subject of Trinity, rarely losing an opportunity to make a gibe at the institution as a repository of the undead, maintaining a suffocating influence on Dublin life through its resolute philistinism. He was determinedly repudiating the assured world of the Dublin haute bourgeoisie, where Synge was objectively located (whether he wanted to be or not).[12]

The two apprentice Irish Protestant bohemians, then, had cause for mutual distrust. And when Yeats used Synge's life as subject for his art (because Yeats's prefaces and autobiographies are nothing if not art), he deliberately abstracted Synge from that background, making him an icon for artistic loneliness, integrity, authenticity and rejection. Some of this is relevant, but it does not fit the Synge known by his family or by Molly Allgood. He was also someone whose art sprang from his life, if not as automatically and directly as his family biographer Ned Stephens thought. But Yeats was determined to show not only that Synge liberated himself from surrounding influences in order to create great art, but also that he, Yeats, had a part in this transformation.

'Placing' his friends in different sections of *A Vision*, he wrote of AE: 'I no more accept his visionary painting, and his visions of "nature spirits", as true to phase, than I accept the gloomy and selfconscious verse and prose of Synge before he learned to write in dialect.'[13] He put Synge in Phase Twenty-three (with Rembrandt, Michelangelo, Balzac and, oddly, Daniel O'Connell), where the creative genius ('CG') was greatest. But 'of all phases, it most misuses its faculties'.[14] And, in an interrogation conducted through his wife's automatic writing, he clarified that for Synge 'Personal life can enter the art but the art is from without'.[15] Synge, it was decided, had to undergo 'an aesthetic transformation, analogous to religious conversion, before he became the audacious joyous ironical man we know'. It was important to Yeats that he himself should have been an agent of that transformation. Synge's qualities and his progress were much in his mind as he tried to pin down the process of creative genius in *A Vision*; he visited the Wicklow

valley of Glenmalure in March 1918, probably because it was where
The Shadow of the Glen was set, at the very time when he and his wife
George were conducting the most intensive automatic-writing sessions.
By then Synge was nearly a decade dead, and the process of his assump-
tion into the Yeatsian heroic frieze was well advanced.

III

What had fixed him there was the great theatrical collaboration with
Yeats and Gregory. It was symbolic – though possibly no more – that
Synge had visited Coole Park in 1899, when he returned to Ireland
from Paris, at the very time when the Irish Literary Theatre was coming
into being; this enabled Gregory to claim he had been there from the
beginning.[16] Though he was an observer, he does not really become a
presence until *The Shadow of the Glen* was produced in 1903; it is the
third volume of Hogan's and Kilroy's indispensable history of Irish
drama, covering the period from 1905, that is called *The Years of
Synge*.[17] In these years, he was at the centre; 'we three always', as
Gregory reminisced to Yeats after his death. In 1905 he was part of the
rather draconian takeover by that triumvirate – though his strategy had
differed from Yeats's, and there were resentments below the surface.[18]
In crises like Marie Walker's alienation from the Fays, Yeats was all for
vehement offensive tactics, while Synge more wisely wanted 'TO LET
THE HARE SIT' (*CL* I 149). Yeats, unheeding, sent Synge dictatorial
letters about the need for someone to take a decisive and 'dangerous'
line, and in the process alienated Walker for good.

Synge said, quite correctly, that Yeats was too impetuous to deal with
the actors; he 'had everything by the wrong end and was quite hostile,
but when I explained everything to him he quite came over ...'.[19] He
takes the same judicious line when writing to Yeats himself ('It would
probably be best for you to come the day before meeting so that
Russell may not have time to fight with you' [*CL* I 161]). He sounds
both older and wiser than Yeats; he also appears more at ease in dealing with people.

This was especially true when they had become – as the actors now
were – employees.[20] It may have been true, as W.G. Fay declared, that
democracy was unworkable in a theatre; and Yeats may have been the
Machiavelli who arranged the change of organizational structure.[21] But

it still was noticeable, and perhaps rather unfortunate, that the three directors were all Ascendancy Protestants. Given the fact that those who seceded from it tended to argue along nationalist lines, and went on to present deliberately nationalist works, the original, reorganized company was inevitably seen as non-'national'.[22] This was probably unfair to Gregory – whatever about Yeats. But thus they were identified. And Synge's close artistic and theatrical connections with Yeats and Gregory rather misrepresented him; as Declan Kiberd has pointed out, up to the time of the *Playboy* riots many of Synge's inclinations were closer to those of the Gaelic League.[23] But he did dislike professional *Gaeilgóirí* and pious chauvinists; and the fact that Yeats had used *The Shadow of the Glen* (among other strategies) to dish James Cousins's play *Sold* set the middle classes against Synge for good.

It is also significant, if hardly surprising, that in their private communications the Abbey triumvirate allowed themselves a certain note of asperity about Catholic pieties – especially evident in Gregory's letters (now in the Berg collection) and Yeats's journal of 1909, by which time he had decided that the 'sense of form … the power of self-conquest, of elevation' were all Protestant characteristics in Irish life. In this, Synge's self-transformation and his artistic discipline were important influences. As for Synge himself, he might allow Christy Mahon to mock Catholic celibacy; but whether he would have subscribed to Yeats's more sweeping theories may be doubted.

And there were other differences between the directors. Gregory never liked *The Playboy,* though she stoutly defended it; she lost few opportunities, in interviews with journalists, of claiming that she had originated the kind of language used by Synge in his plays, and she was not always very supportive. (Witness her comment to Synge the day after the opening of *The Well of the Saints*: 'What happened to you last night? We thought you had committed suicide.'[24]) When it came to Yeats and Synge, she was completely sure whose side she was on: as when she counselled Yeats to refuse to let *The Pot of Broth* be put on with *The Playboy* in 1907. It was, she told Yeats, 'Synge setting fire to your house to roast his own pig'.[25] Nor did she keep these feelings to herself, telling Synge in December 1906 that Yeats's dramatic work 'was more important than any other (you must not be offended at this) as I think it our chief distinction'.[26]

From the other side, Synge admitted Yeats's practical ability, as Stephen MacKenna recalled. 'He had … a curious admiration for Yeats on the practical side of things; he said once Yeats is a genius in bossing carpenters and judging the good qualities of nails and the price of a wooden platform; Synge pined for this power' (*CL* II 135n1). But in terms of day-to-day running of the theatre, Yeats was less admirable as a colleague. Synge recorded sardonically in 1908, 'The Fays left us early in January and since then Yeats and I have been running the show i.e. Yeats looks after the stars and I do the rest' (*CL* II 140). More seriously, Synge increasingly resented Gregory's and Yeats's determination to impose a high proportion of their own plays on to the programme. In 1907, he tells Molly, they show an American producer 'ONE play of mine "Riders", five or six of LG's and several of Yeats. I am raging about it' (*CL* II 316). It should be said that Gregory's undemanding plays were the bread and butter of the repertoire. But to Synge their prominence was a recurrent annoyance, and it made him consider withdrawing his work from the Abbey tours. He resented Yeats's lack of tact, as when he sweepingly dismissed *Riders to the Sea* as 'quite useless for the provincial tours' (*CL* II 38–9). He had distinct reservations about Yeats's plays, and his poetic satire on AE's Celtic art contains some sharp digs at Yeats too.

> Adieu, sweet Angus, Maeve and Fand,
> Ye plumed yet skinny shee
> That poets played with hand-in-hand
> To learn their ecstasy.
>
> We'll stretch in Red Dan Sally's ditch
> And drink in Tubber fair,
> Or poach with Red Dan Philly's bitch
> The badger and the hare. (*CW* I 38)

His target here is the sexlessness of Celtic Twilight views of Irish reality, and a certain strain was put on his relationship with his fellow Ascendancy directors towards the end of his life because of his love affair with the bewitchingly different Molly Allgood – who was, as someone who knew her once remarked, 'the image of Pegeen Mike'. This not only spelt trouble for Gregory's vigorous notion of *noblesse oblige*; it was also in marked (and earthy) contrast to Yeats's relationships with women.

Annie Horniman, who paid the piper, was, in a sense, one of Yeats's women, and she deeply disapproved of Synge; when she tried to detach Yeats from the Abbey and bring him to Manchester and pastures new, it was in her mind to get him away from Synge as well as from Gregory.[27] In December 1906, when Yeats was trying to keep Horniman well disposed by manoeuvring William Fay into a different (and subordinate) position, Synge took a very contrary line.[28] Horniman told Yeats on 31 December: 'Over and over again the road has forked before you; at this moment Fay, in the form of Mr Synge, points one way, and I and your interests point in the other.'[29] To her credit, she supported *The Playboy* when the storm over it broke a couple of weeks later; though she continued to bombard Synge with abusive letters on yellow paper. (He said mournfully that he could never look on daffodils with any pleasure again. When he died, in the cold spring of 1909, Yeats remembered this as he walked to the graveside, and noticed Annie Horniman's floral tribute: a large wreath of daffodils.)

Despite these pressures and resentments, the triumvirate of directors stuck to each other; and even after Synge's shattering death, his theatrical presence remained. In 1915 Yeats said: 'Synge has left us a glorious heritage, and I have worked to make the theatre a Synge theatre.'[30] This did both of them justice. He had even, evidently, decided that *Riders to the Sea* was possible for provincial tours after all.

IV

To be fair, Yeats had long hailed Synge as a dramatic genius; and he was right. But there were several reasons why Synge's work spoke so powerfully to Yeats, and some of the most interesting of them concern qualities other than literary merit. For one thing, it provided, like folklore, a way into Irishness: a purchase upon native tradition. Part of the appeal of folklore, for Gregory, Hyde and O'Grady as well, was that through its study you could demonstrate and claim 'Irishness' at the very time when this was being defined more and more restrictively.[31] Synge revealingly put his discovery of Ireland as a substitute for a lost Protestant religion. 'Soon after I had relinquished the Kingdom of God I began to take a real interest in the Kingdom of Ireland. My patriotism went round from a vigorous and unreasoning loyalty to a temperate nationalism and everything Irish became sacred.'[32] His conflation of 'Protestantism' with 'loyalty' (meaning 'loyalism') is important: it indicates an automatic identification between political culture and religious belief, always a close identification for conventional Irish Protestants. (Lily Yeats was told by the Dean of St Patrick's that a mutual acquaintance 'has no religion but is an out-and-out Protestant in everything else'.[33]) But even a Protestant who had lost his religion was still a Protestant in other, Irish ways; at least in the beady perceptions of the Arthur Griffiths and D.P. Morans of the world. Yeats too had found this, to his cost. For him, and possibly also for Synge, the discovery of the 'folk' and explorations of 'the people' in their 'unspoiled' mode went with a contempt for the new middle classes – expressed early on by Yeats in his antipathy to the plays of Boyle and Cousins, and articulated by Synge in his much-quoted letter to Stephen MacKenna after his western tour with Jack Yeats.[34] Such attitudes crystallized for both men after the *Playboy* riots; but, in a way, they were always implicitly there.

For Yeats, Synge was from the time of his first Abbey play sanctified as an Irish hero. For one thing, he had become 'baptized of the gutter', and set himself against his class, as Yeats had decreed must be done in the first issue of *Samhain*. (This went with the fellowship of bohemianism.) But what really accomplished his canonization was the *Playboy* riots. For this demonstrated that Synge, having given himself to the people, was turned on by the pack, and died prematurely. Yeats had already noted Goethe's remark that Irish Catholics always seemed to him like a pack of hounds, dragging down some noble stag – though he tended to drop the word 'Catholics' and read it as 'Irish' (as well as strategically forgetting that the reflection was inspired by O'Connell). And this interpretation of Synge linked him very powerfully with the figure already coming to prominence in the iconography of Yeats's imagination as the emblem of Irish nobility: Parnell. Another rebel from the Wicklow Protestant Ascendancy, torn down by the common people in the name of Catholic morality, after a career spent trying to elevate their cause. For Yeats, the death of Synge (like the death of Parnell) became central to his energy and his vision, and part of his politics. When he describes Synge in the nursing-home turning around and saying 'it is no use fighting death any longer',[35] the adversary is, for Yeats, not so much Hodgkin's Disease as the forces of outraged middle-class Irish philistinism. The circumstances of Synge's death were reinterpreted by Yeats to put him in the category of Parnell, Wilde and Casement.[36]

This was because Yeats had, in a sense, fitted out Synge for the part since the first controversies aroused by his work. The attack on *The*

Shadow of the Glen was a vital part of this process, since it was led by William Martin Murphy, the traducer of Parnell. Yeats's great polemic on the subject, entitled 'The National Theatre and Three Sorts of Ignorance', made the connection practically specific. It was also an important stage in the development of Yeats's idea that Irish national-ist politics might be corrupted through anti-intellectualism. 'Extreme politics in Ireland were once the politics of intellectual freedom also, but now, under the influence of a violent contemporary paper, and other influences more difficult to follow, even extreme politics seem about to unite themselves to hatred of ideas.' The figure of Cuchulain in *On Baile's Strand* was specifically linked by Yeats to Parnell;[37] and Synge is in there too. His work and the reaction to it had crystallized Yeats's idea of Parnell as 'that lonely and haughty person below whose tragic shadow we of modern Ireland began to write';[38] these qualities were applied to Synge as well, along with the images of passion, and of an aristocratic will to serve the people – cruelly repaid. It is significant that Yeats's epigram, 'On those that hated *The Playboy of the Western World*', written at the same time as his preface to Synge's poems, used the image of Don Juan in Hell – again, a Parnellite image. And it is from the time of the *Playboy* riots that Yeats began frequently invoking Parnell in interviews and reflections.[39]

An important aspect of this Parnellite archetype was that 'the people', implicitly, had proved themselves unworthy of the hero; thus Synge, in Yeats's view, knew better than his audience, and was in a sense too good for them. This is hinted at in an interview Yeats gave to a newspaper in 1909, at the time of the crisis over Shaw's controversial play *The Shewing-Up of Blanco Posnet*. Yeats compared Shaw's work with that of Synge. The satire of Blanco Posnet, he said, was directly comprehensible and therefore not offensive (Yeats always enjoyed putting down Shaw); but

Synge's work, on the other hand, is precisely the work that is dangerous with an Irish audience. It is very hard to understand, and, therefore, the very desire to do so makes them impatient with it. They have gradually come to know what he means, and to accept his work without resentment. But it has been a long fight. To him everything was capricious and temperamental, and he could not tell his secret quickly.[40]

For Yeats, then, Synge became (like Parnell) the figure of a great gentleman. In other ways too his Ascendancy aura was subtly stressed. The asperity in his character was Swiftian; and he was a solitary, like

Swift and Berkeley, seeking solitude 'as befits scattered men in an ignorant country'.[41] Thus Synge played a part in Yeats's evolving theory of
aristocracy. It is significant that Yeats's Italian journey with the
Gregorys in 1907 was taken in the aftermath of the *Playboy* riots – in
fact, as a sort of convalescence from that excitement. For it was on this
journey that he discovered Castiglione, Urbino, and the idea of noble
discourse in culture and aristocratic patronage of the arts which he later
applied, ludicrously but effectively, to eighteenth-century Ireland.

What Synge was coming to represent to him was the uncompro-
mising attitude that went with elite authority tempered by good manners: always an Anglo-Irish preoccupation.[42] Oddly, Synge also
preached the importance of manners in his letters to Molly, and 'wearing a sort of masque after a while, which is rather a needful trick' (*CL*
I 351); though Yeats was not to know that Synge also told her 'people
like Yeats who sneer at oldfashioned goodness and steadiness in women
seem to want to rob the world of what is most sacred in it' (*CL* II 22).
And in manners, too, Yeats knew Synge had an enviable edge over him.
He was not only able to speak French, but he could relate easily to the
lower classes (including actors) in a way Yeats could not: he could keep
his temper, and hold his counsel, which Yeats never managed. This
stemmed from insecurity – whereas Synge could unaffectedly fall in
love with Molly Allgood, one of Yeats's arguments to Maud Gonne
against marrying John MacBride was that she would lower herself
socially by doing so.[43] As Max Beerbohm remarked when reviewing *The
Shadow of the Glen*, Synge possessed an incapacity to be vulgar. The way
he struck a visiting Australian in 1904 was exactly as Yeats himself
longed to appear. 'He was full of race and good breeding, courteous,
sensitive, sincere ... a simple man; but there was something strange and
alluring about him, an indescribable charm expressed in his voice and
manner, and, above all, in his curious smile that was at the same time
ironic and sympathetic' (*CL* I 84 n.1). Again, this recalls an idealized
figure from *The Speckled Bird*; or, indeed, John Morley's description of
Parnell: 'Uniformly considerate, unaffectedly courteous, not ungenial,
compliant rather than offensive. In ordinary conversation he was pleasant, without much play of mind; temperament made him the least discursive of the human race.'[44]

Yeats read and marked this description; like the Australian's portrait
of Synge, it evoked a great gentleman. And Yeats knew it described
qualities he did not have. He was not unaffected, not considerate, not

compliant, not controlled; his temperament made him the *most* discursive of the human race. He feared in himself his own tendencies to vulgarity – his hysterical overreactions, his agonized self-examination, his obsessive insecurities. All these qualities he tried to school out of himself.[45] Much later, in 'Coole Park, 1929', he remembered how he 'ruffled in a manly pose/For all his timid heart', and put this in immediate apposition to Synge's 'slow and meditative' qualities. Ironically, this undemonstrative, detached quality of Synge's was something that Yeats 'in real life' often resented, as did Augusta Gregory. After Synge's death they privately commiserated with each other over the way he never complimented them or their work. 'I have often envied him his absorption,' Yeats wrote, adding mysteriously, 'as I have envied Verlaine his vice.' Maybe he meant that both were mechanisms for blocking out the distracting world, which was always too much with him.

Synge, however, could remove himself through a certain aristocratic discipline, like Parnell; and this became Yeats's ideal, and influenced his half-envious, half-affectionate view of the younger playwright. Synge's influence, like Parnell's, matured in Yeats's mind and his work. A Synge-like voice emerged in the Crazy Jane poems – their rhythm as well as their content. It is echoed in *Purgatory* (where the references to the old man's son being born from a tumble with a tinker girl in a ditch recall a controversial exchange in the first version of *The Well of the Saints*). The conflation of myth and bawdy realism in Yeats's late work recalls poems of Synge's like 'Queens'; and what Yeats called Synge's 'hunger for harsh facts, for ugly surprising things' (*CW* I xxxiv) has direct relevance to his own work throughout the 1930s. It went back to what W.J. Lawrence in 1907 had interpreted as 'the Swift-like horror of humanity that renders so much of the work of the Irish National Theatre Society repulsive'.[46] (This was in contrast to the wholesomeness of the Ulster Literary Theatre.) By 1930, when Swift had joined Parnell, Synge, Wilde, Casement and Berkeley in Yeats's Ascendancy gallery, this endorsement was exactly what he wanted. Synge had contributed this element early on – which we nowadays see as a celebration rather than a horror of 'humanity'. It continued to represent for Yeats something admirable, with which his own dramatic work never quite connected. So, on a wider level, personally and psychologically, did Synge himself.

As a coda, some reflections about fishing. This was one of the things that Synge did most, and did best. It is beautifully caught in Ned Stephens's evocative description of fishing with his uncle:

We usually went to Annamoe bridge and each fished alternate pools as we went down the river past the rectory. John carried his old brown rod, which used to lie against the chimney-piece in the back drawing-room, as he did not trouble to take it down unless we were going to fish at a distance. He had an old leather fly book in his pocket, a spare cast round his hat, and a fish basket on his back, but he used no other equipment. The trout in the Annamoe river were not so large as to make a landing net necessary and John never thought of waders. He wore his usual knickerbockers, home-knit stockings, and strong shoes and was quite indifferent as to whether he walked on the bank or in the water. I often watched him excited and intent, standing with his feet firmly set apart among slippery stones and crouching slightly while he watched cast after cast on the end of a rapid as it slid in decreasing waves to calm in a deep pool.

When it was too dark to see our tackle we walked home, often in silence except for the measured squelch of water from John's shoes. It was pleasant to slide fish out of his basket when we reached home and lay them evenly on a plate under the lamp. I caught very few, but John said that the gift for catching fish would come to me with practice and would seem to come quite suddenly ...[47]

Fishing is a matter of sensitivity – especially trout-fishing. It needs leisure and skill; it sets the countryman apart. This means that it is often taken as an index of gentlemanly status, although this can be over-interpreted. There is a striking passage in the Irish critic Denis Donoghue's memoir, *Warrenpoint*, where he describes being, as he thought, condescended to in Cambridge by the Anglo-Irish scholar Tom Henn. Henn told Donoghue, then a gauche young lecturer, that he was off to the ancestral home in Clare to fish. Donoghue inquired whether he would catch salmon. Henn said yes, he expected to 'kill' some salmon. Donoghue, decades afterwards, agonized at the correction, the condescension, the pulling of rank which he read into this exchange.[48] In fact, it is simply a country usage, derived directly from the Gaelic: the condescension is that of the countryman to the townsman, not, as Donoghue thought, the Anglo-Irish Protestant to the working-class Catholic. But it demonstrates the sensitivity of the question.

Yeats would have loved to be able to fish. He posed as a fisherman at Coole, writing with elaborate casualness about going out to fish, and was described by fellow guests as arraying himself in full and magnificent costume (including a sky-blue mackintosh). He wrote of trout-fishing as an image of solitude and disdain ('And maybe I shall take a trout/If but I do not seem to care'[49]); it was also, quintessentially, a gentleman's pursuit and a gentleman's skill. Unfortunately, in the marshy lakes of Coole, all he could pursue were plebeian pike. But staying there with his new wife in 1918, he was still trying. He attempted to impress

her by suggesting they go mayfly-fishing for trout. They struggled to a
stream with their equipment, where it slowly became clear that he had
no idea what to do next. Finally he gestured vaguely at the cloud of
summer insects darting above the water and asked her helplessly which,
she supposed, might be the mayfly? This ignorance revealed, they abandoned fishing, sat on the bank, and he told her about Florence Farr's
love-life instead. They probably both preferred this.

But he still wished he could fish. A few years before, he had thought
of Synge, already abstracted into a pure Ascendancy icon, when he was
writing 'The Fisherman'.[50] Both Henn and Nicholas Grene have drawn
attention to Synge's presence in that poem as 'The dead man that I
loved'; he is compared implicitly to the hangers-on of Dublin pub culture who now pass for literary figures. But he is also suggested by the
central image of the confident, skilled, solitary fisherman, in his

> … grey Connemara cloth,
> Climbing up to a place
> Where stone is dark under froth,
> And the down-turn of his wrist
> When the flies drop in the stream;
> A man who does not exist,
> A man who is but a dream …[51]

Synge was still in Yeats's mind when in 1930 he called on the Swift/
Berkeley/Burke tradition whose task was to 'preserve that which is
living and help the two Irelands, Gaelic Ireland and Anglo-Ireland, so
to unite that neither shall shed its pride'.[52] Synge also came from an
eighteenth-century tradition of intellectual toleration and Protestant
elitism; and he had his part to play in the celebration of Gaelic Ireland.
This, in a way, is what 'The Fisherman' was about: and it was also about
Yeats's despairing aspiration to play such a part himself. It shows us,
too, how in the forty years since their Paris meeting Yeats (who had
then posed as Synge's mentor) reversed their positions. He had made
Synge a mentor and an inspiration for himself – utterly different from
the seedy magus-figures of his Paris period but, in some ways, just as
unreal an idealization. And, like those figures, his image of Synge was
necessitated by the insecurity which accompanied Yeats's own genius;
and which, for all his efforts, stayed with him throughout his life.

FRANK McGUINNESS

John Millington Synge and the King of Norway

Synge learned his literary politics from a supreme and dangerous tac-
tician of the game, W.B. Yeats. The author's preface to *The Playboy
of the Western World* is an admirably ingenious manifesto, implicating
Synge profoundly in the forging of a national language, a notional language, neatly deflecting the charges of condescension and betrayal that
would attend the play in performance. Synge outlines that from Mayo
to Kerry to Dublin, Geesala to Carraroe to Dingle Bay, here is the language of his people, preserved in his play, the Gaelic names of the
townlands themselves resonating strangely through the confident
English of the text, echoing a past that in its 'wildest sayings and ideas'
finds parallel only in the writings of 'the Elizabethan dramatist'. This
beautifully, but cunningly, marries the two traditions of Celt and Saxon,
and the benevolent matchmaker is J.M. Synge himself. Read thus, the
preface is one of the most astonishing pieces of cultural self-promotion
ever produced, surely worthy of Yeats's star pupil. It prompts only one
interesting question: what was he hiding?

*

The preface is a magnificent piece of self-promotion for it is an even
more magnificent piece of self-denial. Synge presents himself as a writer
possessed by historical voices, both naïve and native, innocent in a
world that they know by instinct. A communal conscience and character emerge through the language of the text, identifying, removing the

tangential, creating a spokesman for that communal conscience. Joyce rightly feared Synge. Here was the real rival in the fight to the death. It is still debatable as to who won, for in the literary history of this country there is one corner that is forever Ireland, and you will find it through 'a chink in the floor of the old Wicklow house where I was staying, that let me hear what was being said by the servant girls in the kitchen'.

Servants in the kitchen, a chink in the floor. The Japanese believed in the gods beneath our feet. But Wicklow is not Japan, so what was beneath Synge's feet that he so passionately, truly believed? Projecting himself forward as the voice of the people may have caused confusion, and it is possible that in hearing this voice he may instead have been hearing his own. The preface is an assertion of a tradition. It seeks to provide a critical guide for the reading of Synge's writing, giving to that writing an ecstatic celebration of 'striking and beautiful phrases' and a visionary warning that such celebration will soon end, since, 'In Ireland, for a few years more, we have a popular imagination that is fiery and magnificent, and tender ...'.

Synge makes for himself a mystical role, and while that intense love of life, the poignant simplicity of that 'few years more' in the light of his coming death, can imbue the preface with an almost unbearable sorrow, we are dealing here with propaganda, not poetry. In Synge's plays sanctity is there to be rejected. The blind, eventually, cherish the blind. To hell with blessings. Such delicate sourness does not, unfortunately, distinguish the preface. 'In a good play every speech should be as fully flavoured as a nut or an apple', and in Synge's great plays he serves up rancid nuts and rotten apples cultivated by his characters. In the preface Synge absolves himself and blesses his audience. It is a comfort, but it is also a charade. And he knew it, a little. Condemnation in the preface is confined to foreign writers, Mallarmé, Huysmans, with their sonnets, prose poems, elaborate books, and Zola, 'dealing with the reality of life in joyless and pallid works'. One other name is added, casually, astonishingly, to the list of the condemned. Ibsen.

Joyce consistently paid full homage to Ibsen, but he was a novelist, and perhaps the surest proof of this is his play *Exiles*. Brilliantly written to formula, the gilded cage of its construction weighs it down. Joyce had learned everything from Ibsen's theatre apart from terror. I am not denigrating *Exiles*. It is an excellent first play, and Joyce's abandonment of drama is beyond question the twentieth-century theatre's, or more correctly perhaps, cinema's loss. And yet as a piece of theatre, it stands inferior in its potential, in its prophetic signs of what is to come, to another apprentice piece by another writer, proving therein that writer's debt to Ibsen. The writer is Synge; the play is *When the Moon Has Set*. His reluctance to discard this unfinished shard, his desire to see it published, these may be interpreted in various ways, but I'd like to think that at least it was an acknowledgement of, or even an apology to, Ibsen.

In her exemplary edition of Synge's plays Ann Saddlemyer suggestively pinpoints a related passage to the play from Synge's essay 'A Landlord's Garden in County Wicklow': 'The desolation of this life is often of a peculiarly local kind, and if a playwright chose to go through the Irish country houses he would find material, it is likely, for many gloomy plays that would turn on the dying away of these old families, and on the lives of the one or two delicate girls that are left so often to represent a dozen hearty men who were alive a generation or two ago.'

This, in nearly all its particulars, is a description of the setting for Ibsen's play *Rosmersholm*, the home of the family Rosmer. Great men, prominent men, the Rosmers have controlled their district. They are civil servants, clerics, military men. From every wall their portraits stare upon the living. This is a haunted, or in Synge's terminology, lonesome space. White horses appear at times at Rosmersholm, and they signal the arrival of death. A family servant, Mrs Helseth, is the source of this supernatural knowledge. The present owner of Rosmersholm, John Rosmer, is a widower. His late wife Beata had sunk into madness and drowned herself. Before her death Beata had been attended by a young woman, Rebekka West, who now lives in platonic harmony with Rosmer. Their union troubles the more reactionary elements of society, for a fierce intellectual war is raging between the conservative and liberal parties. The inheritor of conformist ideology, Rosmer, under Rebekka's influence, joins the liberal side. He proposes marriage to Rebekka. Astonishing herself, she refuses. She feels the pull of the dead. Beata has committed suicide at her bidding. Rosmer asks Rebekka to do the same. She agrees, they make a pact of death, and both drown, watched by Mrs Helseth, who sees the white horses, wrapped in Rebekka's white shawl, observed by the living dead of Rosmersholm. Prior to the suicide, Rosmer has been visited by a former teacher, now a half-mad philosopher, Brendl, who in his strange images ultimately urges the pair of repressed lovers to action.

This, in skeletal outline, is what happens in *Rosmersholm*, where the dead spill out the secrets of the living, as they do to tragic effect in the drownings of *Riders to the Sea* and to comic effect in the resurrection of Old Mahon in *The Playboy of the Western World*. But the first strong connection between Ibsen's play and *When the Moon Has Set* is the big house, the sinister portrait, and the visit of madness. Neither Ibsen nor Synge is alone in these theatrical images. From the Greeks we inherit the stage as a place of strange plague. The dangerous portrait is in a direct line from the poisonous skulls of Jacobean drama. Since Shakespeare, madness is second nature to all European playwrights. In placing *When the Moon Has Set* beside *Rosmersholm* I am not positing the former as a pale copy of the latter. Rather it is as if Ibsen himself has visited Synge's dramatic imagination in the manner of the dead clinging to that house of *Rosmersholm*, shaping the interior designs, conveying a manner of telling the tale that goes beyond the expositions of the living – the recurrent motif of Ibsen's text is 'let us sit and talk'. This theatre encourages instead whisperings beyond the grave where dead souls and past selves conspire to control the future. It seeks to confront its characters with the shock of the old.

The Protestant furies pursuing the lapsed clergyman John Rosmer and the freethinking Rebekka West will ensure that this John is no beloved disciple nor that this Rebekka be mother to a new chosen tribe. The curse of childlessness that befell Rosmer and his wife increases in biblical wrath to take the lives of the lovers. They stand alone before their makers and are found wanting by them, even if they die together as a last act of heroic daring, obtaining at the last the all-consuming courage of the Viking sagas, pitting a pagan indifference against Christian scruple and orthodoxy. The marriage ceremony conducted privately between Rebekka and Rosmer might also be blessed by the ritual that ends *When the Moon Has Set*: 'We have incarnated God, and been a part of the world. That is enough. In the name of the Summer, and the Sun, and the Whole World, I wed you as my wife.' The fundamental opposition between the lovers of the two plays is that if Rosmer and Rebekka love to death, then Colm and Eileen in Synge's play love to life. Synge struggles through the play to release a spirit of affirmation, as if in defying the story of the dead old man in the bed, he and his characters will defy the powerful influence that controls the creation of the play itself.

The ironic reversals of detail between the plays have about them a calculated haphazardness that points to anxiety. In one line deleted from *When the Moon Has Set* the game gives itself perfectly away: 'I suppose it is a good thing that this aristocracy is dying out. They were neither human nor divine.' Then what are they? Malignant forces, deciding the fates of those after them, composing dirges to themselves, demanding power over what's past and present and to come? Ibsen pitted the pagan against the Protestant. Synge cleverly confuses the Catholic with the Protestant, rejecting the sterility of their implacable opposition, depriving both of any spiritual energy, seeking to create instead a new communion of saints. He christens the characters of this new morality with the names of ancient holy men and women – Colm from Columba, Bride from Bridget – and Eileen from Eibhlín will be a new redeemed Eve, fertile mother of a race liberated from sin as she liberates herself from her nun's vows of chastity: 'I have left my veil in the room where your uncle is lying … I seem to be in a dream that is wider than I am. I hope God will forgive me. I cannot help it.' The past will be buried, the dead defeated, or rather, silenced.

In escaping the sorrowful destiny of the mad virgin Mary, a Costello of Spanish descent who was reared with the nuns and rejected sexual passion with Colm's dead uncle, Eileen frees herself from moral tyranny. Rebekka walks into the mill race just as Nora in *A Doll's House* walks away from her husband Torvald – believing herself to be a free spirit. Eileen differs from these women in one great respect. She is still utterly under the tyranny of men. And this is why *When the Moon Has Set* does not take flight. The desire to soar is too great to succeed.

Yeats saw it as a blemish on the perfect body of Synge's work. The need to establish Synge's genius and the meshing of that genius to the National Theatre required this work's early exclusion from the collected plays. These decisions are understandable, but it is surely time to insist on the play's rightful place in the Synge canon, and even to argue a case for it being perhaps the crucial text in Synge's development as a writer. The careful and cunning rewriting of the play, the concentrating of its two acts into a single speed of action, the glorious creation of Mary Costello, all indicate the increasing power of the playwright, a power not least signalled by the capacity, the maturity to abandon it unfinished. At its final stage of composition it had served its purpose. A productive exercising of the muscles, it contained sufficient effort to feed and develop plays yet to come. It also spelt the end of Ibsen's obvious influence. The formulae of the well-made play, the swerves from naturalism to symbolism, the restrained schemes of character, they have been tried, tested and failed. Mary's great cry for her unborn children will be transformed:

I was afeard it was my little children – for if I was never married your honour, and have no children I do be thinking it's alive they must be if I never had them itself ... There are five children, five children that wanted to live, God help them, if the nuns and priests with them had left them be ... They're always nice your honour, with clean faces, and nice frocks on them, and little sticks in their hands. But I wouldn't like them to begin to die on me, for I'm not like the rest of you ... and it's queer things I do be seeing the time the moon is full.

It will of course turn into Maurya's universal and particular lament at the end of *Riders to the Sea*. The idyllic marriage of Colm and Eileen will give way to the violent marriage of Martin and Mary Doul, the aborted marriage of Pegeen and Christy and the broken marriage of Deirdre and Naisi. Eileen shares two characteristics with Rebekka West. She prettifies the house, being 'clever with her fingers', and in both plays it is the maid who laments the young woman's leaving with almost similar sentiments: 'It's lonesome you'll be leaving the lot of us behind you, and you after bringing a kind of a new life into this house was a dark quiet place for a score of years, and will be dark again maybe from this mortal night.' Mrs Helseth in *Rosmersholm* pleads with Rebekka to stay in similar manner, for the sake of John Rosmer. But Synge's women are to grow in stature, for he heard the great cry of pain that is at the very heart of *Rosmersholm*, and acted accordingly. At one stage of the play Mrs Helseth, after underlining how there are no children at Rosmersholm, asks Rebekka if she has ever heard Rosmer laugh. Rebekka slyly replies that people don't laugh much in these parts. It is an observation with which Rosmer concurs. He defends his conversion to liberalism with the pained self-accusation that he and his ancestors have systematically, consciously, killed joy in this district. It is joy that he longs for, that desire now controlling his life.

That passionate desire, that energetic longing, propels the imaginative journey of many of Ibsen's later plays. It is as if in joy there lies a lost language of magic, of marvels, a language where, to return to Synge's preface, 'the imagination of the people and the language they use, is rich and living, [and] it is possible for a writer to be rich and copious in his words, and at the same time to give the reality which is the root of all poetry, in a comprehensive and natural form.' The ageing Ibsen laments the loss of his first love, poetry. Remember his plaintive protest, 'I am more of a poet than a social commentator.' The young Synge hears the sigh of the haunted Ibsen. The older man is searching for a lost youth, the younger is searching for a lost race. They are hampered by the obstacles that in truth neither such youth nor such a race ever existed. However, a writer's ambitions were never thwarted by such fantasies as the truth, and so Synge's reply to Ibsen's request is *The Playboy of the Western World*.

At first glance *Peer Gynt* might be said to satisfy Synge's criteria for a theatre of 'wildest sayings and ideas', particularly in its first three acts. Words erupt from the mouth of Peer, spinning his yarns, weaving his fantasies, believing his own lies. He sees himself as 'master of all fights', is heedless to his standing as village idiot, and above all, when he talks to himself does so with a conviction and intensity that bear no mark of self-consciousness. In short, Peer Gynt is arrogant, articulate and alone. He is a perfect counterpart to Pegeen Mike. They share a snobbishness of extraordinary proportions. Peer revels in the pride of being John Gynt's son, a man who has drunk his prosperity dry. This pride gives an edge to his fantasies, making them his biological as much as his imaginative right. His dreams are letters to himself, formally addressed to the Emperor Peer. Pegeen begins *The Playboy of the Western World* writing a letter, talking to herself, revealing herself to us. What does the letter tell? It tells of preparations, preparations for plenty. There are signs of celebration, a yellow gown, a fine pair of boots, and a hat, 'suited for a wedding day'. A wedding, a bride and groom, the sacrament of human love. The letter then in its subtext speaks of love, and where or to whom is this love to be sent? It is sent to the sender, to Pegeen Mike herself, very much introducing herself as her father's daughter, as Peer is his father's son, for this is Margaret Flaherty, the woman of her father's house.

In the play's opening scene Synge presents his actor with an irresistible yet intimidating invitation to play – to play, as Peer Gynt plays, with a conflicting mixture of self-assertion, subtly, imperceptibly almost, qualified by a sense of repression. The finery of gown and boots, hat and tooth-comb gives way to more mundane matters, 'three barrels of porter in Jimmy Farrell's creel cart', porter in that amount only coming to a shebeen, premises of Mister Michael James Flaherty. A woman prepares for marriage sitting in her father's place of business. Love and money go hand in hand, and they are accompanied by fear, with the arrival of the timid rabbit, Shawn Keogh, scared of his own shadow, and even more scared of Pegeen's.

Theirs is a world of shadows, his and Pegeen's, and in the shadowy hinterland beyond the stage a wake takes place, Kate Cassidy's. A wedding and a funeral wait in the wings of *The Playboy of the Western World*, preparing us for gains and losses, speeches and silencings. Love, money, fear, a wedding and a funeral – these obsessions link *The Playboy* and the opening acts of *Peer Gynt*, Peer's early career commencing as it does with the theft of the bride, Ingrid, and concluding in Act Three with the death of his mother's Åse, a death that is also the end of young Peer. Like Peer, Christy will attempt to steal a bride. Like Peer, he will receive the attentions of country girls. Like Peer, he will set out to conquer the world. But we will never know how he ends. Peer ends defeated. A sense of utter loss informs *Peer Gynt*. And *The Playboy* ends with Pegeen's terrible cry of grief: 'I've lost him surely. I've lost the only playboy of the western world.' Christy may then share sexual and semantic natures with Peer Gynt, but Pegeen is his kindred spirit, for they are in a pain that only the poetry of self-recognition can identify.

To match the terror of Pegeen's last keen for herself and her life, Peer addresses a falling star:

> Brother star, greetings from Peer Gynt.
> We're light, we dim, we die in darkness.
> Is there none out there,
> Not one in the whole multitude,
> Not one in the pit, none in heaven?
> Poor soul, go back to nothing,
> Vanish into mist.
> Earth, full of wonders, forgive
> That I tramped your grass in vain.
> Sun, full of wonder, you've wasted your light
> Touching a house whose owner was never home.
> Earth, and Sun, most beautiful,
> Why did you shine at my mother's birth?
> Spirit mean and nature wasteful,
> It is rough to pay for your birth
> With the price of your life.
> Let me rise to the highest peak.
> I want to see the sun rise again.
> I want to look on the promised land
> Until I am tired. I will see to it

> That snow drifts over me. Write above it,
> No one lives here. Afterwards – afterwards –
> Let life go on its own way.

Synge ends his play on Pegeen's despair. Ibsen lets Peer lie down to sleep and dream again in the arms of his lost love, Solveig:

> My own soft boy, sleep and sleep,
> My hand's my eyes to wean and see.
>
> The boy sat on his mother's knee,
> The two played through life's long sleep.
>
> The boy drank from his mother's breast,
> In life's long sleep, God grant him joy.
>
> The boy did breathe his mother's breath,
> Through life's long sleep, my tired boy.
>
> My own soft boy, sleep and sleep,
> My hand's my eyes to wean and see.
>
> My hand's my eyes to see and wean,
> My own soft boy, sleep and dream.

By the time of composing *Rosmersholm*, with its double suicide, Ibsen had come a long way in his depiction of heterosexual love and its destructiveness. By the time of writing *The Playboy of the Western World* Synge had come a long way from the fragile Sister Eileen in his understanding of heterosexual women and their loneliness. Ibsen had most effectively revolutionized European theatre by the moral, political and, in pure acting terms, technical demands he had made of women. Synge benefited from him there, beyond question. He also ultimately benefited from the sheer span of Ibsen's achievement, giving as it did to theatre a restored sense of its own danger and daring, confronting and challenging the most passionately held beliefs of the society it serves to subvert. The pious propaganda in awe of the Irish peasantry is of course shattered by the savagery of the actual play. Wild sayings and ideas, striking and beautiful phrases, give way to the primal force of a dirty deed.

Revenge triumphs over romance. Loss is the consequence of love. A scream ends the sweet mouthings. Synge, like Ibsen, is a true poet of the theatre for he realized the silence that lies at the heart of darkness, and spoke it on the stage.

*

'Afterwards – afterwards –/Let life go on its way'; the year after Ibsen's death at the eastern corner of Europe, came a play located in a western corner that revitalized Irish drama after the tragic death of Wilde. Did Synge know the scale of his achievement? Early on in *The Playboy of the Western World* Christy is belittling his story, and Pegeen, that Irish Hedda, complains revealingly, encouragingly, irresistibly, 'And I thinking you should have been living the like of a king of Norway or the Eastern world.' That is the way with kings. It takes one to know one, be he of the eastern or western world.

ANGELA BOURKE

Keening as Theatre: J.M. Synge and the Irish Lament Tradition

When John Millington Synge died in 1909 at the age of thirty-eight, his six plays remained as a deeply original contribution to the European theatre. He had also given the history of theatre one of its enduring images: the keening woman, lamenter of the dead. In *Riders to the Sea*, it is Maurya, mother of the drowned young man, who mourns most poignantly, swaying back and forth on her stool as she weeps and speaks. At the end of the play, she is joined by a chorus of old women who enter in silence, 'crossing themselves on the threshold and kneeling down in front of the stage with red petticoats over their heads' (*CW* III 21). They too begin to keen, 'swaying themselves with a slow movement' (*CW* III 23). In his last play, *Deirdre of the Sorrows*, written when Synge knew that he had not long to live, the keening woman is Deirdre herself, left alone to mourn when her lover and his brothers have been killed, and performing her heartbroken lament over their bodies. Even in his relatively lighthearted *The Shadow of the Glen*, a man's body, dead or apparently dead, is the focus of the play, while the ritual of Irish funeral custom provides most of the action.

Synge's use of keening in his drama is closely related to his descriptions of two funerals he witnessed in the Aran Islands, in Galway Bay, around the turn of the century. During his summer visits to Inis Meáin, the middle island, between 1898 and 1902, he observed what was still a living tradition, an essential part of that isolated society's strategy for maintaining and repairing its own fabric. Death rituals are among the

67

oldest and most persistent manifestations of human culture: from the
cremation urns and grave-goods of archaeological excavations to the
funeral homes of today, all societies observe formalities in their response
to death. 'Keening', from the Irish *caoineadh*, is the Irish version of an
international practice. All over the world there are societies in which
loud public lamentation is expected at funerals, and where mourning
the dead is specifically women's work, carried out according to closely
prescribed convention. In Europe at the beginning of the twenty-first
century, public lamentation has all but died out, but a hundred years
ago this kind of mourning was common in Greece, Corsica and
Finland, as well as in the west of Ireland. It survived longest on the
periphery, as more tight-lipped and private ways of coping with
bereavement spread from metropolitan centres.

Aside from the vividness and memorability of his dramatic images,
Synge's keening women deserve study for two reasons. For students of
the Irish-language tradition, his prose and drama, including his stage
directions, offer relatively recent and richly detailed accounts of the
contexts in which the poetry of *caoineadh* was composed and performed. Meanwhile, an acquaintance with that poetry and with earlier
descriptions of keening should afford students of the theatre an insight
into Synge's dramatic project. This essay will argue that in the ritual of
death in the Aran Islands, both the wake and the practice of *caoineadh*,
Synge found a theatre: a whole technique of setting a period of time
aside from time, and of articulating space, gesture, words, voice, and
even costume, in a way that would cause people to view the world differently. Performance has been defined as 'an activity which generates
transformations',[1] and I want to suggest that Synge saw the art of
caoineadh in just this way. I suggest that it was precisely the theatrical-
ity of *caoineadh* that caught his imagination, that he was uniquely alert
to it, and that this tradition of women's oral poetry in performance
provided him with a vessel in which he would carry his own creativity
onto the stage.

Synge's talent as dramatist and prose writer has tended to obscure
the meticulousness of his ethnographic scholarship; in matters of Irish
learning he is often regarded as a gentleman amateur and dilettante.
The Anglo-Irish society in which he was born and raised did not see the
language or culture of ordinary Irish people as worthy of serious study,
while the self-appointed cultural police of the Gaelic League viewed
him with deep distrust. The League had been founded in 1893, with

the aim of reviving Irish as the spoken language of the whole country. It was immensely influential in the cultural politics of the time, but Synge was no revivalist. His acquaintance with Irish has usually been downplayed as a result, although, as Declan Kiberd has demonstrated, it was quite extensive.[2] The School of Divinity at Trinity College Dublin offered Irish as part of the curriculum which prepared young men for the ministry. Synge studied with Professor James Goodman, an elderly clergyman whose father had been rector in Dingle, Co. Kerry, and who had had grown up in the Gaeltacht: a scholar, uileann piper, and notable collector of traditional music.[3] Having by this time rejected his mother's evangelical Protestantism, Synge did not become a clergyman, but he was awarded the Irish Prize at Trinity in 1892. During his visits to the west, therefore, he was able to converse with the people of the islands, listen to the stories Pat Dirane and others told, and understand what was going on from day to day.

He would have known something about the Irish practice of lamentation before he heard women in Aran give voice to it. In the years before he began to make regular visits to the islands, Irish readers of English had been introduced to *caoineadh* as a source of romantic poetry. Thomas Crofton Croker's *Researches in the South of Ireland* (1824) and *The Keen of the South of Ireland* (1844) had drawn attention to the traditional oral lament many years before, but it acquired a retrospective glamour when *The Last Colonel of the Irish Brigade*, Mrs Morgan John O'Connell's account of her husband's distinguished ancestors, appeared in 1892.[4] This two-volume work included in an appendix a copy of *Caoineadh Airt Uí Laoghaire*, with a translation into English. *Caoineadh Airt Uí Laoghaire* was the long and elaborate *Lament for Art O'Leary*, as it came to be known in English, said to have been composed by Eibhlín Dubh Ní Chonaill (aunt of Daniel O'Connell, 'The Liberator'), when her twenty-six-year-old husband was shot dead on horseback at Carraig an Ime (Carriganimmy), between Millstreet and Macroom, Co. Cork, in May 1773. It had been preserved in various versions, in oral tradition and in manuscript, but was now published for the first time.

For nineteenth-century romantics, Eibhlín Dubh (black-haired Eibhlín) fitted the role of eighteenth-century heroine better than most makers of laments. The typical lamenter or *bean chaointe* was a poor elderly woman who had witnessed many deaths and had time to assimilate all the conventions of the lament tradition,[5] but Eibhlín was scarcely thirty years old when she composed her lament; she was not poor, and the man she mourned was not her son or foster-son, but the husband with whom she had eloped only a few years earlier. *The Last Colonel of the Irish Brigade* refers to her throughout as 'Dark Eileen'. With its strong echo of the 'blood-drenched nationalist fervour' of James Clarence Mangan's 'My Dark Rosaleen' (1846), this was a bold stroke in the creation of an Irish romantic heroine.[6]

Mrs Morgan John O'Connell did not know Irish, but she sought the aid of the distinguished writer, teacher and priest An tAthair Peadar Ó Laoghaire, who had himself grown up in the area where Art Ó Laoghaire lived and died.[7] He made the translation she asked for, but also kept a copy of the original, which he emended, possibly from independent acquaintance with oral versions. In 1896, his friend and disciple Osborn Bergin, a classicist just beginning to make his mark as a Celtic scholar, edited his text for the Gaelic League's *Irisleabhar na Gaedhilge/The Gaelic Journal*, observing that *Caoineadh Airt Uí Laoghaire* was still widely known in the oral tradition of Munster, and appealing for further versions. Bergin, who at twenty-two was two years younger than Synge, wrote:

The foregoing is a poem of great power and beauty, and of the deepest natural pathos – the Lament for Art O'Leary, by his wife. It is doubtful if any literature contains so true and powerful an expression of the devotion of a high-minded woman to a noble husband, as shown in her grief after his death.[8]

Bergin's interest, like that of most of the Irish-language scholars who worked on *caoineadh*, was primarily textual and antiquarian. It was also not a little elitist. Synge lived more in the present, preferring garrets, cottages and the open air to libraries. He was interested in legends, folktales and oral poetry, but even more intrigued by the people on whose lips he heard them. At the Aran funerals, as he sets himself to observe word and action simultaneously, we can already observe the three-dimensional imagination of the playwright at work. He sees and hears, not as a textual scholar, but as an ethnographer.

In *The Aran Islands*, finished in 1901, Synge drew together the notes and photographs he had taken during his visits. The delicate precision and fine understanding of his observation are quite remarkable. Here is his first account of a funeral:

After Mass this morning an old woman was buried. She lived in the cottage next mine, and more than once before noon I heard a faint echo of the keen. I did not go to the wake for fear my presence might jar upon the mourners, but all last evening I could hear the strokes of a hammer in the yard, where, in the middle of a little crowd of idlers, the next of kin laboured slowly at the coffin. To-day, before the hour for the funeral, poteen was served to a number of men who stood about upon the road, and a portion was brought to me in my room. Then the coffin was carried out sewn loosely in sailcloth, and held near the ground by three cross-poles lashed upon the top. As we moved down to the low eastern portion of the island, nearly all the men, and all the oldest women, wearing petticoats over their heads, came out and joined in the procession.

While the grave was being opened the women sat down among the flat tomb-stones, bordered with a pale fringe of early bracken, and began the wild keen, or crying for the dead. Each old woman, as she took her turn in the leading recitative, seemed possessed for the moment with a profound ecstasy of grief, swaying to and fro, and bending her forehead to the stone before her, while she called out to the dead with a perpetually recurring chant of sobs.

All round the graveyard other wrinkled women, looking out from under the deep red petticoats that cloaked them, rocked themselves with the same rhythm, and intoned the inarticulate chant that is sustained by all as an accompaniment. (*CW* II 74)

The detail is striking, testifying to careful and tactful observation. The elderly women, walking in procession with red petticoats over their heads, and rocking their bodies to the rhythm of the *caoineadh*, are obviously the models for Synge's chorus in *Riders to the Sea*. Elsewhere he explains that their homespun woollen petticoats were dyed red with madder, and that when it rained they would throw an extra one over their heads, with the waistband around their faces. A photograph from the Irish Folklife Division of the National Museum, taken sometime before 1930, shows three elderly women wearing petticoats over their heads this way as they walk along a road, while a fourth wears a Galway shawl. Anne O'Dowd explains that the heavy woollen Galway shawl in brown and fawn, with a wide patterned border, began to be introduced to the islands about the turn of the century, replacing 'an older form of cloak or shawl which the women themselves invented by sewing a *crios* or woollen belt for decoration to a spare *cóta* or skirt. This they placed on their head allowing the full width of the skirt to drape over their shoulders and down their bodies, back and front, thus giving the appearance of a cloak.'[9]

The primary impact of his description is visual, but Synge has also paid attention to the words the women spoke. It is important to note that he describes only the *accompaniment* to the *caoineadh*, by women other than the chief keener, as inarticulate. 'Keening' has entered the

English language from Irish, and usually suggests a sort of high-pitched moaning – a cry without words, even an animal sound – but the Irish *caoineadh* was anything but inarticulate. As well as stylized sobbing and wailing – the *ochón* or *olagón* of Synge's 'perpetually recurring chant of sobs' – it included a whole tradition of poetic utterance, such as we find in *Caoineadh Airt Uí Laoghaire* and other texts from the eighteenth and nineteenth centuries. It is impossible to know now how much of this poetic tradition was still to be found in Aran at the turn of the century, but this was what Synge called 'the leading recitative'. According to him, each old woman, as she took her turn, cried out *to* the dead. *Caoineadh* was an oral-formulaic poetic composition, produced in performance, in broadly the same way as Homer's epics must have been, by combining and recombining traditional motifs according to a traditional metre.[10] The lamenter addresses the dead person directly, asks him to get up and come home, reproaches him for dying, praises his beauty, his generosity and the splendour of his home, and piles image upon image of the desolation that will now follow his death.

As late as 1955, visiting Inis Mór (as Árainn, the largest island, has come to be known) with a battery-run tape recorder borrowed from the BBC, Sidney Robertson Cowell was able to record two short samples of *caoineadh*. One of the women who features on his *Songs of Aran* is Bridget Mullin, born in 1868, who had taken part in Robert Flaherty's celebrated 1934 film *Man of Aran*.[11] 'Many people mentioned her to me as the leading professional keening woman of the islands,' he writes. 'She was able to sing fragments of songs for me in her strong old voice, and when I asked her if she could sing the Caoine for me she began to tell over a long series of family tragedies: her father, her husband, her brothers and her sons all dead in Ireland or America, "crying them" with the age-old ritualistic plaint as she thought of each in turn.' As a young woman, Bridget Mullin would have been present at funerals such as Synge witnessed.

The person lamented in remembered examples was usually a man, and the woman who keened him praised him lavishly, with descriptions of his beauty, generosity and noble lineage, and anger at his enemies or the natural forces that had caused his death. Nowadays, when war and natural disaster strike less-developed societies, television and other visual media seek out and find lamenting women, and skilled lamenters know how to draw media attention to their political and humanitarian causes. In the Irish tradition too, *caoineadh* was a vehicle for the dramatic and effective expression of grievances, both personal and political.[12]

Some of the value of Synge's description lies in his ability to bridge a gap of interpretation. Observers from inside and outside the Irish-language tradition have offered very different views of *caoineadh*. Those from within leave texts, remembered or transcribed, usually with only the scantiest information about how, where, when and by whom they were composed or performed; whereas outsiders give descriptions. Most of these stress the exotic and incomprehensible in what the visitor saw and heard: the cacophony of cries, the wild behaviour. Almost invariably, they ignore the poetry. It is normal for members of a culture to assume that what is familiar to them is familiar to everyone, but it is also a commonplace of colonization that the language of the colonized sounds simply like noise, and that highly structured events can seem like chaos. Both sets of evidence are valuable, however, and for a full picture they must be combined.

Diarmaid Ó Muirithe has assembled the comments of travellers in Ireland on the funerals they witnessed.[13] The first was Gerald of Wales, Giraldus Cambrensis, in the twelfth century, but most were Elizabethans, anxious to find examples of barbarity and otherness in their newly colonized lands to set against images of civility at home.[14] Fynes Moryson, Edmund Spenser, and Richard Stanyhurst referred to the 'shrieking, howling and clamping of hands' (Moryson), 'despairful outcries and immoderate wailings … altogether heathenish' (Spenser), and 'howlings and barbarous outcries' (Stanyhurst). But the *caoineadh* was already centuries old by Elizabethan times, and had been by the time Giraldus wrote, four hundred years earlier, for it is mentioned in several medieval texts.

In the eighth century, an Irish cleric named Blathmac composed two long poems in which he asked the Virgin Mary to intercede for him with her son. Schooled in the conventions of formal secular poetry, he offered something of his own in return. He deplored the fact that Christ had not been keened upon his death, as every great leader should be, and offered to make good the deficiency if Mary would do as he asked. He described what should be done:

… every individual of the host of men and women is mourned; no cry meeting cry was raised over the body of Christ, the bright and gentle one.

Every splendid household beats hands over their lord; beating of hands over the body of pure Christ was not permitted to apostles.[15]

Clapping of hands is mentioned as part of mourning behaviour by Fynes Moryson in 1617 and in many modern texts in Irish. In Synge's second funeral description he tells us twice that the mourners beat upon the wood of the coffin with their hands:

The young man has been buried, and his funeral was one of the strangest scenes I have met with. People could be seen going down to his house from early in the day, yet when I went there with the old man about the middle of the afternoon, the coffin was still lying in front of the door, with the men and women of the family standing around beating it, and keening over it, in a great crowd of people. (*CW* II 160)

Later, as the grave was being opened, Synge witnessed an action that has since been captured more than once by news photographers in eastern Europe. The mother of the dead man lifted a skull from the earth – the skull of her own mother – and took it away, keening over it. His description continues:

When [the grave] was nearly deep enough the old woman got up and came back to the coffin, and began to beat on it, holding the skull in her left hand. This last moment of grief was the most terrible of all. The young women were nearly lying among the stones, worn out with their passion of grief, yet raising themselves every few moments to beat with magnificent gestures on the boards of the coffin. (*CW* II 161)

Here is a description from 1683, of the same behaviour at a funeral in Kildare, where the observer notes how laments were repeated many years after the deaths that gave rise to them:

When they come at the church-yard ..., perhaps 5, 10 or 20 years after their husband, friend or relation has been buried, they repair to their graves, where they kneel over them, knocking and beating upon the grave and praising the party, repeating the former kindnesses have passed between them, intreating that they would attend and give ear to them, then in an odd tone sorrowing and lamenting their loss complain and tell them how they are misused and by whom injured and thereon pray their help to right them ...[16]

According to Synge in the first passage quoted above, and in his stage directions for Maurya and Deirdre, the lamenting woman rocked or swayed back and forth as she cried. Mr and Mrs Samuel Carter Hall, in their three-volume account of their travels in Ireland in 1840, write that at a wake, women ranged themselves on either side of the body, then: 'They rise with one accord, and moving their bodies with a slow motion to and fro, their arms apart, they continue to keep up a heart-rending cry.' They describe the funeral of a widow's son near Killarney as 'the most touching and sad, though interesting funeral we ever attended':

... Long before we could see any portion of the crowd, we heard the *keen* swelling on the ear, now loud and tremulous, anon low and dying, dying away. Keening has fallen into disuse in this district; but the Kerry keen was more like what we imagine the wild wail of the Banshee to be, than a demonstration of human sorrow.

The body had been put in a plain coffin – what, in England would be called a shell; and this was put upon a very common hearse, not unlike a four-poster bed, drawn by an active, but miserable-looking horse. The widowed mother, shrouded in her blue cloak, sat beside the coffin; and when the keeners cried the loudest *she rocked her body to and fro*, and clasped [*r.* clapped?] her hands, as if to mark the beatings of her stricken heart.[17]

The Halls' account bears out Synge's and those of other travellers, but betrays no inkling that the crying of the keeners consisted of intelligible words.

Crofton Croker's *The Keen of the South of Ireland* gives English translations of the lament-poems which people repeated for him. No Irish originals are included, but a knowledge of the metre and formulae of *caoineadh* gives clues that allow the outlines of the originals to be reconstructed. He too noted that the keener rocked back and forth, and added that she mumbled to herself, the same line over and over, before she began to keen in earnest. He suggested that she was assuring herself of the order of her words.

The metre of *caoineadh* is simple: short lines with end-rhyme and two, three, or sometimes four stressed syllables in each. In selecting her first line, the *bean chaointe* determined the end-rhyme and the number of stresses in the several lines which would follow. She seems to have taken her metre from the rhythm of her body's movement, and may very well have used the rocking and repetition to induce an altered state of consciousness. The first line of each passage of poetry was typicallly an affectionate address to the dead person (though it could also be an exclamation of grief, or a call to someone else present), and the descriptions which survive suggest that it worked like a mantra – repeated over and over, with eyes closed – to shut out distractions and enable the keener to focus her mind and emotions, to access that part of her memory where the most vivid and intense imagery and formulae of lament were stored.

In *Riders to the Sea*, Synge's stage directions tell us that when Cathleen says 'There's no sense left on any person in a house where an old woman will be talking forever', Maurya 'sways herself on her stool' (*CW* III 13). Later, when Bartley's body is brought in, stage directions stipulate that 'The women are keening softly and swaying themselves with a slow movement' (*CW* III 23). When Maurya begins her famous speech – not a speech at all perhaps, but a chant, because these are the words of a *caoineadh*, 'They're all gone now and there isn't anything more the sea can do to me ...' – she is 'speaking as if she did not see the people' (*CW* III 23). Synge places her in the trance-like state observed by many other commentators, giving her words their full, chilling authority, and recalling his description of the Aran women by the open grave as each 'possessed for the moment with a profound ecstasy of grief' (*CW* II 74).

In *Deirdre of the Sorrows*, when Deirdre looks into the grave, 'She crouches down and begins swaying herself backwards and forwards, keening softly. At first her words are not heard, then they become clear' (*CW* IV 261). This recalls Crofton Croker's comment that at first the lamenter mumbled and could not be heard, but that presently her voice rose. The speech that follows Deirdre's crouching and swaying is her keen: a direct address to the dead, in which she recalls the comforts of her life with them and the desolation of a future without them:

It's you three will not see age or death coming, you that were my company when the fires on the hilltops were put out and the stars were our friends only. I'll turn my thoughts back from this night – that's pitiful for want of pity – to the time it was your rods and cloaks made a little tent for me where there'd be a birch-tree making shelter, and a dry stone: though from this day my own fingers will be making a tent for me, spreading out my hairs and they knotted with the rain. (*CW* IV 261)

At this point in the play, 'Lavarcham and [the] Old Woman come in stealthily on right', but, stage directions tell us, Deirdre does not see them. She continues keening, oblivious and apart: 'It is I Deirdre will be crouching in a dark place, I Deirdre that was young with Naisi, and brought sorrow to his grave in Emain' (*CW* IV 261). This 'apartness' of the lamenting woman – the dissociation and total concentration which cut her off from those who can hear her – obviously made an impression on Synge, as on other commentators; his stage directions show his awareness of its dramatic quality.

Of course Synge did not invent the role of keener for Deirdre:

medieval and early modern versions of her story consistently depict her lamenting Noisi (Synge's Naisi, modern Naoise), as indeed Emer laments Cú Chulainn. Here again, we can observe the continuity of the tradition, as keening women over many centuries are described as drinking the blood of the dead. Some of the most striking lines of Eibhlín Ní Chonaill's lament for Art Ó Laoghaire tell us that when Art's horse came home without him, she leaped into the saddle and rode to find him. I translate from Seán Ó Tuama's edition of the Irish text:

> My best-loved friend,
> I didn't credit your death
> till your mare came home,
> with reins trailing down,
> your heart's blood on her head,
> and on the fine saddle
> where you sat and stood up.
> I took one leap to the doorway,
> A second to the gate,
> A third into the saddle.
>
> I struck my hands together
> and pressed the mare to gallop
> as fast as she could travel,
> and found you lying here
> by a low furze bush
> without pope or bishop,
> without priest or cleric
> to read a single psalm,
> but only one old woman
> who spread her cloak across you –
> your blood was flowing from you:
> I didn't stop to wipe it;
> I drank it from my hands.

Ó Tuama notes a mention of the drinking of blood in Spenser's *A View of the Present State of Ireland* (1596).[18] In the Irish sagas Emer drank Cú Chulainn's blood too, and when Deirdre found that Naoise was dead, she demanded to be allowed to kiss him, and proceeded to suck his mouth and drink his blood (*'Ligidh domhsa mo chéile a phógadh'* ... *agus do ghabh ag caoineadh Naoise agus ag sughadh a chuid fola*).[19] By the time he came to write his Deirdre play, Synge was dying. Perhaps it was her identification as a keening woman that prompted him to feel he could make his own version of Deirdre. He wrote the part for his fiancée, Molly Allgood, who had already created the role of Pegeen Mike. She would be left alone to mourn when he was gone.

Synge knew Irish: unlike the Elizabethans, or Mr and Mrs Hall, he understood some or most of the words spoken by the women he heard lamenting in the Aran Islands; unlike Crofton Croker, he did not have to depend on translations provided out of context. The speeches he puts into the mouths of women characters who keen in his plays accord with what we know of *caoineadh* from the oral tradition. He does not build these speeches out of formulae as a *bean chaointe* would – he was writing in English, and the traditional formulae of *caoineadh* are in rhymed and rhythmic Irish – but the atmosphere, the tone and the force of what Maurya says, or what Deirdre says, accord perfectly with the tradition.

In writing these parts, Synge drew on his empathetic witnessing of individual women's performance at funerals. His lines enter into grief and express it without condescension, but they do more. Over and above the subjective emotion they express, Synge's keening women give structure to his plays. It has long been taken for granted that the Irish-language tradition knew little or nothing of drama, although the English-language mumming tradition is quite widespread in Ireland.[20] Viewed in the light of mumming, however, the three-dimensional model of lament performance, pulled together like a ship in a bottle by the various strings of native and outsider testimony, begins to look remarkably like a theatre.

The body in its coffin was the centrepiece of the funerals Synge witnessed. Men and women arranged themselves around it, coming closer and moving away by turns. Texts of *caoineadh* which record the words of the *bean chaointe* show many traditional formulae which enjoin those listening to come forward or stand back, as the woman who led the lament controlled the space within which it was performed. 'Room to rhyme' is the demand of folk performers in other contexts: if the crowd in a marketplace or a farm kitchen will stand back and give them space, the mummers will provide an entertainment. This is the basis of theatre: the bargain players make with their audience. The crowd consents to a part of the shared space being set aside – made sacred, out of bounds – as a stage, or framed area. The players will have licence there to behave in ways outside normality. The lamenter, too, behaves in ways that are not those of every day.[21] According to descriptions in songs and sagas, and in lament-texts themselves, she might be bare-headed and barefoot, with her hair loose or dishevelled, her bodice open or ripped. She might curse and criticize, or speak openly of sex and childbirth. She might hold a skull in her hands, or drink the blood of a person dead by violence. She used her voice to maximum effect – young women practised to get the proper blood-curdling effect – and her art was recognized by her neighbours and by herself. Like the shawled women in eastern Europe and North Africa who turn their grief-stricken faces towards the lenses of the Western media, the Irish *bean chaointe* knew the power of her own performance. As late as the 1940s in the Aran Islands, women who had discarded the fashion of red petticoat as cloak would bring it out again for wakes and funerals.[22] Synge would have understood why.

J.M. SYNGE

On an Island

You've plucked a curlew, drawn a hen,
Washed the shirts of seven men,
You've stuffed my pillow, stretched the sheet,
And filled the pan to wash your feet,
You've cooped the pullets, wound the clock,
And rinsed the young men's drinking crock;
And now we'll dance to jigs and reels,
Nailed boots chasing girls' naked heels,
Until your father'll start to snore,
And Jude, now you're married, will stretch on the floor.

NUALA NÍ DHOMHNAILL

Ar Oileán

(aistriúchán ar 'On an Island' le J.M. Synge)

Tá cuirliún pioctha agat, is cearc glanta,
léinte seachtar fear stáirseáilte,
mo philiúr pulctha, mo bhraillín sínte,
an báisín líonta chun do chosa a sciúradh.
Tá na cearca sa chúib agat, an clog tochraiste
is próca uisce na bhfear óg rinseáilte.
Is anois, a shiúirín, téanam ag rinnce
beidh bróga tairní ag leanúint sál cosnnochta na gcailíní,
go dtí faoi dheireadh beidh do Dhaid ina shrann codlata
is anois nó táir pósta, caithfidh Jude síneadh ar an urlár.

DECLAN KIBERD

Synge's Tristes Tropiques: The Aran Islands

Like *Gulliver's Travels*, J.M. Synge's personal documentary on the Aran Islands is composed of four parts, each devoted to a separate voyage, and each more fragmented and problematic than its predecessor. The self which narrates its adventures grows ever more uncertain as a direct consequence of what is experienced. Although both works are written in an autobiographical mode, they also have a distinctly anthropological thrust, as the author asks a question: just how valuable a creature is mankind in a world where animals may be worth more than humans? What Synge found in the writings of Pierre Loti about Breton fisherfolk – 'a terrified search for some sign of the persistence of the person' (*CW* II 395) – may also be found in his own book. There can be few more harrowing scenes in Irish writing than that funeral described in *The Aran Islands* during which a female mourner snatches the skull of her dead mother from a newly opened grave and proceeds to lament as she cradles it in her lap (*CW* II 161).

The subsistence economy of the islands might seem to deny their inhabitants the chance of becoming individuals, in a culture where both dead and living share the same limited repertoire of phrases, clothes and equipment. Synge's even more terrifying discovery, however, is that there are no individuals persisting on the mainland: only those *types* mass-produced by a thoroughly anglicized society. His visits to Aran, ostensibly to study the island culture, will prompt him to deliver a fierce critique of a mainland which is losing contact with its own dynamic traditions, to make way for a double-chinned bourgeois vulgarity.

He was not the first member of his family to go to Aran. His uncle, Reverend Alexander Synge, had established a Protestant mission in the place in 1851, hoping to combat the 'dirt and ignorance' and to convert the people.[1] He made himself deeply unpopular on Inis Mór by putting a stop to a Sunday ball-game and by employing a motorized fishing boat in competition with the frail canvas currachs used by the islanders. His fishing succeeded but his mission failed. Forty-seven years later, his nephew arrived at Cill Ronáin, the main village, not so much on a mission as on a pilgrimage. John Synge was by then already an agnostic, whose childhood faith in 'the kingdom of God' had been replaced by a devotion to 'the kingdom of Ireland'. He sought from nature a fulfilment which his uncle might have thought possible only in religion. 'Our pilgrimages', wrote the nephew, 'are not to Canterbury or Jerusalem, but to Killarney and Cumberland and the Alps' (CW II 351).

The Anglo-Irish had long been interested in the islands, not for their soil (which was scarce and infertile) but for their prehistoric remains. Sir William Wilde (father of Oscar) had made a study of these. In 1857 he was leader of an expedition by the Ethnological Section of the British Association to 'the great Firbolg fort of Dun Aengus', which, according to its official report, 'was most judiciously selected as our banqueting hall on the occasion'. The gentlemen in their frockcoats and top hats must have been a strange sight for those islanders who watched from a respectful distance, as the bizarre *déjeuner sur l'herbe* took its course. At the close, a decanter of sherry was passed around and Sir William proposed that the Provost of Trinity College Dublin preside over the after-dinner meeting. This was addressed by such leading antiquarians as Drs Petrie, O'Donovan, O'Curry and Stokes.

The father of a future dramatist was quick to seize upon the theatrical potential of the setting: 'I believe that I now point to the stronghold prepared as the last standing-place of the Firbolg aborigines of Ireland, here to fight their last battle if driven to the western surge.' The local aborigines, if they were following this fustian, must have been relieved that here was not another sabbatarian killjoy seeking to ban their ball-games. Sir William did, however, in a calculated aside to eavesdroppers, rebuke them for permitting their ancient sites to decay as they clambered over them in pursuit of rabbits. And he had a better material reward to dangle before them: 'It has been one of my fondest hopes to render Aran an object of attention, and an opposition shop, if I may say so, to Iona.' Eugene O'Curry then spoke in Irish, asking the islanders to mingle freely with the gentlemen. The banquet concluded with a jig, 'in which the French Consul joined con amore'.[2]

When J.M. Synge set foot on Aran in 1898, he came with a different agenda: to learn Irish and to take instruction from the people on their cultural codes. He was no day-tripper or antiquarian, much less a hot-gospeller. Every Sunday, while the inhabitants of the middle island Inis Meáin attended mass, he climbed the local Dún there to meditate on his own natural religion. This prompted the visiting priest to joke over breakfast: 'if you ever go to Heaven, you'll have a great laugh at us' (CW II 163). Synge shared the life of the islanders, the dangers of the sea and the precariousness of a world without doctor or nurse (a real risk for a chronic asthmatic).

Being shy, he had brought with him a fiddle and a box-camera, hopeful that these could provide talking-points with the locals. The camera was the first ever used among them, prompting some to marvel at how the photographs allowed them to see themselves, as if for the first time. One of the younger men, who taught Synge Irish and was himself an advanced reader, quarrelled with the photographer, wishing to appear in his Galway suit rather than the homespuns 'that become him far better' (CW II 134). One could read Synge's comment as an echo of Sir William Wilde's insistence that old ways be preserved, but the same point about the greater beauty and practicality of homespuns had already been made by Douglas Hyde in his call for deanglicization.[3]

Synge was in fact an exponent of that left-wing pastoral which in later decades would go by other names: sociology and anthropology. His reports from the Congested Districts for the *Manchester Guardian* attempted to awaken its readers to the 'penury' of an area which had been the subject of government blue books. In many ways, his writing anticipated the George Orwell of *The Road to Wigan Pier*, while his plays might be said to have prefigured the art of Roddy Doyle, seeking moments of communal solidarity among a people whose poverty is exceeded only by their richness of language.[4]

There are two kinds of pastoral. The first is the more familiar, conservative kind, in which a leisured aristocracy plays at being poor in a spurious attempt to wish real class differences away; the second is the more unusual, radical sort, in which a real peasantry may be depicted as having qualities often thought peculiar to aristocrats.[5] *The Aran Islands* fascinates because it draws simultaneously on both traditions. Synge's own spiritual autobiography is written into the narrative in a familiar Orientalist mode, involving some key elements – a romantic landscape as backdrop to the play of the writer's own consciousness; a betrayed friendship with a sensitive local youth; a near-wordless infatuation with a native girl who leans across his knees, innocently admiring the photographs; and a sad, melancholy withdrawal from a place which seems more and more lost in a dream.[6] The scientific and objective element in Synge's personality, which had led to his agnosticism, also declared itself in his anxiety to tell things exactly as he found them, 'inventing nothing, and changing nothing that is essential' (*CW* II 47). That blend of old-fashioned romanticism and vigilant empiricism would be found in many other left-wing pastorals later in the twentieth century: it is what links the Orwell of *Homage to Catalonia* with the Julia Kristeva of *About Chinese Women* or the reports of Margaret Mead from Bali.

Synge's photography displays the same ambivalence. It runs the obvious risk of exposing him as a mere 'tourist in other people's reality'[7] and one, moreover, who may have the effect of reducing the islanders to tourists in their own. In confiding that they were seeing themselves in his snapshots for the first time, some of the more sophisticated islanders seem already to have fallen for a world of mere representations as somehow superior to the world itself. The young man who shuns the homespuns wants to look more like the sort of youth who should normally appear in a picture album: already, he inhabits a landscape where nothing is finally 'real' until it has been photographed. This is why traditionalists in such communities feared that a camera might take their souls away: that, quite literally, is what cameras often did, converting people into objects who could be 'possessed' by the virtual world of representation. The Balinese told Margaret Mead that 'we have no art: we just do everything as well as we can';[8] and most of the people of Inis Meáin were similarly suspicious that all representations might be misrepresentations.

On an island where everyone seems to be an artist, there can be no need for art with a capital A. The old carrier of local tradition, Pat Dirane, creates a comical scene which is at once a representation of mockery and a mockery of representation:

Today a grotesque twopenny doll was lying on the floor near the old woman. He picked it up and examined it as if comparing it with her. Then he held it up: 'Is it you is after bringing that thing into the world', he said, 'woman of the house?' (CW II 70)

The portable camera, by miniaturizing experience, runs the risk of transforming it into mere spectacle, by ripping each moment out of its wider social process: and a truly artistic photograph may be beautiful but deeply untruthful, illustrating the gap that can exist between a fine image and a painful reality, 'between a gallous story and a dirty deed' (CW IV 169). The youth who refused to be pictured in homespuns may already have seen too many facile exercises in sentimentality. By 1934 Walter Benjamin was complaining that the camera had succeeded 'in turning abject poverty itself, by handling it in a modish, technically perfect way, into an object of enjoyment'.[9] Isolated snapshots can deprive a moment of its meaning by removing it from the flow of experience: without a text or context, such photographs may appear like images in the memory of a total stranger and 'lend themselves to any use'.[10] This is why the poet Charles Baudelaire was so shocked by 'Daguerre's cheap method of disseminating a loathing for history'.[11] He believed that such pictures would take the place of memory and rob persons of a capacity for judgement, leaving them in the grip of sensations rather than experiences.

That is the fear which haunts younger islanders once they enter the culture of the mainland in Galway: that they will forget their own kindred in the very act of seeming to recall them with the aid of a form of technology. A letter from 'Michael' (actually Synge's friend Martin McDonagh) sent back to Synge on Inis Meáin ends with enquiries about his own family:

What way are my mother and my three brothers and sisters, and do not forget white Michael, and the poor little child and the old grey woman, and Rory. I am getting a forgetfulness on all my friends and kindred – I am your friend. (CW II 112)

Synge is amazed that Michael should rebuke himself for forgetfulness, just after asking for each of his people, but that is precisely the point. Michael fears that the act of writing the enquiry down will give him a sort of permission to forget it. To those brought up in an oral culture, writing itself is a technology which, like the camera, 'records in order to forget'.[12] The fear of forgetting is so deep in Michael that when later he sees Synge in a Galway street, he is too shy to accost him in the crowd, 'so I followed you the way I'd see if you remembered me' (*CW* II 122). In other words, his natural assumption is that even friendly persons from a modern society do not necessarily have a developed capacity to recall old comrades.

Synge was well aware of the dangers of the camera, but to someone who felt himself a mere interloper among a welcoming people, the machine helped to register that mingled sense of intimacy and estrangement. As Susan Sontag has observed of the camera:

It offers, in one, easy, habit-forming activity, both participation and alienation in our own lives and those of others – allowing us to participate, while confirming alienation.[13]

The risk of succumbing to conservative pastoral was obvious. The *flâneur* of the boulevards walking solitary among scenes of Parisian blight in the 1890s might transfer himself to the islands, where his photographic eye would survey all with a detachment which suggested a transcendence of class interest and the achievement of a universalist perspective. But Synge was hardly such a *flâneur*. He seems in fact to have taken few, if any, photographs in Paris; and his object on the Aran Islands was to share with the people those pictures of them that he had made. Far from surveying them, he wished to help them survey themselves.

Moreover, by providing each photo with a comprehensive context of other photos, and ultimately with the text of *The Aran Islands*, he attempted to return each snapshot to its developing history. In many ways, the narrative technique of *The Aran Islands* is photographic, a fast succession of briefly realized scenes, each overlaid on the previous one; and there are moments when Synge worries that his own verbal snapshots may lose their hold on reality, appearing as if in the memory of another man. Nevertheless, the sequencing is so richly layered as to render the pressure of a truly felt experience. Walter Benjamin argued that this was the best way to undo the violence of photography, with words and with other photographs, on the linked assumption that the better the picture, the fuller the context that could be created.[14]

The pictures taken by Synge do not have an invasive quality. They were clearly done only with full permission of their subjects, such as the mother and daughter at their cottage door or the man scutching straw on a stone. Such people were able to achieve the expressive coherence of a properly posed study, focusing all their lives into the captured moment rather than hurrying past it. The longer exposure encouraged subjects to 'grow into' the frame. Above all, however, they show that Synge saw himself not just as a reporter to the rest of the world, but 'as a recorder for those involved in the events photographed'.[15] In that way, he incorporated the pictures into communal memory, his own but also that of the islanders. It might even be argued that, as some of the islanders had their few earthly possessions seized by bailiffs in the course of evictions, these snapshots were all that remained in the physical world to ratify the reality of their past lives.

Apart from his camera, Synge also brought the first alarm clock to the islands. He left it with the people, prompting one to boast that no two cocks could equal it (CW II 106). Before that, the keeping of time had been at the mercy of the direction of the wind. When the northerly blows in *The Aran Islands*, the south door of the house is opened and the fall of the shadow on the kitchen floor indicates the time of day; but if a southerly comes, the north door is opened and the people are at a loss. When Synge tells them what o'clock it is, they are dissatisfied, wishing only to know how many hours of daylight remain. For Gaelic League meetings on Sunday afternoons, a bell must be rung because the hours are not recognized. The islanders do not possess any sundial and the older among them hardly understand in more than a vague way the convention of the hours.[16]

The Aran Islands is a study of the onset of modernity on the islands, for, after Synge's departure, people will count off the hours and learn to show their facial profile to greatest advantage. However, this is a modernity which the author and many of the islanders largely deplore. Synge's one serious breach of trust with them occurred when he published one of Martin McDonagh's letters without permission in *The Gael* of April 1901. Those islanders who were, like Martin, on the cusp between tradition and modernity felt themselves particularly exposed to the possible ridicule of the outside world. Some commentators believe that many islanders held a grudge against Synge for using their artefacts in this way.[17] The row was a remarkably early instance of an immense problem in both ethnography and literary modernism: the removal of cultural objects, whether African statuary or Latin American music, from their original settings and their reproduction in Western works of art. Once the place of the priest had been assumed by the artist, it was always possible that the pilgrimage which began as a search for Truth would settle for Spectacle, bringing home all kinds of loot to the artist's own stamping-ground.

A cynic might want to read *The Aran Islands*, like *Heart of Darkness*, as but a further example of such booty, despite their authors' eloquent warnings against the appropriations of imperialism. Although the solid administrators of empire thought of themselves as polar opposites to the feckless bohemians, both often agreed on their right to expropriate any native artefact which might be turned to use in a modernist work. Since life for the modernists was justifiable as an aesthetic phenomenon or else not at all, any such activity was permissible. Synge was deeply troubled by this possibility. Early in *The Aran Islands* he records a local storyteller's remark that Jeremiah Curtin earned £500 for a book of that teller's own stories. The islanders, however, seem unbothered by money relations among themselves, seeing cash as an affliction of the outside world. One old man even encourages Synge to take out an insurance policy on his life in Dublin and earn himself £500 – the exact amount gained by Curtin for retailing the stories.

What the people whose cultural artefacts were so appropriated actually thought of these developments remains a mostly unrecorded chapter in the history of modernism.[18] Those who travelled far enough to sense what had been done were often as angry as Martin McDonagh. In recent decades, Indian potters have witnessed on television the use to which European artists put their centuries-old traditions, copied after cursory visits – and they have voiced deep resentment.[19] The license claimed by an artist like Synge in his dealings with the islanders did not trouble the authorities in Dublin, but when he exercised the same sort of freedom in the capital itself, things were different. 'The Story of the Faithless Wife' from *The Aran Islands*, when dramatized as *The Shadow of the Glen*, led Arthur Griffith to protest and Maud Gonne to walk out of the Abbey, and lines culled from *Amhráin Ghrá Chúige Chonnacht* helped to detonate a riot during the opening week of *The Playboy of the Western World*.

Synge was anxious to patch up his quarrel with Martin McDonagh and felt genuinely humiliated by his own insensitivity. By February 1902 he was forgiven in time for a fifth visit later that year (*CL* I 53). All the same, he never returned after that. In his own mind, Aran was a world elsewhere, his Tristes Tropiques. Again and again in his narrative, an 'Eastern' note is sounded, as if to confirm affinities already sensed by Yeats. Ethnographers had long thought of Irish as one of the latest examples of an Indo-European language, and that tradition is still vibrant in Bob Quinn's *Atlantean*, which pursues many analogies suggested by Synge.[20] Synge himself found that the recital of ballads on Inis Oírr 'has the general effect of a chant I once heard from a party of Orientals' while the red petticoats of the women project 'a glow of almost Eastern promise' (*CW* II 141, 58).

Synge's documentary is also akin to Orientalism in being an anthology of selected texts, a set of parts submitted as exemplary of the whole culture, in the manner of sample collections of the nineteenth century. The elements identified by Edward Said in *Orientalism* are all present. Apart from those already discussed, there is also the sense that the visitor can feel more for the natives than they can ever feel for him. Here the writer is mocked for being unmarried and over thirty (as Edward Lane was ribbed in the East[21] and Brian Merriman in *Cúirt an Mheáin Oíche*). The hopelessly confused, subjective moods of a listless young European sophisticate are brought into objective clarification by the spectacle of the primitive world laid out before him.[22] And the contention that the old place is debilitated and wan, like a beautiful but depressed woman who can be restored to vitality only by a male deliverer, is a truism not only of the *aisling* poem but of the Orientalist.[23]

Most striking of all, however, is the intertextual nature of such writing. What seems a first-time discovery of a pristine world turns out to be 'a form of copying'.[24] The main template for Synge was an essay called 'The Isles of Aran' and published in *The Savoy* by Arthur Symons in 1896. Through the earlier years of the 1890s, Synge had been trying to emulate Symons's work as a critic of French literature. When Synge and Yeats first met at a Parisian hotel in 1896, the poet had just come from a visit to the Aran Islands, made in the company of Symons, who wrote it up in the article. The visit had been deeply frustrating for Yeats, who felt hampered by his lack of Irish. He passed the baton to Synge:

Go to the Aran Islands. Live there as if you were one of the people themselves; express a life that has never found expression.[25]

That last sentence is wonderfully ambiguous. It could recall the famous lines of Karl Marx on the French peasantry, applied by Edward Said as an epigraph to *Orientalism*: 'They cannot represent themselves, they must be represented.'[26] In truth, of course, the people of Aran had been expressing their values through Irish for over a thousand years.

Yeats's sentence might be more tellingly read as applying to Synge, whose struggle for self-expression through the 1890s had been doomed to incoherence and mawkish sentimentality. Words like 'glory' and 'primitive' and 'sacred' recur through the writings of those years as vehicles of an introverted and formless art. In *The Aran Islands* and in his plays, by way of contrast, they seem to have found an objective social context. As Yeats so piercingly explained:

Whenever he tried to write drama without dialect he wrote badly, and he made several attempts, because only through dialect could he escape self-expression, see all that he did from without, allow his intellect to judge the images of his mind as if they had been created by some other mind. The objectivity he derived from dialect was technical.[27]

Still, *The Aran Islands* was a form of copying. Even the opening account in Symons's essay, sighting the island as 'a grey outline', is repeated in Synge's 'dreary rock'.[28] For Symons the attraction of the people lay in the fact that 'their life of the present was the most primitive life of any part of Ireland',[29] just as Synge (upping the ante just a little) would find on Inis Meáin a life that is 'the most primitive that is left in Europe' (CW II 53). Symons found the people of the middle island more charming and simple, a view echoed by Synge, who called them 'a simpler and perhaps a more interesting type'.[30] Synge also followed Symons in the spelling 'Inishmaan'.

'There is not even a policeman,' Symons had written, 'so sober, so law-abiding, are these islanders.'[31] Synge extended that perception in ways that will be presently discussed. Symons was especially struck by the red petticoats and blue shawls, drawn closely about the wearers, 'as women in the east draw their veils closer about their faces'.[32] All that would be recycled, as well as Symons's perception that shyness and eagerness impelled the women and children in equal measure. The upright carriage of the men was attributed by both to the light pampooties used among the rocks.

Symons imagined a prehistoric setting – 'the long-oared galleys of ravaging kings'[33] – and also an affinity between natural and human moods. Likewise, he met in sequence with the two storytellers, Old Mourteen on Inis Mór and an old man on Inis Meáin (who told of how a murderer from Connemara had been sheltered on the islands). It was predictable, of course, that such repetitions would be found in accounts left by visitors who came in close succession. Synge's is a far more detailed and compelling version, but the closeness of phrasing and general approach strongly suggests a direct influence.

The other possible textual influence is a little more surprising: Oscar Wilde's 1891 essay on 'The Soul of Man Under Socialism'. Symons in 1896 had judged the islanders so law-abiding that there was no need of a policeman. Two years later in *The Aran Islands*, Synge finds that his predecessor had got things the wrong way round: it was not crime which brought the police but the police who had brought with them the idea of crime. One islandman, Patrick, has sold his 'honour' for money (by acting as bailiff) in a straightforward confrontation between the new English law and the old Irish tradition. Knowing that the sort of eviction which his own brother had sanctioned on their family estates was now to be carried out against defaulting tenants, Synge feels 'a strange throb' to see the boats being lowered (*CW* II 88). What he is about to witness is the primal fall, the colonial occupation of Ireland re-enacted. His use of the word 'civilisation' is now as nauseated as was Symons's:

After my weeks spent among primitive men this glimpse of the newer types of humanity was not reassuring. Yet these mechanical police, with the commonplace agents and sheriffs, and the rabble they had lured, represented aptly enough the civilisation for which the homes of the island were to be desecrated. (*CW* II 89)

The police here are rather like the 'improved specimen' of black humanity in charge of a steamer in *Heart of Darkness*. The outrage to home and hearth is the catastrophic onset of modernity. The scene-painting is done in broad brush-strokes: while the police sweat and gasp, islanders walk about as cool and fresh-looking as the gulls.

A few pages on, Synge retells another parable of law versus tradition: the story of the murderer who was protected by the people and then spirited away to America. Succour was offered not just because the English law was despised, but because the people (never criminals, though always capable of crime) knew that 'a man will not do wrong unless he is under the influence of a passion which is as irresponsible as a storm on the sea':

If a man has killed his father, and is obviously sick and broken with remorse, they can see no reason why he should be dragged away and killed by the law.

Such a man, they say, will be quiet all the rest of his life, and if you suggest that punishment is needed as an example, they ask, 'Would any one kill his father if he was able to help it?'

Some time ago, before the introduction of the police, all the people of the islands were as innocent as the people here [on Inishmaan] remain to this day. (*CW* II 95)

The ethic here is existential: one is punished less *for* one's sins than *by* one's sins.

To that liberal critique of capital punishment is linked a rooted distrust of the corrective efficacy of state institutions. Synge declares it absurd to apply the same laws to the islanders as to the criminal classes of the cities; and he observes very caustically that the introduction of police has brought an increase of crime to Inis Mór. Worse still, the old faction-fights, which were conducted according to a self-regulating code, are now liable to lead to endless litigation, as the law displaces tradition. There was a time, he reports, when a miscreant islander could be entrusted with a letter to his mainland jailer – a story to expose the silliness of punitive incarceration (as did the story of mainland miscreants in Galway sent as a punishment for a month's imprisonment on Inis Mór).

All of these passages connect powerfully with the major contentions put forth in 'The Soul of Man Under Socialism':

The less punishment, the less crime. Where there is not punishment at all, crime will either cease to exist, or if it occurs, will be treated by physicians as a very distressing form of dementia, to be cured by care and kindness.[34]

Wilde declared himself sickened not by the crimes committed by the weak so much as by the punishments inflicted by the virtuous,[35] and he contended that society is more brutalized by punishment than by crime. The best form of government is, of course, none at all (a blessed condition usually enjoyed by the islanders, except during official 'visits'), because anarchism 'does not try to force people to be good. It knows that people are good when they are left alone.'[36] In writing as much, Wilde might himself have been coping with a distressing memory of Irish evictions. 'English law has always treated offences against a man's property with far more severity than offences against his person,' he lamented, 'and property is still the test of complete citizenship.'[37] The real perfection of persons lies not in what they have but in what they are. Just as the culture of money leads an islander to sell his honour, so the law of property 'had made gain not growth its aim'.[38] On the more developed Inis Mór, Synge is appalled by the effects of the new money economy on some men's bodies:

The charm which the people over there (on Inishmaan) share with the birds and flowers has been replaced here by the anxiety of men who are eager for gain. The eyes and expression are different. (*CW* II 116)

The Aran Islands might be read as a document in the history of 1890s anarchism, with the community on Inis Meáin presented as a version of the commune, a utopian zone where most of the discontents of civilization seem to be annulled. The journey out is a voyage back in time:

It gave me a moment of exquisite satisfaction to find myself moving away from civilisation in this rude canvas canoe of a model that has served primitive races since men first went on the sea. (*CW* II 57)

Synge is introduced as a man who had been in France 'a month from this day' (*CW* II 58): the Commune there may be only a memory, but on Inis Meáin it clearly flourishes. Art has ceased to be a decadently specialized pursuit; instead, every man and woman, 'in this simple life where all art is unknown', can realize the impulses of artists. Each item of furniture has a personal character, and even canoes or baskets, being made of local materials, exist as a natural link between the people and an unalienated environment.

Wilde had questioned whether the full expression of a personality was now possible on anything other than the imaginative plane of art, and his remedy was that 'the public should try to make itself artistic'.[39] This is the state enjoyed (but without deliberate effort) by the people of Inis Meáin, who live against a majestic seascape:

The continual passing in this island between the misery of last night and the splendour of today, seems to create an affinity between the moods of these people and the moods of varying rapture that are frequent in artists, and in certain forms of alienation. (*CW* II 74)

It is almost as if the artists and alienists of Montmartre have found at last a spiritual home. Even the danger of life at sea and on rock 'makes it impossible for clumsy, foolhardy, or timid men to live on the islands' (*CW* II 94). The storytellers, like Wildean dandies, 'can tell as many lies as four men' (*CW* II 100), which is only to say that stories have strengthened their imaginations.

Work in a communal setting has none of the character of sweated labour, being instead 'full of sociability' (*CW* II 130). At the thatching

of a cottage roof, the whole experience is more like a festival, and the
man whose house is being redecorated is seen as a host rather than an
employer. There is no contractual trade relationship. The energies of
art seem to animate the people, who are perfectly unaware of the
modern world of specialist endeavour, a world in which each employee
discharges the same tasks over and over. Not so on the islands, where
people become strong individuals (despite poverty) through the sheer
versatility of their activities:

It is likely that much of the intelligence and charm of the people is due to the
absence of any division of labour, and to the correspondingly wide development of
each individual, whose varied knowledge and skill necessitates a considerable activity of mind. Each man can speak two languages. He is a skilled fisherman, and can
manage a curagh with extraordinary nerve and dexterity. He can farm simply, burn
kelp, cut out pampooties, mend nets, build and thatch a house, and make a cradle
or a coffin. His work changes with the seasons in a way that keeps him free from
the dulness that comes to people who have always the same occupation. The
danger of his life on the sea gives him the alertness of a primitive hunter, and the
long nights he spends fishing in his curagh bring him some of the emotions that
are thought peculiar to men who have lived with the arts. (*CW* II 132–3)

Such versatility is repeatedly contrasted with the monotony of indus-
trial culture. When he encounters a suit of miserable black clothes
among vibrant islanders, Synge is quite sure that it has come from the
mainland.

The refusal of the people to simplify themselves for the purposes of
bourgeois efficiency is clear in their attitudes to names and naming. A
child of one year is given no official name, not having left the fireside
(*CW* II 111), but the emergence of individual personality is traced by
the naming process. The common European method of employing a
surname to indicate stable devotion to a singular profession (smith,
cooper, thatcher) will not do here 'where all have the same calling'
(*CW* II 135): 'When a child begins to wander about this land, the
neighbours speak of it by its Christian name, followed by the Christian
name of its father' (*CW* II 134). Sometimes, the mother's name, or a
hair colour, are used. At the local primary school the official name of
each child is called ('Patrick O'Flaherty'), and the children whisper the
island translation ('Patch Seaghan Dearg') before the boy responds.

The reason for this is that, in a predominantly oral culture, there can
be no sense of distance between a name and what it signifies. A word
must be accorded the reverence given to the person it names, because

words offer a hold on reality. There is little abstraction in the speech recorded in *The Aran Islands*, for this is a noun-centred language in which each word clings to its uniquely appropriate object. Such an idiom has the childlike directness which Wilde expected to find in a wholly realized personality.[40] It is a personality which, like Synge's, delights to describe a thing or a person as if it is being seen and rendered for the first time. In his love letters to the Abbey actress Molly Allgood, Synge told her that he was able to see her in a way that no man had ever done, a claim repeated by Martin Doul in *The Well of the Saints* as he sweet-talks the ravishing Molly Byrne. It was with such speeches in mind that Yeats praised Synge for writing as if he were Adam and this the first morning of creation.[41]

Such childlike concreteness of language assumes a strong sense of context. A pig in such a discourse is never just a pig but 'the pig with the black feet', or a rope will be 'the rope that Michael got in Connemara'. The words become part of the object which they render, and the object is wholly affixed to the word. This is why the islanders, despite Synge's own doubts, can never imagine that Irish could die out, for in their minds potatoes could not be planted nor hay saved without the magical words that ensure that those deeds are done. 'They have only the Irish words for all that they do in the fields' (*CW* II 149), explains one man, before articulating why Irish must seem to die before being perpetually reborn: 'It can never die out, and when the people begin to see it fallen very low, it will rise up again like the phoenix from its own ashes' (*CW* II 150). That is a paradigm of island life, for Synge never feels himself more vibrant than when he is dicing with death, buffeted by massive, rolling waves in a frail currach.

That vitality is conditional upon an aesthetic of shock and disorientation. A setting filled with jeopardy and premature death calls forth a defiant, answering assertion of life. Hence the flaming red petticoats which stand out against the monochrome grey tints of rock and sky. Another example is the poitín: this brings 'a shock of joy to the blood' and 'seems predestined to keep sanity in men who live forgotten in these worlds of mist' (*CW* II 73). The poitín is often taken before men submit themselves to the terrors of the sea. Yet another example might be the wild laments of usually silent people in the presence of pain or death. In these howls of defiance may be found an attempt to purge violence by acceptable means. A passage deleted from the published text saw Synge return to the 'murder' theme: '... the island without this simple red relief would be a nightmare fit to drive one to murder in order to gloat a while in the fresh flow of blood' (*CW* II 54n1).

'A sick man picturing health' was Yeats's description of Synge, who thanked him for sending him to Aran with a telling response: 'Style comes from the shock of new material.' Many passages erased from the final text attempt to capture that sense of shock, as a version of the challenge posed by an exacting work of art or by a strikingly radiant woman:

It is well arranged that for the most part we do not realize the beauty of a new wonderful experience till it has grown familiar and so safe to us. If a man should be supposed to come with a fully educated perception of music, yet quite ignorant of it, and hear for the first time let us say Lamoureux's Orchestra in a late symphony of Beethoven, I doubt his brain would ever recover from the shock. If a man should come with a full power of appreciation and stand for the first time before a woman – a woman perhaps who was very beautiful – what would he suffer? (*CW* II 97n1)

The ultimate shock, however, of which these were just minor versions, was the enigma of arrival on Aran: the sense that here was a world founded on a philosophy of life utterly at variance with any he had previously known.

It was strange for a young man used to Dublin and Wicklow to walk across a landscape quite bereft of trees, and stranger still to cross an island without a single wheel in use. Even more shocking was the cheerful indifference of the inhabitants to all the traditional Victorian distinctions – between a thing and a name, between feeling and reason, between pagan and Christian. Soon after his landing, Synge was amazed to learn that far from attacking fairy faith (as most priests on the mainland were now doing), the people of Inis Mór had effortlessly assimilated it to Catholicism. They held that when Lucifer saw himself in a mirror (again the bogy of representation), he declared war on God and was thrown out of heaven, along with the bad angels. As they fell towards hell, an archangel interceded asking mercy for some 'and those that were falling are in the air still, and have power to wreck ships, and to work evil in the world' (*CW* II 56). Not only do the islanders refuse to separate pagan and Christian notions, but they 'make no distinction between the natural and the supernatural' (*CW* II 128). The dead are as present to them as the living. One island girl regards Synge's ability to fan the flames of a fire by holding a newspaper against the mouth of the chimney as a sure sign that he is a sorcerer: 'it's to hell you'll be going by and by' (*CW* II 114).

No distinction is made either between the scientific and the magical: the one simply is the other, for anything which the people cannot understand is assumed to be the work of spirits or fairies. If pagan belief can be assimilated to Christian, the traffic may flow in the opposite direction too, as when the *De Profundis* prayer is recommended to ward off evil spirits. The spirit of *Dracula* rules, even to the extent that a child taken by fairies is replaced by one with 'a wound on its neck' (*CW* II 51). The locals understand that Protestants do not believe in such things 'and do be making fun of us' (*CW* II 180). Nevertheless, they steadfastly assume that a child thus 'taken' was away, body and soul, with a surrogate in its bed, much as Cuchulain in the saga was replaced by his sidhe-father, when he took a rest in mid-battle with the men of Connacht.

By placing himself in such an unfamiliar environment, Synge as a Protestant-bred gentleman was deliberately exposing himself to such shocks. Even the distinction between animal and human – so precious to the Victorians yet so precarious after the revelations of Darwin – was soon broken down and in very strange ways. The islanders strike Synge as animalistic, yet rather aristocratic as well, a surprising combination:

The absence of the heavy boot of Europe has preserved to these people the agile walk of the wild animal, while the general simplicity of their lives has given them many other points of physical perfection. Their way of life has never been acted on by anything more artificial than the nests and burrows ... they seem in a certain sense to approach more nearly to the finer types of aristocracies – who are bred artificially to a natural ideal – than to the labourer or citizen, as the wild horse resembles the thoroughbred rather than the hack or cart-horse. (*CW* II 66)

Again the implication is anarchist: only those beyond the world of wage slavery can enjoy a life where work is play because play is work, a life free of the discontents of civilization. In the heroine of *Deirdre of the Sorrows* – a girl placed by the king in the wild woods as a preparation for the noble calling to be his queen – Synge recreated that unusual mix first encountered on Inis Meáin, where 'a touch of the refinement of old societies is blended, with singular effect, among the qualities of the wild animal' (*CW* II 66). The young women with red bodices and white-skinned legs seem to have the beauty of tropical seabirds 'as they stand in a frame of seaweeds against the brink of the Atlantic' (*CW* II 76) – an image that would be reworked by James Joyce for Stephen

Dedalus's vision of a girl wading on Dollymount Strand in *A Portrait of the Artist as a Young Man*.

Soon the narrator of *The Aran Islands* embraces the possibility of becoming animal himself, finding companionship in cormorant and crow: 'Their language is easier than Gaelic, and I seem to understand the greater part of their cries' (*CW* II 73). By Part Three he seems 'to exist merely in my perception of the waves and of the crying birds' (*CW* II 130). Not one whit degraded by such affinities, Synge takes the view that 'it is this cosmic element in the person which gives all personal art, and all sincere life, and all passionate love a share in the dignity of the world' (*CW* III 176). For him a full expression of any personality entails a recapitulation of all human experience from prehistoric man to modern living. It would scarcely be too much to say that it is the attempt to re-enact that very evolution which is another of Synge's reasons for sojourning on Aran. The tragic knowledge which he must accept on this journey is the inculpation of his own people, the Anglo-Irish, in the fall from a communal culture into a world of private property, a lapse from the majesty of tradition to the pedantry of the law.

In Part Three Synge begins to recognize that, if humans may have animalistic qualities, animals can themselves, especially in moments of vulnerability, seem sadly human. The pigs of Inis Meáin shriek 'with almost human intonations' (*CW* II 137) as they are loaded for export to England. A kindly woman strokes a particular favourite to keep it still while the boats are launched. Suddenly, Synge realizes with a guilty start that what he is witnessing is but another version of that primal scene, the fall from grace that would lead inexorably to eviction and emigration. The pigs are all too human, all too Irish:

They seemed to know where they were going, and looked up at me over the gunnel with an ignoble desperation that made me shudder to think that I had eaten of their whimpering flesh. (*CW* II 138)

Too honest to deny the truth, Synge knows that his very presence as a sojourner on the island, as in his Parisian garret, is made possible by eviction scenes such as this. In one of the notebooks which he kept on the islands, he penned a blackly humorous dedication: 'To the little Irish pigs that have eaten filth all their lives to enable me to wander in Paris, these leaves are dedicated with respect and sympathy' (*CW* II 138n1).[42]

Becoming one with animals is, of course, no final answer. Even they seem to have no common language, no shared codes which might transcend those moments of pain and humiliation. All that they ultimately share with humans is a capacity to withstand an apparently endless sequence of shocks. Of the islanders, Synge observes:

They have the same emotions that I have, and the animals have, yet I cannot talk to them when there is much to say, more than to the dog that whines beside me in a mountain fog.

There is hardly an hour I am with them that I do not feel the shock of some inconceivable idea, and then again the shock of some vague emotion that is familiar to them and to me. (*CW* II 113)

It is the same blending of ideas or attitudes more often considered to be opposed which shocks Synge again and again. The artistic life of the islands is at once primitive and reminiscent of certain forms of alienation. The world so conceived evokes not only the ancient mythological cycle of Cuchulain but also the anarchist values of left-bank Paris.

Synge often appears to conspire in turning the Inis Meáin community into a version of the Latin Quarter. He takes pleasure in teaching French phrases to learners. The newspaper trick to fan the fire prompts him to tell the incredulous young woman of 'men who live alone in Paris and make their own fires that they may have no one to bother them'. 'They're like me so', she responds, 'would anyone have thought that!' (*CW* II 114). The women of the island remind Synge of those self-sufficient ones whom he had known as dancers and writers in Paris – but these are 'before conventionality', unlike the bohemians whose freedom is more knowing and 'who have freed themselves by a desperate personal effort from the moral bondage of lady-like persons' (*CW* II 143n1). Nonetheless, the affinities startle Synge, who finds that the island women 'share some of the liberal features that are thought peculiar to the women of Paris and New York' (*CW* II 143).

The Paris Commune had been put down in 1871, the year of Synge's birth, but it was a living memory to many of the intellectuals with whom he mingled in the city. They would have recalled figures like Louise Michel, the natural daughter of a *châtelaine* who wore a wide red belt with a gun and travelled under cover of male disguise to Versailles, just to demonstrate to colleagues that the trick could be done.[43]

When Arthur Griffith accused the author of *The Shadow of the Glen* of blending hedge-school folklore with 'the decadent cynicism that passes current in the Latin *Quartier*',[44] he may have been a poor literary critic of a fine play but his antennae were picking up its main cultural codings. Synge was hardly one to promote sexual license. In fact, he writes rather admiringly of the delicate balance achieved on the islands between sexual desire and family feeling: 'The direct sexual instincts are not weak on the island, but they are so subordinated to the instincts of the family that they rarely lead to irregularity' (*CW* II 144). People seem to have struck an enviable equilibrium between the moods of romantic love and the impulse-ridden life of the savage. When he visits Michael in his new life in the city of Galway, Synge is impressed by the refinement of his nature, which leaves him as unaware of the presence of half-naked women on a Salthill beach as was the young island woman who leaned innocently across Synge's limbs to study the photographs unaware of his sexual interest. The islanders seem like perfectly balanced androgynes who have transcended all consciousness of gender.

Nevertheless, the life on the islands is a form of civilization, which exacts a psychic cost, especially from the women. The maternal feeling is so strong that it imposes a life of torment on many, who raise children only to lose them to the sea or to the emigrant ship. They have only two redresses: to curtail their feelings towards their children in life and to articulate them with ritual intensity when their offspring are lost. Out of the experience of mortal loss come the *mná chaointe*, those wailing women whose voices seem to call forth a thunderclap over an island funeral. Each of the women, taking up the recitative of the *caoineadh*, seems momentarily possessed by a cosmic grief, of the kind voiced in the lament for her husband by Eibhlín Dhubh Ní Chonaill:

This grief of the keen is no personal complaint for the death of one woman over eighty years, but seems to contain the whole passionate rage that lurks somewhere in every native of the island. In this cry of pain the inner consciousness of the people seems to lay itself bare for an instant, and to reveal the mood of beings who feel their isolation in the face of a universe that wars on them with winds or seas. They are usually silent, but in the presence of death all outward show of indifference or patience is forgotten, and they shriek with pitiable despair before the horror of the fate to which they are all doomed. (*CW* II 75)

Much later, in Part Four, at the funeral of a young man, 'the keen lost a part of its formal nature, and was recited as the expression of intense personal grief by the young men and women of the man's own family' (*CW* II 161). Again this alteration is in keeping with Eibhlín Dhubh Ní Chonaill's treatment of the tradition. Synge may have over-stated this gloomy feature of island life, reading intimations of his own early death into the bearing of fishermen, whom he believed to be under 'a judgement of death' (*CW* II 162); but he was careful to recognize also that 'wild jests and laughter' were another way in which people could express 'their loneliness and desolation' (*CW* II 140).

Another text of the 1890s which influenced Synge's narrative was *The Golden Bough* by James Frazer. When Synge reports, for instance, that a needle is recommended to ward off evil spirits, his explanation comes straight out of Frazer's classic book, augmented by a Breton memory: 'Iron is a common talisman with barbarians, but in this case the idea of exquisite sharpness was probably present also, and, perhaps, some feeling for the sanctity of the instrument of toil, a folk-belief that is common in Brittany.'[45] This would be incorporated into that scene of *The Shadow of the Glen* in which a visiting tramp tells the widow of a dead man that 'there's great safety in a needle' (*CW* III 41).

Synge's indebtedness to Frazer was not just in points of detail, but in overall interpretative schemes. The old man who believed that Irish could never die, since it was used by those who named and sowed pota-toes, was applying a principle which Frazer dubbed Contagious Magic. 'It proceeds', he said, 'upon the notion that things which have once been conjoined must remain ever afterwards, even when quite dissevered from each other, in such a sympathetic relation that whatever is done to the one must similarly affect the other.'[46] In fact, many of Frazer's cate-gories – measurement of time; puberty and marriage; magic; murder – are seen to recur like leitmotifs through Synge's documentary.

Was Synge an anthropologist *avant la lettre*? Like the anthropolo-gists of Cambridge and the Collège de France, he followed in tracks beaten first by Christian missionaries and antiquarians. Frazer had argued that there were three phases in the history of civilizations: the magical, the religious and the scientific. Synge generally seemed to view the Aran Islanders as caught between the first and second stage. Frazer, of course, considered himself an evolutionary scientist: from that priv-ileged vantage-point, he could study more primitive peoples. These peoples were unable to distinguish the natural from the supernatural, and so were at the mercy of events that they could not understand or control. By 1900 the illusion of an imminent and absolute control over nature was widespread among scientists: some even offered shares in an Axis-Straightening Company which promised to abolish irregular weather patterns and seasonal fluctuations by the year 1950.

Frazer worked from his armchair at Cambridge University. In his awesomely detailed book he employed his categories to 'fix' the primitives of the globe as satellites around a still centre of Western science. They were 'a spectacle surveyed and dominated by the viewing taxonomist'.[47] Synge's approach was rather different. He worked and wrote in the field, carrying notebooks, camera and typewriter wherever he went. He was radically disoriented (shocked, in fact) by what he found; and *The Aran Islands* shows that he asked as many questions as he answered. If there is an implied 'Western' norm at the start of Part One, it is well and truly broken into fragments-without-commentary by the end of Part Four.[48] Just as he recognized the ways in which the islanders' Irish permitted them to disrupt standard English syntax, so Synge exposed himself willingly to the shocks of inconceivable ideas. His, therefore, was not only an Orientalist practice, but also a sort of reverse Orientalism, which accepted the capacity of the 'Orient' to intervene in the 'West'. Although he continued to write the standard English which he himself spoke, it takes up less and less space in each part of his narrative, while the Hiberno-English of the islanders emerges as a discourse perfectly calibrated to study the culture of the mainland.

In the decades after Synge, anthropologists would find that there were basically two ways in which to report a landscape: as a moody backdrop to the writer's self-fashioning or as an objectively documented world. In the first mode, the ego often risks overwhelming the world; in the second, the danger is that the world will annihilate the self that does the reporting. The brilliance of *The Aran Islands* is its astute interweaving of both methods: passages of spiritual autobiography or vivid dreaming are followed by island recitals or accounts of actual conversations. Sometimes, the two styles are employed in the same paragraph, with the empirical used to undercut and contain any excessive tendencies to romanticism:

Yet it is only in the intonation of a few sentences or some old fragment of melody that I catch the real spirit of the island, for in general the men sit together and talk with endless iteration of the tides and fish, and of the price of kelp in Connemara. (*CW* II 74)

While pathetic fallacy is permitted in certain scenes (as when thunder peals over a funeral), on other occasions it is denied (much as Lavarcham denies it in the closing lines of *Deirdre of the Sorrows*).

Synge said that whatever is highest in poetry is always achieved where the dreamer is reaching out to reality, or where the real man is lifted out of it (*CW* II 347), and that is the technique at work in *The Aran Islands*. Near the end of Part One, he recounts a dream in which his body seems to dance involuntarily to a siren-sound and he loses the distinction between self and soul. It is a characteristic 1890s moment, Dracula-like in intensity, when 'I knew that if I yielded I would be carried away to some moment of terrible agony' (*CW* II 99), but his limbs move in spite of him and he surrenders self. The predicted agony and self-disgust follow; and then the cryptic sentence: 'I am leaving in two days' (*CW* II 100). This is the return to the real and a fitting punishment. But is the dreamer really culpable? After all, the dream seems unwilled, a proof of the psychic memory that plays itself out in certain locations.

In saying as much, Synge has effectively signed away his pretensions to scientific rigour and willingly conscripted himself back into the world of magic. Later anthropologists would, of course, say the same of Frazer, whose own tendency to taxonomize everything in triads seemed itself a form of white magic, 'as if the evolutionists sought mythical solutions to the problem of myth'.[49] Synge, at least, remained open to the possibility that he might be no more than another dreamer reaching out to another 'reality'. His imagining of Inis Meáin as a woman anticipates Bronislaw Malinowski's relation to the Western Pacific as a female body, 'beautiful but odious to the touch'.[50] Here is Synge:

With this limestone Inishmaan however I am in love, and hear with galling jealousy of the various priests and scholars who have lived here before me. They have grown to me as the former lover of one's mistress, horrible existences haunting with dreamed kisses the lips she presses to your own. The thought that this island will gradually yield to the ruthlessness of 'progress' is as the certainty that decaying age is moving always nearer the cheeks it is your ecstasy to kiss. How much of Ireland was formerly like this and how much is today Anglicized and civilized and brutalized? (*CW* II 103n1)

That passage was suppressed from the published version of *The Aran Islands*, perhaps because it got too close to the truth, portraying Synge as a kind of necrophiliac and re-enacting yet again the one shock which terrifies him above all others: the fall into colonialism. Malinowski suppressed *all* semblance of colonial types from his texts, in the attempt to render the primitive life before the colonial encounter. In effect, he wished away the very project of which his own anthropology formed a part. There is thus a strange congruence between the agendas of anthropologists and those of certain nationalist or Anglo-Irish writers, committed to the recovery of a pre-invasion identity. Synge was more honest, including in the finished text two graphic accounts of this fall, in the transportation of the pigs and in the eviction scenes, both emphasizing the barbarous ways in which the new dispensation is imposed.

If Synge employed a quasi-religious vocabulary (pilgrimage, glory, radiance) to describe his voyage to Aran, that may have been a suitable terminology with which to introduce his withdrawal from the 'big world' for a period of penance and struggle in the wilderness. The anthropologist is, among other things, a latter-day ascetic, who may have a conversion-experience in the waters and the wild. In her essay 'The Anthropologist as Hero' Susan Sontag writes:

It is mainly poets, novelists, a few painters who have *lived* this tortured spiritual impulse, in willed derangement and self-imposed exile and in compulsive travel. But there are other professions whose conditions of life have been made to bear witness to this vertiginous modern attraction to the alien.[51]

Her subject is Claude Lévi-Strauss, but she might equally be describing Synge, for he also exposed the few ideas which survived his clashes with religion to the corrosive doubts of an island code which challenged them to an extreme degree. The heroism is of the usual kind, calling for physical courage and endurance, as well as for a vigilant intelligence, and beyond these, a willingness to heal one's alienation from 'society' by completing it utterly.

The anthropologist is one who solves his alienation by exacerbating it to a point where he will be a nomad, a stranger to his own people:

What he does is to offer an exquisite, aristocratic version of this neutrality. The anthropologist in the field becomes the very model of the twentieth-century consciousness: 'a critic at home' but a 'conformist everywhere'.[52]

Synge took a similar position: an artist must never be like his country's idea of itself and should feel free to set up as one of its foremost critics. The price is never to feel at home anywhere and it is a price paid on Inis Meáin by a young island woman who has spent some time on the mainland before returning. 'The disillusion she found in Galway has coloured her imagination' (*CW* II 114), he reports, even though she is not yet halfway through the teenage years. When he asks whether she would prefer to return to a town on the mainland, she answers with the fellow-feeling of another whom life has made an anthropologist: 'Ah, it's a queer place, and indeed I don't know the place that isn't' (*CW* II 114).

Identification with such a figure of romantic estrangement is absolute. In contemplating her, Synge seems to be encountering the enigma of islands which are so estranged yet so homely, so young and yet so old. She moves 'from the gaiety of a child to the plaintive intonation of an old race that is worn with sorrow. At one moment she is a simple peasant: at another she seems to be looking out at the world with a sense of prehistoric disillusion' (*CW* II 114). Synge appears to have fallen in love with the girl, who is in his eyes possessed of a more developed consciousness than any other islander. She is the one who thinks the lonely men in Parisian apartments (including the writer, of course) are 'like me so', and yet she is also the one who considers that his fire-stunt will earn him a place in hell. In her ambivalence about modernity, she embodies his conflicted feelings about the islands, for mingled with his genuine fascination is a horror of his subject, a repulsion felt at some point by most anthropologists from the primitive itself:

On some days I feel this island is a perfect home and resting place; on other days I feel that I am a waif among the people. I can feel more with them than they can feel with me, and while I wander among them, they like me sometimes, and laugh at me sometimes, yet never know what I am doing. (*CW* II 113)

One of the delusions of much anthropology was that the native lacked the self-consciousness and self-awareness of the visitor, the recognition that there are many ways of being in the world other than one's own. On the contrary in *The Aran Islands*, this is an awareness which the people have in abundance, whether Michael in Galway or the returned Yank or the girl who left the mainland. What they also possess, however, is a willingness to anthropologize the mainland society, in that mode of defamiliarization favoured by literary modernism, to the point at which the mainland reader feels less and less comfortable in his or her culture. The islands which began in peripheral vision eventually become *normative* in the fourth part.

All anthropologists seek to record the moment when the techniques of 'our' society are brought to bear in a study of 'theirs', but the fascination which draws a person towards study of a culture may in the end cause that culture to overwhelm many aspects of the self. That is what happens, slowly and very gradually, through the successive parts of *The Aran Islands*. Yet the minimal self which survives at the end is supposed to be purified, and therefore narratable. As the documentary disintegrates into fragments, the autobiographical portions recede and the more objective sections take precedence. The encounter with the island girl comes to nothing after she consigns the interloping sorcerer to the devil. Synge was a translator of Petrarch and, as David Richards has wickedly suggested, 'there is something of the petrarchan lover about the anthropologist in his passion for a subject which cannot or will not satisfy his desire but leaves his questions unanswered'.[53] Synge knows that he will always be a waif and an eavesdropper in that place, reading over the shoulder of an Inis Meáin youth the texts which belong more to the boy than they ever can to him. Yet even in that experience, the corruptions of the modern world may intrude: the boy, already committed to a writerly English, would prefer the translation which the islanders study to have used 'golden' rather than 'gold'.

Many anthropologists like Malinowski kept personal diaries of their experiences, while drawing up their field-notes in the publishable, official narrative. Synge bravely conflated the two modes of writing. If the autobiographical sections are imagined as removed from the earlier parts of *The Aran Islands*, what remains reads a little like the opening chapters of a nineteenth-century novel with its network of social relations, its omniscient author whose presence is nonetheless subsumed into narrative, and its vision of an older world frozen before the irruption of outside forces of which some inhabitants are still poignantly ignorant. The attraction of the book for its first generation of readers, like the seductive charm of *Cuchulain of Muirthemne*, may have derived from its blending of the novelistic and the mythico-personal.

The methods of novelistic realism never seemed really to fit such transitional communities. One reason was that 'realism' offered the semblance of actual experience, a stunningly exact version of a reader's known world, whereas a place like Inis Meáin interested readers because it was the very opposite of their quotidian location. Yeats's novel of Aran life never fully materialized, not just because of his ignorance of Irish but for that more formal reason. In Synge's own judgement,

Emily Lawless's Aran novel *Grania* was a failure: to write a novel of such a life would necessitate years spent among the people, as well as a deeper recognition of Aran's *strangeness*. 'You cannot make a pet book of a book everybody reads', he avowed, nor 'a pet place of a place everyone visits' (*CW* II 103n1). He was far too shrewd to attempt a full-blown novel, but smart enough to employ some of the devices of novelistic realism – character study, reported conversation, chapter sequences – in order to secure the reader's submission to his story.

Synge used the 'primitive' world of Aran much as Lévi-Strauss would employ that of *Tristes Tropiques*, as a basis from which to offer a critique of progress. This was a truly radical anthropology, far more unsettling than that of *The Golden Bough*, a Victorian folly in which the imagination of 1890, by invoking a violent and sexy prehistoric world, could 'free itself from too much history by reconstructing its remote past in speculative reformulations of human evolution'.[54] Synge might seem to have been doing that in a classic Anglo-Irish strategy. Deeper down, below the textual surface, he was reversing Frazer's practice: whereas the Cambridge don was sceptical of ancient religion and a celebrant of progress, the visitor to Aran took the opposite line. The insurgent counter-appeal from the native Irish to the more sympathetic minds among the ruling class had found another willing answerer, a process about which T.S. Eliot would soon issue a strong warning: 'In so far as the culture is *lived*, the student will tend to identify himself so completely with the people whom he studies, that he will lose the point of view from where it was worthwhile and even possible to study it.'[55]

With an attitude like that, it is hardly surprising that Eliot found Synge's poetic use of language a 'dead end' for drama. Eliot's use of myth was far more controlled than that of Synge, who saw tradition as a force that might further disrupt the present,[56] rather than one that could afford it order and protection. In Synge's plays and prose the Gaelic tradition is a challenge to progress far more daunting than any auto-critique which the shock-troops of literary modernism would mount themselves.

Ultimately, the anthropologist is a type of the hero, because he is attempting the impossible. Synge recognizes that he can never fully know or narrate the islanders: and, at about the same time as he reaches this conclusion, he also begins to abandon the attempt to narrate himself. His own identity needs to undergo a period of reformulation, in the light of what he has learned, before seeking further self-expression;

but he knows that it would be an act of criminal folly to become yet another in the long line of mainlanders who have tried to reform the islanders. It takes an heroic constitution to live out this tragic anthropology, as Lévi-Strauss avers:

The paradox is irresoluble: the less one culture communicates with another, the less likely they are to be corrupted, one by the other; but on the other hand, the less likely it is, in such conditions, that the respective emissaries of these cultures will be able to seize the richness and significance of their diversity.[57]

For that reason, Synge is driven back to the mainland, in the knowledge that what he has learned may be of help in reforming his own society. His own society is, he can now see, the only one that he can reform without destroying. He cannot claim the islands: they rather have possessed him, and may yet speak through him, helping him to express a life of his own that has not yet found expression.

Synge's heroism also lay in his willingness to flirt with the possibility of his own collapse, to dice with the possible dissolution of that ego with which he had come armed against the natives. The dream of ecstasy and abandonment, which offered such a dissolution, was quickly punished with another long spell on the mainland, for the self can never be fully given up, even if it can be recreated. The anthropologist, according to Lévi-Strauss, has no axe (Christian, Freudian, rationalist) to grind, for his real object is to save his own soul by 'an act of intellectual catharsis'.[58] That catharsis, like the conversions of ancient saints, occurs out in the field, where it is marked by a turning-point and a revolution in the heart. For Synge as for Lévi-Strauss, that was the recognition that there was no real difference between mythical and scientific thinking: science was just the magic of the modern world.

Even Synge's submission to the Orientalist strategy of the anthology, in which fragmentary parts must imply an absent whole, was itself a form of magic, not at all unlike that ritual process in which a part of the human body is worshipped as a synecdoche for the whole person. The modernized teenage girl on Inis Meáin turned out to be at once sophisticated and prehistoric, for the one quality cannot exist without the other which it helps to define.

Beyond the excitement of these discoveries lies a sense of human tragedy and loss which, no matter how much he tries to deflect it with storytelling, keeps erupting into Synge's narrative: the fall into colonial expropriation. That fall can only be undone if one pays the necessary price of abandoning all ideas of human progress, those crazy ideas which had brought the police and the tax-collectors to the islands. Appropriately, Synge refuses to append a map (that characteristic device of a colonial surveyor) to his text. The only way to free the Aran Islands is to vacate them and to recognize the spot as the no-place or utopian commune that it is for those still living happily on it. 'It is not drawn on any map', observes Herman Melville of a similar spot in *Moby-Dick*: 'True places never are.'[59]

TOM PAULIN

Riders to the Sea: *A Revisionist Tragedy? Some notes for an imaginary production*

first studied Synge at school in Belfast in the mid-1960s. It seemed
to me then that *Riders to the Sea* was a timeless drama about the
people whom I also read about in *The Aran Islands* – one of those texts
like *On the Road* which appealed so strongly to my generation (I have
a friend who read it as a 6th-former in Wales, saved his wages after leaving school and then went to live on Inishmore for a year). Over the
years I began to see – or to think I saw – a different pattern in the play.
The perception of that pattern was shaped by reading a lot of Irish history – the deepening of the Troubles in the North of Ireland meant
that many people went back to Irish history in search of a way of
understanding what, if anything, the historical situation we were living
through meant. From teaching the play as a beautifully constructed
miniature classical tragedy, I turned to teaching it as a coded historical
drama which represented Irish history in both a tragic and a revisionist
manner – one associates revisionism with various forms of irony, from
the laid-back to the savage, but a revisionist tragedy is, I believe, an
appropriate oxymoron. I made a set model in order to communicate to
my students how the stage props work to build the shadow of the gallows which falls across this play, as it also obsessively falls across *The
Playboy of the Western World*.

What follows is an informal account of the play – I find it very difficult to write about drama, and because this play has changed for me

over the more than thirty years I've known it, I find it difficult to fix my response to it. It is part of the dreamtime that was Belfast in the mid-60s, but it is also something that has taken on other resonances as the Troubles have affected my response to this masterpiece which stimulated Lawrence, a great admirer of Synge, to write 'The Odour of Chrysanthemums' and then to adapt that story into his fine play *The Widowing of Mrs Holroyd*.

In 1998, the bicentenary of the 1798 uprising, I imagined how a theatre group might tour Ireland presenting a triple bill. First they would stage Yeats's *Cathleen ni Houlihan*[1] and the audience would see Bridget, Michael's mother, in the opening scene undoing a parcel while the noise of cheering comes in from outside. That noise of cheering they would hear recur in the company's third play, *The Playboy of the Western World*, while the parcel recurs in the second play, *Riders to the Sea*.

The noise in *Cathleen ni Houlihan*, the audience would remember, is that of the French army landing at Killala, but early in the play Patrick says 'they are cheering again down in the town. Maybe they are landing horses from Enniscrone. They do be cheering when the horses take the water well.' When Christy is victorious in the racing on the strand in *Playboy* we remember this moment. Just after Michael in *Cathleen* says 'I see an old woman coming up the path', Peter goes over to a large box in the corner, opens it and puts the bag in and fumbles at the lock. When Nora and Cathleen in *Riders* put the bundle of clothes in a hole in the chimney corner we remember this action.

The actor playing the old woman in *Cathleen* plays the Widow Quin in *Playboy* and Maurya in *Riders* – this means that the spooky moment when she looks through the window at Michael in *Cathleen* will reverberate and complicate the part of Maurya. The song the old woman sings –

> I will go cry with the woman,
> For yellow-haired Donough is dead
> With a hempen rope for a neckcloth,
> And a white cloth on his head

– that song and the reference to Donough that was hanged in Galway, as well as the gallows in the next song the old woman sings, are picked up in the frequent references to hanging in *Playboy*, and in the very subtle use of stage props in *Riders* – the four new boards and the rope.

Similarly the old woman's historical narrative is caught up in *Riders*. She says:

there was a red man of the O'Donnells from the north, and a man of the O'Sullivans from the south, and there was one Brian that lost his life at Clontarf by the sea, and there were a great many in the west, some that died hundreds of years ago, and there are some that will die tomorrow.

Maurya in *Riders* says: 'there were Stephen and Shawn were lost in the great wind, and found after in the Bay of Gregory of the Golden Mouth, and carried up the two of them on one plank, and in by the door'. They are like Roman heroes brought out of battle on a shield. What seems to be a natural disaster is in fact a historical disaster. It is towards a historical disaster that Michael moves when he drops the bundle of his new clothes, his wedding clothes, and rushes out of the cottage following the old woman's voice. In *Riders*, we realize, the name of the young man who once wore the clothes in the bundle is also Michael. Synge turns the moment round when he has Bartley going out and refusing to heed the old woman, his mother's injunction to remain in the cottage. On one level he is a rebel going out to join a rebel army, like Michael; on another he is a pragmatic forward-looking businessman who is refusing to stay by the superstitious backward-looking hearth. If poetic images can convey contradictory movements of thought and feeling, so can dramatic scenes.

In the opening scene of this imaginary production of *Riders* the set designer has added the halter, the bit of new rope, Bartley asks for when he comes in. The audience see that:

—the new boards and the new rope chime

—beside the fire there is a hole where the bundle is put later

—the bundle consists of a shirt and one stocking – as audience we think of baby clothes, so the hole by the chimney is a womb – on the other hand we think of a dead body and a grave

—the spinning wheel makes the three women into the three fates

—the pot over on the fire makes them into the three witches in Macbeth who are wreckers – 'though his bark cannot be lost, /Yet it shall be tempest tossed.'

For the audience, superstition is aroused when Nora and Cathleen put the ladder against the gable. We are most of us scared of walking under ladders – I don't know why, but the associations with executions are strong. The United Irish general Hugh Munro, I recall, was hanged from the lamp bracket outside his house in Lisburn. He mounted the ladder placed against the wall, said 'I die for my country,' and leapt to his death. Patriotic woodcuts sometimes show ladders with the hangman leading a noosed rebel up to his death.

Synge, being a Protestant, knew that the ladder had another significance – it is Jacob's ladder, a masonic symbol. Maybe it's meant to communicate two opposite things here? Superstition and a mindset that is for freedom and equality, and is opposed to superstition (I am conscious, though, that there is an essay by Roy Foster which argues convincingly that Irish Protestants have been and remain deeply superstitious). What I hope this production would communicate is an ironic doubleness of intention. The play is written in prose, but it reads like a verse play: 'Is the sea bad by the white rocks, Nora?' Ten syllables, six stresses, not an iambic pentameter, but a perfect line of verse, a beautifully poised sentence sound, to use Robert Frost's phrase for the vernacular in poetry.

Maurya says to her son, her only surviving son, 'You'd do right to leave that rope, Bartley, hanging by the boards.' We hear that word 'hanging' again (it runs so much through *Playboy*), but Bartley ignores his mother and takes the rope. Maurya says, 'It will be wanting in this place, I'm telling you, if Michael is washed up tomorrow morning, or the next morning, or any morning in the week; for it's a deep grave we'll make him, by the grace of God.'

Maurya is trying to restrain him from going on the sea, but he is moving, he thinks, towards life and activity, while she is dedicated to memory and the dead. We remember that the actor playing her in *Cathleen ni Houlihan* draws Michael towards death in battle or by hanging. We remember too that that old woman in *Cathleen* – Cathleen ni Houlihan herself – was played by Maud Gonne in the first production. Maud/Maurya/Cathleen would commemorate a bicentenary, Bartley wouldn't – he is Craig the would-be pragmatist and modernizer to her backward-looking de Valera. (There is a famous story that when Craig and de Valera met in 1921 to try to reach a compromise, Craig was frustrated at having to listen to de Valera's long account of seven hundred years of Irish history, a subject Craig judged irrelevant to the business of the meeting.) This pragmatism exists on one level; on another, Bartley is like young Michael in Yeats's play going out to die, and his mother is trying to prevent him.

Then Maurya says: 'It's hard set we'll be surely the day you're drowned with the rest.' Dramatically this functions as a kind of curse. Bartley lays down the halter, takes off his old coat and puts on a newer one of the same flannel – we remember the new wedding clothes in *Cathleen ni Houlihan*, we remember the hidden bundle in this play. Now we see that the new boards, the new rope, the new or newer coat chime with each other. The old woman in the Yeats play has the walk of a young woman at the end, while in *The Playboy of the Western World* the Widow Quin and Pegeen are contrasted – youth and age, birth and death are brought together. In John Crowley's 1998 Royal Shakespeare Company production the whole cast of *Riders* had a hooley at the end – in a subtle echo of the end of Behan's *The Hostage*, there was dancing and music as Bartley came back to life.

Now Cathleen says to her mother: 'Why didn't you give him your blessing – sending him out with an unlucky word behind him and a hard word in his ear?' This makes Maurya responsible, like the old woman in Yeats's play. Then Cathleen realizes they've forgotten to give Bartley the bread – another bundle, for the bread will be wrapped in cloth. Now the bread is taken out of the black pot oven – out of another hole. As she takes it out of the oven Cathleen says 'It's destroyed he'll be, surely' – the colloquialism 'destroyed' has an ominous literal meaning. Maurya is sent out to give Bartley the bread and to break the 'dark word' and say 'God speed you.' Cathleen says give her the stick. What stick? asks Nora. The stick Michael brought from Connemara, Cathleen says. The introduction of the name of the drowned Michael is deliberate here; it increases the ominousness of the scene, it works against the idea of care and comfort and the blessing of a traveller on the road; like the ladder which Nora immediately goes over to, it is a symbol of bad luck.

Now the two young women take the bundle from the loft and Nora gets a knife to cut the string – they are the Fates slitting the thin-spun life. Nora should stand by the wheel – at this very moment Bartley must be drowning.

When Christy is tied up with ropes in *Playboy* we remember this scene – his father loosens the ropes and he escapes. In a sense he is like a rebel who escapes execution or like a rebel escaping through death from history into eternity and myth. The boards in *Riders* aren't simply coffin boards: one of them represents the boards which a condemned man walked onto carrying a handkerchief. The noose was placed round his neck. When the condemned man dropped the handkerchief, the hangman kicked the board away. Are you ready, sir? said the hangman to Emmet. Not yet, not yet. In a sense the stage in *Riders* is a scaffold – its horizontal wooden boards are what Prospero means by 'this bare island'.

When Maurya re-enters keening, she tell us that something choked the words in her throat and stopped her saying 'God speed you.' Bartley says 'The blessing of God on you', but she can say nothing – this is like the scene Macbeth recounts just before he murders Duncan and the two grooms:[2]

MACBETH	One cried, 'God bless us!' and 'Amen' the other,
	As they had seen me with these hangman's hands:
	List'ning their fear, I could not say, 'Amen,'
	When they did say, 'God bless us!'
LADY MACBETH	Consider it not so deeply.
MACBETH	But wherefore could I not pronounce 'Amen'?
	I had most need of blessing, and 'Amen'
	Stuck in my throat.

The effect of this is to make Maurya a guilty party, so that when she remembers that when her son Patch was drowned 'I was sitting here with Bartley and he a baby lying on my two knees' – the bundle and the drowning theme, birth and death, are joined.

When Bartley's body is brought in on a plank with a bit of sail over it the bundle is again present, but there is a comic moment later when the bread bundle is given to one of the men to eat while he is making the coffin.

For all its apparent naturalism, for all its transcendental tragic effect, this play is a dream vision of Irish history, of repetitive cycles of death and suffering. As I write, a coffin containing the body of Eamon Molloy, one of the disappeared, is being taken from an ancient, disused graveyard in Co. Louth. There is a purple cloth – an alb – over it.

ANTOINETTE QUINN

Staging the Irish Peasant Woman: Maud Gonne versus Synge

INTRODUCTION

Kathleen ni Houlihan, Nora Burke and a surnameless Bride are the heroines of three one-act dramas performed or published in three of the first years of the Irish National Theatre movement: Lady Gregory's and W.B. Yeats's *Kathleen ni Houlihan* (April 1902), John Millington Synge's *In the Shadow of the Glen* (October 1903), and Maud Gonne MacBride's *Dawn* (October 1904).[1] This essay provides a new context for the political controversy over *In the Shadow of the Glen* by placing the play at the centre of a series of dramas which focus on the plight of a peasant woman and are set in or in the environs of a peasant cottage.[2] To reread the play in this theatrical context highlights the ideological investment in the staging of Irish women, especially peasant women, in the emergent national theatre. Maud Gonne, who was first and foremost a dedicated and resourceful national propagandist,[3] played a key part in attempting to control or mistress-mind the dramatic construction of the Irish female. In her related roles of president of the nationalist women's organization, Inghinidhe na hEireann, and vice-president of the Irish National Theatre Society, actress, audience, reviewer and dramatist, she directed, enacted and scripted the appropriation of the peasant woman as a nationalist property.

Inghinidhe na hEireann (Daughters of Ireland), the political and cultural nationalist organization she founded in 1900, provided the base from which Maud Gonne attempted to control the staging of Irish women.[4] While this sisterhood was not merely an extension of herself and included many gifted and enterprising women, it enabled her in her capacity as president to speak with collective authority and to summon up talented collaborators for her various propagandist ventures. The Inghinidhe sponsored and financed the première of *Kathleen ni Houlihan*. Maud Gonne herself created the title role, the other actresses were also drawn from the Inghinidhe's ranks, and the society's banner, a sunburst on a blue background, was conspicuous near the stage during the first performances.[5]

The following year, the president of the Inghinidhe and one of its honorary secretaries, Máire Quinn, walked out from the première of *In the Shadow of the Glen*. This gesture of protest was followed up by Maud Gonne's verbal onslaught on the play in the columns of the *United Irishman* and her resignation as vice-president of the Irish National Theatre Society. *Dawn*, the one-acter she published in the *United Irishman* a year later, enters a dialogue with both *Kathleen ni Houlihan* and *In the Shadow of the Glen*, returning to the issue of the staging of Irish peasant women and implicating the nationalist women's organization in the revision of their role. The title, *Dawn*, alludes to the symbolic sunburst device on the Inghinidhe banner; its heroine, Bride, derives her name from Brigid, who, in her dual character of goddess and saint, was the organization's patron; the lyrics for the play were composed by an Inion, Ella Young;[6] and acting rights were reserved for Inghinidhe na hEireann.[7]

Kathleen ni Houlihan had forged a continuity between the new theatrical medium and the established nationalist visual and literary traditions through its feminization of the nation. *In the Shadow of the Glen*, one year later, represented an unwelcome innovation, the liberation of the Irish female from her iconic role into human vulnerability. Synge's characterization of female desire and destiny as personal and individual was fundamentally antagonistic to the nationalist agenda. That the play should have been produced by the National Theatre Society and coupled with the politically orthodox *Kathleen ni Houlihan* signified a lack of ideological purity and purpose on the Society's part which was anathema to nationalist propagandists such as Maud Gonne. Ironically, her failure to oust Synge's Nora from the national repertoire was in some measure due to her own failure to conform to the nationalist female ideal in her private life. Her public were to prove as intolerant of her marital unorthodoxy as she had been of Nora Burke's.

Synge and Maud Gonne had started out as friends and political fellow-travellers.[8] Both were rebels against their own class, Irish Protestant Ascendancy and English garrison respectively, with a shared sympathy for the Irish poor and a shared hostility towards landlordism; and both were deeply concerned with techniques of representation. Yet within months of their first meeting in December 1896, when both were living in Paris, the irreconcilable ideological differences between them were already evident to Synge. He had first met Maud Gonne in the company of Yeats and had became a founder member of their new political organization, l'Association Irlandaise, inaugurated in her apartment on New Year's Day. The objective of the Association was to establish an Irish nationalist propagandist presence in Paris with a view to enlisting French sympathy for the cause of Irish independence. On St Patrick's Day 1897 Synge joined other members of the group when they drew attention to France's historic role in combating English rule in Ireland by laying a wreath at the statue of Hoche, commander of the French forces at Bantry Bay in 1796.

This excursion to Versailles anticipated Gonne's and Yeats's extensive participation in the centenary celebrations of the 1798 rebellion in Ireland, which would also recall Franco-Irish military cooperation and would lead, inter alia, to their collaboration in the staging of *Kathleen ni Houlihan*. According to Gonne, l'Association Irlandaise 'never did much effective work, except sending votes of congratulation (or the reverse) to political groups in Ireland', though its official organ, *l'Irlande Libre*, served to publish inflammatory articles on famine and eviction in Ireland for republication in other journals. Synge's resignation from the Association in April appears to have been largely based on his aesthetic recoil from the propagandist aims and content of this journal. His first profound disagreement with Maud Gonne was over the representation of Ireland to foreign audiences. Yet he was concerned to maintain an appearance of national solidarity in face of this audience and offered to continue attending the Association's weekly meetings as an unofficial and silent member until he left Paris in May. So the first political rift between Synge and Maud Gonne was not made public at his request and on this occasion, too, their friendship survived ideological difference. It was manifest to Synge, however, and he made it clear to Gonne, that he could not support her 'revolutionary and semimilitary' nationalism and that his 'theory of regeneration for

Ireland' was 'widely' different from hers. How different would become apparent in their public clash over the dramatic representation of the lives and loves of Irish peasant women.

NATIONALISM AND GENDER

Maud Gonne founded Inghinidhe na hEireann in reaction to the exclusion of women from politically nationalist societies.[9] Its gendered title and adoption of sisterhood as an organizational model signified a conscious defiance of the male monopoly of political activism and of the homosocial bonding promoted in nationalist ballads and songs.[10] Apart from their subversive claim to agency within militant nationalism, the Inghinidhe were ideologically orthodox. They were liberal feminists asserting equal metaphorical rights within the existing tropes of nationalism where the figuration of Ireland as a mother, and the nation as a family, were established signifiers of community and common lineage.

However, the inscription of femininity within the nationalist movement was contested. While the Inghinidhe's adaptation of the familial metaphor, which served to naturalize the idea of the nation and represent it as an organic unity, appears ideologically orthodox, it conflicted with the prevalent Victorian middle-class family ideology adapted by the largely middle-class Gaelic League, founded in 1893. Though the League included some women activists among its ranks, it idealized mother and home as the repository of spiritual, moral, and affective values, and it constructed women as the bearers and cultural reproducers of the future nation:

... the characters of the future citizens of the country are built up in the chimney corner, where a woman tells stories in the twilight to wide-eyed listeners.
... the spark struck on the hearthstone will fire the soul of the nation.
If we make our hearthsides Irish we make Ireland Irish ...
If the Gaelic League could get a thorough grip of the cradles all over the country, and keep that grip, its work would be assured ...[11]

Home for the League was the site of a nationalist pedagogy, an Irish alternative to the official colonial system of education designed to make 'a happy English child' of every pupil. The Irish language, still spoken along the western seaboard, was presented as a home language, a mother tongue, transmitted to the nation's children along with an Irish cultural heritage of history and folklore. A nationalist pedagogy which conflated women's roles with their maternalism could prove unaccommodating to political activists such as the Inghinidhe, who positioned themselves as daughters rather than mothers. Mary Butler, author of the Gaelic League pamphlet *Women and the Home Language*, contrasted the 'gentle, low-voiced women' inculcating nationalism at the hearth with the 'shrieking viragoes or aggressive amazons' who sought a public platform.[12]

Some present-day feminists would object to Inghinidhe na hEireann's choice of nomenclature because, in colluding with the figuring of Ireland as female, they were helping to deflect attention from the very real distress of many Irish women.[13] In their journal, *Bean na hEireann*, launched in 1908, the Inghinidhe did protest against the romanticization of the 'pretty barefooted, red-petticoated cailin' whose 'picturesque' appeal derived from her poverty, and they attributed the large-scale emigration of rural women to their 'bleak and colourless life of endless drudgery'.[14] Their involvement in the three plays under consideration here, however, reveals that a clear demarcation between the responsibilities of pastoral feminism and cultural nationalism was not apparent to them when peasant women and peasant homes were first represented in the national theatre.

Intent on giving women public agency in the nationalist project, Inghinidhe na hEireann were almost immediately drawn into controversy over the representation of women in Irish drama. *Dawn*, written for the sisterhood, is Maud Gonne's experiment with a dramatic mode designed to reconcile the pastoral, familial, and nationalist concerns which had become disconnected in *Kathleen ni Houlihan* and in *In the Shadow of the Glen*.

TOWARDS A NATIONALIST WOMEN'S THEATRE

Recent emphasis on print culture in the dissemination of nationalist ideology has distracted attention from the importance of spectacle in the creation of the imagined political community.[15] Almost from the outset of the new Irish dramatic movement, nationalists perceived the potential of theatre as a mode of inventing and enacting cultural difference. In the early-twentieth-century debate between those who, like W.B. Yeats, championed the dramatist's artistic rather than ethnic

responsibilities and those who, like Arthur Griffith,[16] favoured a repre-
sentatively national drama, the new theatre's importance as successor
to the popular *Spirit of the Nation* ballad in nationalist consciousness-
raising was among the issues discussed.[17] Inghinidhe na hEireann were
in the vanguard of those who perceived the cultural importance of con-
structing an Irish alternative to the imported popular culture of theatre
and music hall. Among the organization's principal aims was 'To dis-
courage the reading and circulation of low English literature, the
singing of English songs, the attending of vulgar English entertain-
ments at the theatres and music hall …'.[18]

In their attempt at countering colonial popular entertainment, the
Inghinidhe experimented with inventing an Irish popular theatre,
mounting *ceilithe*, magic-lantern shows, *tableaux vivants* and one-act
plays, and sometimes combining all these in a single evening's performance. The *ceilidhe*, an innovative theatrical form, was a concert where
the repertoire of music, songs, and recitations was exclusively Irish and
the stage set was an Irish peasant kitchen. The peasant home was
thereby recruited as an ideological site in urban theatre. Magic lantern
shows were often devoted to realist propaganda, based on photographs
of political prisoners, evictions, British burning of homesteads in the
Boer war. (This coincides with the inclusion of silent film as part of
music hall entertainment in Ireland.) By contrast, the spectacles staged
in the *tableaux vivants* were a selection of symbolic images representing scenes from Ireland's pagan or Christian past or from nationalist
ballads or Moore's *Melodies,* and were accompanied by the reading of
a narrative or poem, the singing of a ballad, or the playing of instru-
mental music. The *tableau* form, in which Alice Milligan, a member of
the Inghinidhe, had achieved considerable expertise during the 1798
centenary celebrations, marked a significant progression toward the
emergence of a national drama, translating an existing iconography
onto the stage or inventing new visual symbolism and amalgamating
both with such established forms of nationalist discourse as historical
narratives, legends, and ballads.[19] Milligan herself made the transition
from *tableau* to drama proper with her one-act plays on Irish historical
and legendary themes, including *The Last Feast of the Fianna* (1900),
the first play to use Irish saga material.[20] Inghinidhe na hEireann, which
had drawn on the talents of Milligan to design and produce *tableaux
vivants*,[21] was the first nationalist organization to recognize the desir-
ability of training an Irish theatre troupe to perform specifically Irish

plays, to which end they co-opted the Fay brothers to provide training and direction. Some of the future leading ladies of Irish theatre – Máire Quinn, Máire Nic Shiubhlaigh and Sara Allgood – learned their craft with the Inghinidhe. A sympathy with the language movement, signified by their choice of a Gaelic name, also led the Inghinidhe to pioneer the production of Gaelic drama in Dublin. Under their auspices Father Dinneen's *An Tobar Draoideachtha* (The Magic Well) was first publicly performed in 1900; the following year saw the first Dublin production of P.T. MacGinley's *Eilis agus an Bhean Deirce* (Eilis and the Beggarwoman), and of Alice Milligan's *The Deliverance of Red Hugh*, in which she experimented with both Gaelic and English speaking parts to highlight the colonial intervention in Irish history.[22] Yeats, whose own plays were still being played by English actors, left the performance of *The Deliverance of Red Hugh* with his 'head on fire', excited by an Irish theatre that staged specifically Irish themes in Irish accents.

It is probable that Inghinidhe na hEireann's experimentation with a theatre that amalgamated Irish music, poetry, history, and iconography influenced a play such as *Kathleen ni Houlihan,* which includes all these elements. Its dramatic incarnation of Ireland as Shan Van Vocht and queenly maiden may well have derived from the genre of the nationalist *tableau*. To Maud Gonne and the Inghinidhe, the Gregory–Yeats play must have seemed a continuation of their own theatrical experiments and they were happy to sponsor the first performances.

'KATHLEEN NI HOULIHAN'

Kathleen ni Houlihan, set in a cottage kitchen in Killala at the time of the French landing in 1798, stages two conflicting narratives of Irish peasant womanhood. Mrs Gillane and, potentially, Delia, her son's pretty, well-dowered bride-to-be, represent a realist, maternal order, the values of hearth and home. The Poor Old Woman, Kathleen, also dressed as a peasant,[23] represents a contrary order of being – symbolic, nomadic, virginal, sacrificial rather than procreative, not subject to the imperatives of generational replacement, metamorphosing magically from age to youth. Two forms of continuity are opposed: continuity in the corporeal dimension expressed through reproduction and inheritance; continuity at an ideological level in which an old symbol (Sean

Bhean Bhocht/Kathleen) is revitalized through her success in obtaining adherents in the dramatic present (1798) and in the present tense of the play's production, just over a century later. *Kathleen ni Houlihan* concludes with a diptych of Irish peasant womanhood. The notorious transformation scene – in which the old crone who has lured away the bridegroom turns into a beautiful young girl with the walk of a queen – occurs offstage;[24] onstage, two bereft women, mother and jilted bride, comfort one another.[25] Inghinidhe members played both sets of contrasting female roles: the charismatic Kathleen who subverts the values of cradle, hearth, and smallholding, and the realist peasant women who lose out to the symbolic woman-nation. Nationalists, far from being perturbed by this dramatization of the split between the materialist and familial priorities of peasant conservatism and the abandonment of *kinder* and *küchen* advocated by physical-force nationalism, were elated by the triumph of the woman-nation. *Kathleen ni Houlihan,* which subordinated the interests of women to a sacrificial paradigm of male patriotism and invoked a literary tradition of political allegory, was enshrined as the exemplary nationalist play. It was appropriate that a scheduled performance at the Abbey Theatre during Easter Week had to be cancelled because the Rising, which the play adumbrated, had actually occurred.

It is now well attested that Lady Gregory scripted the roles of the realist peasants in *Kathleen ni Houlihan,* the Gillane family and Delia,[26] but to what extent was the role of Kathleen, which was authored by Yeats, authorized by Maud Gonne? All the part of Kathleen really needed, Lady Gregory famously quipped, was 'a hag and a voice'.[27] Would the play have proved as successful if the part had originally been played by any old hag? Or was it Maud Gonne's creation of the title role that was largely responsible for the play's mystique?

Kathleen ni Houlihan, now probably the best-known female symbol of Ireland, was by no means as familiar as Dark Rosaleen in 1902. She derived from a much less popular poem by Mangan, 'Kathleen-ny-Houlihan', a translation of William Heffernan The Blind's eighteenth-century poem 'Caitilin ni Uallachain'. Her accessibility in the play as a personification of Ireland was largely due to her conflation with the Shan Van Vocht from the popular 1798 ballad. She appears as The Poor Old Woman, not as Kathleen, in the list of 'Persons in the Play', and the authors toyed with the idea of using 'The Poor Old Woman' as the title. Lady Gregory feared that audiences might confuse Kathleen ni Houlihan with the Countess Cathleen from Yeats's earlier play.[28]

The first-night audience had difficulty negotiating the transition from the play's realist representation of peasantry to the figurative role of Kathleen. Yeats reported that they were slow to turn from 'delighted laughter' to an appreciation of the 'tragic meaning' of Kathleen's part. By the third performance they had been educated, and crowds were being turned away from the packed theatre.[29] Yeats's report betrays the risk that he and Lady Gregory were taking in staging Ireland as a female symbol in a realist setting. Without Maud Gonne's collaboration they might not have pulled it off. Edward Martyn commented that 'her sheer talent saved the disaster which otherwise must have come to destroy the high poetic significance of the play by reason of the low comedy-man air adopted by another actor.' That other actor was Willie Fay, and Yeats, in his reply to Martyn, pointed out that the reason for the laughter that greeted him was that Dublin audiences associated him with comedy and were 'ready to laugh before even he speaks'.[30] Fortunately, Fay's associations with comedy, which almost ruined the play, were more than compensated for by Maud Gonne's considerable notoriety in Dublin as an exceptionally ardent and beautiful nationalist. It was her credentials on both counts that authenticated the role of Kathleen, making the final transformation credible.

In 1902 Maud Gonne was at the apogee of her career as an Irish nationalist. A public speaker who was much in demand, she had undertaken lecture tours in France and the United States as well as speaking at many Irish venues. She was a prolific journalist, a prominent pro-Boer campaigner, one of the organizers of the 1798 centenary celebrations, and she was generally prominent in anti-British demonstrations in Dublin. In the role of Kathleen, Máire Nic Shiubhlaigh recalls, she appeared to the young people in the theatre as 'the very personification of the figure she portrayed on the stage'.[31] The *All-Ireland Review* noted the connection between Maud's theatrical role and her more customary role of nationalist orator, making her performance continuous with her politics: 'The well-known nationalist orator did not address the other actors as is usual in drama, but spoke directly to the audience, as if she was addressing them in Beresford Place ... she can scarcely be said to act the part, she lived it.'[32] The play's success in translating a female symbol of the nation from balladry and iconography on to the stage was largely due to Maud Gonne's charisma and her political 'street cred'.

As George L. Mosse observes, theatre which creates 'sexed bodies as public spectacles' helps 'to instill through representational practices an erotic investment in the national romance'.[33] Maud Gonne brought to the part of the *femme fatale* an erotic charge all the more potent for being covert, her disguised beauty colluding with the dialogue, titillating by its promise of a final unveiling. Her late arrival for the première, sweeping through the auditorium in her costume when the audience was already seated, consciously or unconsciously anticipated the play's conclusion.[34]

Moreover, Maud Gonne, who like Yeats was a member of the mystical Order of the Golden Dawn, invested the role of Kathleen with occult force. Yeats was not alone in attributing a 'weird power' to her characterization of Kathleen: Máire Nic Shiubhlaigh described her appearance as 'ghostly', while Joseph Holloway applied the adjectives 'mysterious', 'weird', 'uncanny', 'strange' to her playing and remarked that she 'realised' the role 'with creepy realism'.[35] Through her personal alliance of nationalism and the occult, Maud rendered the woman-nation *unheimlich*, antithetical both to material values and to the home.

The upstaging of real women by the nationalist female icon, which contemporary feminists decry, was not only thematized in the script of *Kathleen ni Houlihan* but was inseparable from its first production. Lady Gregory's co-authorship was ignored on the playbill and neither her co-authorship nor the Inghinidhe's sponsorship was acknowledged in Yeats's post-performance speeches. That the nationalist cause was privileged over the claims of sisterhood is evidenced by the fact that the play went ahead despite the death of Anna Johnston (Ethna Carbery), a vice-president of the Inghinidhe and the first of its members to die.[36] A year later, the Inghinidhe broke away from the newly formed Irish National Theatre Society because they disapproved of the Society's denationalized attitude to female representation as manifested in its staging of *In the Shadow of the Glen*.[37]

'IN THE SHADOW OF THE GLEN'

Synge's indifference to the nationalist preoccupation with historical continuity in the struggle for political independence is evident in his choice of setting for *In the Shadow of the Glen*. Harney's cottage in Glenmalure, on which the Burke cottage is based, had been the headquarters of the 1798 rebel leader Michael Dwyer.[38] Yet that connection, which would have been so resonant to Gregory, Yeats or Gonne, was utterly ignored by Synge as irrelevant to his dramatic purposes. The peasant cottage of *In the Shadow of the Glen* is a private domestic space, unaffected by nationalist politics, and the drama focuses on the personal angst of the unhappily married Nora Burke. In its writing of the body, the play voices a peasant woman's confrontation with sexuality, aging, physical decay, and death. Nora, who had pined for talk, company, sexual fulfilment and financial security, finally sees through social and material comforts to the ultimate futility and horror of being human. Within and without the cottage, life is menacing, but the shadow that overhangs all the characters' lives is not that of British imperialism.

At its first stagings in October 1903, *In the Shadow of the Glen* was played with *The King's Threshold* and *Kathleen ni Houlihan*. Its inclusion in a triple bill with *Kathleen ni Houlihan* normalized the play as part of the emergent national theatre repertoire. Maud Gonne's exit from the première of Synge's play was as conspicuous as her entrance at the première of *Kathleen ni Houlihan* the previous year. In her ostentatious exit, she was accompanied by Máire Quinn who, as well as being an honorary secretary of the Inghinidhe, was one of the cast of the first *Kathleen ni Houlihan*, and by Dudley Digges, who had created the role of Michael Gillane, the peasant turned patriot. Their walkout was a demonstration by the cast of the original *Kathleen ni Houlihan* and its sponsors against the displacement of the woman-nation's troubles by the personal distress of Synge's Nora Burke. It was also an attempt to uncouple *In the Shadow of the Glen* from *Kathleen ni Houlihan* as an acceptable national theatre offering.[39]

The Inghinidhe were not alone in their opposition to Synge's play. Nationalist commentators immediately perceived its staging as a significant theatrical event and regarded it as an unwelcome rival to *Kathleen ni Houlihan*; the new theatre was pulling in two directions and would have to choose between Kathleen and Nora. The controversy over *In the Shadow of the Glen*, in which the right to artistic freedom was pitted against the demand for a nationalist art, turned on the representation of the Irish peasant woman's sexuality. When *The Doll's House* had been mounted in Dublin's Queen's Theatre in June 1903, the audience, according to Joseph Holloway, reacted to Ibsen's Nora with utter indifference, chattering out loud, banging doors, and wandering in and out of the bar at the most inopportune moments, completely impervious to Nora's marital plight or departure from her husband.[40] However,

Synge's Irish Nora outraged nationalists such as Maud Gonne, Máire Quinn, Douglas Hyde, James Connolly, and Arthur Griffith, because its construction of Irish peasant femininity was considered either untruthful or otherwise inappropriate in a national theatre.

Primitivism was positively evaluated by nationalism as part of its anti-imperialist and anti-metropolitan agenda. 'The peasantry', as constructed by the Gaelic League pamphleteer Mary Butler, for instance, were 'by far the most attractive section of the community, by far the least vulgarised and anglicised ... The language is still theirs in many districts, and native customs and characteristics are not yet wholly obliterated among them in any part of the country.'[41] Even when peasant women's sexuality was not co-opted for a nationalist agenda of physical and cultural reproduction, the notion of extramarital peasant sexuality was offensive to puritanical nationalists. Adultery was a particularly touchy topic in post-Parnell Ireland.

The controversy over *In the Shadow of the Glen* conducted in the columns of the *United Irishman* in October 1903 bypassed the complexity of this troubling play and focused on its representation of peasant marriage. Nationalists were intent on closing off alternative configurations of Irish peasant womanhood, and Nora, who did not live up to their expectations of the virtuous, maternal peasant, was dismissed as 'a libel on womankind'. The play was denounced as 'a corrupt version' of the 'Widow of Ephesus' and 'no more Irish than the Decameron'.[42] While the play's opponents as well as its advocates accepted that the arranged and loveless marriage was a fact of Irish life, they differed as to whether marital unhappiness was a suitable theme for the national theatre, and they clashed angrily over its representation of Irish peasant women's sexuality. James Connolly, who later described Irish women suffering under the double yoke of colonialism and patriarchy as 'the slaves of slaves',[43] considered that Synge's play was unsuited to a national theatre whose purpose was to restore 'our proper national pride'.[44] Maud Gonne argued that 'it is for the many, for the people, that Irish writers must write,' and that if 'the Irish people [did] not understand or care for an Irish play' she was 'very doubtful of its right to rank as national literature.' *Kathleen ni Houlihan*, the exemplary national play, 'would be understood and loved by the simplest Irish peasant'.[45] The negative reaction of the peasantry to *In the Shadow of the Glen* could only be hypothesized; Wicklow cottagers were unlikely to have been theatregoers. Mary Butler, without alluding directly to the childless Nora, reminded 'The Daughters of the Motherland' that the onus of nationalizing Irish life falls on mothers and that 'the best of all Irish schools is an Irish mother's knee'.[46] Arthur Griffith, the play's most vehement opponent, maintained that Synge's characterization of Nora was a misrepresentation and that such a lie would neither 'serve Ireland' nor 'exalt Art'. However unhappy the Irish housewife may be, according to Griffith, she does not go away with the Tramp. 'Irishwomen', he asserted, 'are the most virtuous women in the world.'[47]

Griffith was most probably the author of the dramatic riposte, *In a Real Wicklow Glen*,[48] carried by the *United Irishman* on 24 October, a one-act play in which a 'town bred girl' learns the truth about peasant women's sexuality and marriage. Once again, the setting is a cottage. Here the townswoman encounters an elderly widow and a younger married woman, Nora, and is informed that young women forced into loveless marriages with older peasants for the sake of material security achieve some degree of amity with them, busy themselves with their maternal role, and, when their elderly husbands die, marry the sweethearts they were originally compelled to renounce, both partners by then being sufficiently prosperous to marry for love. Griffith's Nora, as a married woman, is insulted and outraged when her former sweetheart wants to kiss her: peasant women in a real Wicklow glen are shown to be paragons of marital virtue.

John Butler Yeats appealed to Maud Gonne MacBride to allow her womanly empathy with Nora Burke's plight to prevail over her nationalism,[49] but she did not relent. Maud, who had a long-standing extramarital relationship with the French political journalist Lucien Millevoye and had borne two children out of wedlock before her marriage to the Irish Boer war hero John MacBride, cannot have been as preoccupied with Irish women's sexual virtue as Griffith. She considered that 95 per cent of married women were less than happy with their lot and was sympathetic to the stance of the New Woman, believing that 'any woman with independent instincts, with the dream of making her individual personality count for something in the world, might just as well shun marriage'.[50]

Moreover, few women in Synge's first audience probably had as much first-hand experience of unhappy marriage as Maud Gonne. In May 1903, just a few months after her wedding to MacBride, she was already confiding in Yeats about her marital unhappiness. Indeed, she may have been resident in Ireland rather than France in October 1903 in order to avoid her husband. Her own conjugal drama was soon to receive a public airing when the *Irish Independent*'s reporting of her divorce case in France in 1905 was followed up by the reports of MacBride's suit against that paper for libel. MacBride was revealed as an alcoholic; he was insanely jealous of Maud's past and present friendships with other men; Maud was a battered wife. Close friends such as W.B. Yeats learned that MacBride had sexually molested other women in her household, including her ten-year-old love child, Iseult.[51] Nora Burke had it easy with Dan Burke by comparison. Maud Gonne's opposition to *In the Shadow of the Glen* would appear to have been political and strategic, not moral.

Dawn was primarily a theatrical response to *In the Shadow of the Glen*. Unlike *In a Real Wicklow Glen*, which limited itself to marital mores, it was an experiment in combining realism with nationalist political allegory in a play focusing on a peasant heroine. Kathleen ni Houlihan was writing back.

'DAWN'

Dawn is a woman-centred play focusing on three generations of an Irish family who have recently been evicted from their home: Bride, a widowed grandmother; her daughter, Brideen, whose husband has emigrated; and Brideen's son, Eoin. It is a plotless drama that traces the increasing oppression of a family and community through eviction and famine to the point where they decide to rebel against their colonial oppressor. The setting is outdoors, a desolate bog, instead of the snug domestic interior of the other two plays. Bride's evictor is a cruel landlord, not, as with Nora, a cruel husband. She and her family live outside the ruin of their former cottage in order to maintain the connection with their home and land, and life in the open is never romanticized as it was by Synge's Tramp. Lady Gregory, Yeats, and Synge had occluded the problem of peasant poverty; *Dawn* foregrounds it. Bride and her family are destitute and Brideen dies on stage of hunger and exposure. The term 'stranger', repeatedly used by Synge to dichotomize the nomad from the 'lady of the house', is now applied to construct the landlord as a foreigner, an oppressive other to the Irish peasant. Maud had refused the part of the Countess Cathleen, the eponymous good landlord, in the play Yeats had dedicated to her.[52] That was not the story about landlordism and famine that she wanted to tell. Her landlord is rendered as a heartless villain, an evictor responsible for peasant misery and hunger who, it is hinted, wishes to exercise his *droit du seigneur* on the dying Brideen.

Dawn is realist in so far as it is factual. It is partly based on scenes its author had observed in 1890 as an aid organizer during evictions in Falcarragh, Co. Donegal, where among the hundred and fifty evictions scheduled to be carried out in one week she had witnessed that of an old woman, her daughter, and two children.[53] Although she resented the presence of foreign visitors who had come to witness the evictions in Falcarragh, angry that peasant misery should be a spectator sport, Maud Gonne was quick to grasp the propagandist value of eviction. She used slides and magic lantern shows of evictions to document her numerous lectures on English misrule in Ireland and, during the Boer war, juxtaposed slides of Irish evictions with those of the burning of Boer homesteads. A photograph of a battering ram at work on a cottage is the only illustration, apart from the author's portrait, in her autobiography, *A Servant of the Queen*.

In *Dawn* the slides with which Maud illustrated her script on lecture tours provide the backdrop to the dramatic dialogue. These scenes, in which the same isolated wrecked cottage in a bog is pictured in three different lights – at evening, night, and dawn – are referred to in the stage directions as three *tableaux*. The customary relation between *tableaux* and slides was that the *tableaux* were photographed so that a technology associated with realism and documentary would bestow a quasi-documentary status on imagined scenes from the Irish past. Maud Gonne reversed this process, converting photographs into *tableaux* in an experiment with staging docudrama.

The cottage on stage throughout *Dawn* is a roofless ruin, a continual visual reminder that domestic space has been violated and destroyed by eviction. The play appeals both to the English middle-class cult of the family and to the Irish nationalist cult of the peasant home by representing eviction as an 'unhoming', primarily a crime against women and children. In her diatribe against Queen Victoria, 'the Famine Queen', Maud Gonne had portrayed her as a hypocritical bourgeoise claiming to uphold family values while condemning Irish peasant women to emigration and possibly prostitution.[54]

For the most part, *Dawn* draws on Maud Gonne's experiences of

Famine and Relief Works in north Mayo in 1898 when she was actively involved as an aid organizer and fundraiser.[55] Her own leadership in mobilizing local resistance against the horrific conditions in Mayo, recorded in *A Servant of the Queen*, is omitted from the play, which instead empowers the peasants themselves. The script records facts that she had personally observed or had had reported to her, such as: only the head of household was eligible for employment on Relief Work construction schemes, even if she were an old woman or a female single parent; a child almost burned to death while its mother was so employed; and the pay was a grossly inadequate three shillings a week per household. Mrs Ryan, the good gombeen woman in the play who gives credit to her starving customers, was based on a local shopkeeper, Mrs Kelly, and was not a fantasy of peasant solidarity.

In her contemporary newspaper coverage of the Mayo famine, Maud represented it as a familial disaster and gave a harrowing account of the plight of mothers and children. Her description of the relief works suggests that the treatment of the labour force bore some similarities to that meted out in Nazi concentration camps: 'What shocked [her] most on the relief works was that women should be employed on them. There they were; old bent women of sixty; young, slight girls of sixteen working away with pickaxes and spades under the pouring rain, or worse, carrying great stones or sods of turf on their backs.' Their food was a piece of Indian cornbread twice a day. Some had no boots and their feet were bleeding.[56] Her newspaper articles end with an appeal to the women of Ireland: 'Oh my sisters, women of Ireland, it is time we shake off our indifference and realise that we have duties of solidarity to each other. It is a slight to all of us that it should be possible to treat any Irish women as these helpless, uncomplaining starving peasant women of Erris are being treated.'[57] Such feminization of famine and the appeal to a common womanhood against the barbarity of official relief schemes made it peculiarly appropriate that *Dawn* should be dedicated to Inghinidhe na hEireann.

During the Mayo famine of 1898 Maud Gonne undertook to be 'the voice of these helpless victims of England's policy'.[58] *Dawn* is a dramatic experiment in giving a voice to the emaciated, depressed victims themselves. Whereas both *Kathleen ni Houlihan* and *In the Shadow of the Glen* had modulated from the comic to the serious, *Dawn* is unrelievedly gloomy. The dialogue, which recounts the hardships endured or witnessed by Bride's family and the local community, dwells relent-

lessly on peasant misery, and the drama topples into melodrama by tele-
scoping too many disasters into too few lines. The play concludes on
an ostensibly upbeat note with the local men mustering for rebellion
and the son who had joined the British army deserting to support the
Irish cause, but its rebels are ragged, pathetic and few in number, and
seem doomed to fail despite their brave words. The play's revolutionary optimism is undermined by its realism, by Maud's memories of
famine-stricken Belderrig where, when people attempted to cheer, it
sounded more like a cry.[59]

In *Kathleen ni Houlihan*, in which peasant and patriotic values were
in conflict, the realist and symbolic dimensions of the drama were
dichotomized. *Dawn*, on the contrary, continually negotiates between
the micropolitics of a local situation and the macropolitics of nationalism. Though based on a near-contemporary Mayo famine it gains much
of its resonance from memories of the Great Famine of the mid-1840s.
Timing and stage lighting are exploited to ensure that familial and local
events are endowed with symbolism, charting a progression from
evening to dawn, despair to revolutionary hope. Bride and Brideen
carry the cultural weight of the nationalist idealization of rural family
life. They represent two versions of nationalist womanhood: the elderly
desexualized mother figure (a grandmother, but not as old as might be
expected), who represents the successful outcome of maternal ideology,
and the youthful sexualized victim of the *aisling* tradition who, though
also a caring mother, is associated, through the apple-blossom bouquet
placed in the hands of her corpse, with pretty, flowery femininity. Bride
also combines the roles of realist victim and nationalist icon, of Mrs
Gillane and Kathleen: in addition to being associated with the values of
family, nurture, continuity, home, and land, she is represented as an
inspirational figure and a visionary. A convert to Catholicism, Maud
Gonne was sensitive to the conflation of Catholic devotion to the
Virgin Mary with a female Ireland; this is suggested by the Marian titles
bestowed on Bride: Bride of the Sorrows (*Mater Dolorosa*) and, in an
aspired-to future, Bride of the Victories (*Notre Dame des Victoires*). The
issue of land and land ownership, so central to the colonial situation,
was dealt with at only a symbolic level in *Kathleen ni Houlihan*, where
the dramatic conflict partly derived from the sacrifice of the family farm
for the 'four beautiful green fields' of Ireland. Innes rightly remarks of
that play that its 'nationalism ... has little to do with the aims of the
Land League, which implied the creation of a bourgeois peasantry'.[60]

Instead of being a disruption of peasant life as in *Kathleen ni Houlihan,* the rebellion with which *Dawn* concludes arises out of communal peasant resistance against the misrule of the colonial landlord. It is a collective response to individual exploitation, not a 'lonely impulse of delight'. The rebels defend peasant family values rather than flouting them. *Dawn* is forthrightly propagandist, appropriating eviction and famine for a militant nationalist agenda. Disappointingly, in a play written for the Daughters of Ireland, it genders political activism as masculine. The daughter, Brideen, dies; it is her son who rallies the all-male group of revolutionaries.

That Maud Gonne felt a sense of personal involvement in the role of Bride is signaled by the nearness of their respective ages: Maud, almost thirty-eight years old at the time of publication, Bride, a forty-year-old. Like Bride, Maud had been regarded as the subject of Brian Ruadh's prophecies.[61] Most obvious is the connection through nomenclature. The name Bride may have alluded to Brigid, patron of the Inghinidhe, but it carried the more immediate reminder of Maud's own married name, Maud Gonne MacBride, with which she signed the play. The young insurrectionary hero, Eoin, Bride's grandson, is virtually a young MacBride, perhaps a tribute to Maud's infant son, Sean. Had she not been preoccupied with sorting out her marital affairs from December 1904, it is probable that she would have acted the role of Bride in an Inghinidhe production of *Dawn.* Might her play then have enjoyed something of the nationalist cult status attaching to *Kathleen ni Houlihan*?

Maud Gonne MacBride's personal circumstances, in particular her legal separation from her husband in July 1905, probably had considerable bearing on the fate of her play. As the *ex*-wife of Major John MacBride, she was no longer the nationalist heroine she had formerly been. When she attended Lady Gregory's *The Gaol Gate* at the Abbey Theatre on 20 October 1906 there were shouts of 'Up John MacBride' from some male nationalists in the audience.[62] Kathleen ni Houlihan had flouted the nationalist code for Irish womanhood and gone part of the way with Nora Burke. Having missed its moment, *Dawn* languished in the obscurity of the *United Irishman* for sixty-odd years before being republished – as one of the 'Lost Plays of the Irish Renaissance' – in 1970, its only republication to date.[63]

CHRISTOPHER MORASH

All Playboys Now: The Audience and the Riot

'Ifeel we are beginning the fight for our lives,' Lady Gregory wrote
to John Millington Synge on 14 January 1907 while his *Playboy of
the Western World* was in rehearsal; 'We must make no mistakes.'[1]
Throughout the early winter of 1907, the Abbey's habitual sense of
crisis was more acute than usual; and, as usual, the principals in this
'fight for our lives' gave every indication of savouring the pleasures of
the complex game they were playing. The Abbey management had
been worried about the new play from the start, closing the rehearsals
to even their most devoted hangers-on, such as Joseph Holloway, who,
of course, knew that something was afoot. 'Mr. [W.A.] Henderson [the
Abbey business manager] was looking gloomy at the Council Meeting
of the National Literary Society', he noted in his diary, 'and I knew
something was wrong at the Abbey.' 'There were too many violent
oaths', Lady Gregory later wrote of the script, 'and the play itself was
marred by this. I did not think it was fit to be put on the stage without
cutting.'[2] Accordingly, she set to work building a firewall around W.B.
Yeats, whose short farce *The Pot of Broth* (which Gregory had largely
written) was originally scheduled to be performed on the same bill with
The Playboy of the Western World. 'It would be an injustice to Yeats to
put a slight thin peasant farce with your elaborate peasant work,' she
wrote cajolingly to Synge, urging *Riders to the Sea* as an alternate cur-
tain-raiser; meanwhile she wrote tersely to Yeats: 'I was determined …
that Synge should not set fire to your house to roast his own pig'.[3]

The Pot of Broth was out, and *Riders to the Sea* was in, but Synge's pig was still going to roast. On 26 January 1907, the opening night of *The Playboy of the Western World*, the auditorium was completely full, with box office receipts of £32.14.10 showing that every possible seat had been sold (in addition to which there were always friends and relations of the managers to be given complimentary seats). *Riders to the Sea* was listened to with reverential silence – a silence demanded not only by the quasi-liturgical nature of the play itself, but also by the theatre management. However, this type of response was becoming increasingly difficult to achieve in the Abbey. Earlier in the 1906–7 season, the Abbey management had introduced, for the first time, a limited number of sixpenny seats in the front of the stalls (now called the pit), partly to boost flagging audience numbers, and partly to meet the criticism that many of 'the people', whom the Abbey was supposed to serve, could not afford to pass through its doors. Under the headline 'The Horniman-Yeats Theatricals: No Low Persons Wanted', the London *Universe* of 14 January 1905 had noted acidly: 'the new theatre, which Miss Horniman has arranged at her own expense for Mr. Yeats and his dramatic sketches, is to be carefully guarded against the presence of the common sixpenny public. In order to prevent "any lowering of the letting value" of the little theatre, prices are to be five shillings, three shillings, one shilling and nothing less. The sixpenny gallery are not wanted.'

Leaving aside the snide remark about 'Mr. Yeats and his dramatic sketches', it is true that the cheapest seat in the Abbey prior to 1906 cost the same as a box seat in the Gaiety, where some of the best touring companies in the world were to be seen. However, changing seat prices at the Abbey also changed the composition of the audience, and within a month of the introduction of a sixpenny pit, in November 1906, Yeats felt compelled to insert a tetchy notice in the Abbey's journal, *The Arrow*, claiming that 'several complaints have reached us, that, at a recent performance of Mr. Synge's *Riders to the Sea*, the effect of the play was all but destroyed, by the opening and shutting of the door to the Stalls', reminding his readers with Wagnerian *hauteur* that 'at Bayreuth, nobody is allowed to enter the auditorium till the Act is over'. Yeats then went on to appeal to Dublin audiences to at least 'endeavour to be seated before the rise of the curtain at 8.15'.[4]

In terms of modifying audience behaviour, this was one more step along a route that included the abolition of half-price tickets after 9.15

(a practice still followed at other Dublin theatres of the time, such as the Queen's Theatre Royal) and the darkening of the auditorium during the performance. Apart from Yeats's more esoteric theories concerning the ritualistic nature of theatre, this increasing regulation of an audience's behaviour was made necessary by plays such as *Riders to the Sea*. The opening moments of *Riders to the Sea*, for instance, begin in almost complete silence, with a rhythmic activity, Cathleen kneading bread; the quiet thump, thump, thump of the bread dough is then amplified slightly and changes timbre when Cathleen moves from the oven to the spinning wheel, and begins to spin with a rhythm which underscores the following conversation:

NORA   [*in a low voice*]. Where is she?
CATHLEEN   She's lying down, God help her, and maybe sleeping, if she's able.
            [*Nora comes in softly, and takes a bundle from under her shawl.*]
CATHLEEN   [*spinning the wheel rapidly*]. What is it you have?
NORA   The young priest is after bringing them. It's a shirt and a plain
            stocking were got off a drowned man in Donegal.
            [*Cathleen stops her wheel with a sudden motion, and leans out to
            listen.*] (*CW* III 5)

Synge borrows the use of the spinning wheel as a rhythm instrument from one of the best known of Schubert's *lieder*, 'Gretchen am Spinnrade' (1814) – a work of which he could not have been unaware, given his earlier studies at the Irish Academy of Music. Like the opening moments of *Riders*, Schubert's song begins with the hushed, metronome-like beat of the revolving wheel, picking up pace until it comes to an abrupt halt as the hushed words reach their climax.

Straining in silence to hear the sound of a spinning wheel was a far cry from what most theatre audiences of the time anticipated, particularly those who were used to paying sixpence for a theatre seat. The opening moments of J.W. Whitbread's phenomenally popular *Wolfe Tone* is far more typical of what Dublin audiences of the time expected. The play opens with a comic Trinity College porter, who is set upon and beaten by a group of students.

            [*Enter STUDENTS from C. Some pass R., some L. Enter SHANE
            dressed as a College Porter C. He sings quietly as he comes down. He looks
            R. and L., then up. Enter two STUDENTS. One knocks his cap over his
            face.*]
SHANE   Murther alive! what's that? [*Other STUDENT hits him in the stomach*]
            Oh! I'm kilt. [*Dances about with hand on stomach*]. Murther, thaves!
            [*STUDENTS laugh and exeunt R ...*][5]

As this business was taking place on the stage of the Queen's Theatre Royal, the audience members were talking to each other, smoking, commenting on the play, applauding or hissing the characters, eating oranges (the traditional fruit in Dublin theatres since the early eighteenth century), calling out witty responses to the action on the stage, or simply wandering around the theatre: in short, they were enjoying the pleasures of theatre-going as they had existed since the late sixteenth century. For such an audience, going to the theatre (regardless of the play) was a form of entertainment, and this is reflected in the practice (never adopted by the Abbey) of charging a few pence extra for early admission. In the place of this traditional active audience, the Abbey was doing its best to create a passive audience who sat silently in the dark, staring intently at the stage, offering up little more than the requisite round of applause when the play was over – all restrictions which a Queen's audience would have considered the equivalent of a custodial sentence.

This was the audience, then, who were beginning to make their way across the Liffey to the new sixpenny seats at the Abbey; more would follow when plays such as Lennox Robinson's *The Whiteheaded Boy* began to take over the forms of the popular theatre. By September 1925 Sean O'Casey would write to Lady Gregory: 'I know that many coal-heavers, dockers, Carters & labourers have been in the Abbey';[6] in the 1940s, the Abbey's Irish-language pantomimes made a further incursion into the last bastion of popular theatre, and the whole process would come full circle when, after the fire of 1951, the Abbey company took up residence in the Queen's, bringing many of the audience back home.

Meanwhile, on the evening of Saturday, 26 January 1907, when *Riders to the Sea* came to an end with the line 'no man at all can be living for ever, and we must be satisfied', there was a short break, during which the orchestra played, just as it would have in the Queen's. Then *The Playboy of the Western World* began. At first the audience were receptive, laughing at most of the right moments, but increasingly uncertain how they were supposed to respond to this strange tale of a young man, Christy Mahon, played by Willie Fay, who wanders into a remote Mayo community claiming to have killed his father. 'I'm thinking this night', says Christy, 'wasn't I a foolish fellow not to kill my father in the years gone by', upon which the curtain came down for the end of the first act. The audience duly applauded, and backstage Lady

Gregory dashed off a telegram to Yeats, who was in Aberdeen giving a lecture: 'Play great success.' In the second act, the adulation heaped on the murderer continued, and the audience's laughter became more uneasy than it had been in the first act. So it continued at the beginning of the final act, increasingly dominated by Old Mahon, the dead father (who is not, of course, dead, having reappeared in the course of the second act). Then, about fifteen minutes from the end of the play, the mood suddenly changes, the humour darkens, and Christy chases his father outside to kill him again (presumably with greater finality). It was at this point that the audience began, like the villagers on the stage, to turn nasty. In quick succession, Christy attacks his father with a loy offstage, and returns to announce that he would have no woman other than Pegeen Mike, even if offered 'a drift of Mayo girls standing in their shifts itself', whereupon one of the female characters on the stage pulls off her petticoat to provide him with a disguise.[7] By now, there was a bedlam of hisses and yells in the auditorium, but fortunately only about ten minutes of performance time left. So it was with considerable relief that the actors playing Christy and Old Mahon finally marched off, leaving Pegeen Mike to lament her loss of 'the only playboy of the western world' before joining them in an anxious backstage retreat to the green room. When the house finally cleared, Lady Gregory sent Yeats the most famous telegram in Irish theatre history: 'Audience broke up in disorder at the word "shift".'

The theatre was dark the next day, being Sunday, and so when Joseph Holloway went out for his afternoon walk on Pembroke Road he met Frank Fay, Willie Fay and his wife, Brigit O'Dempsey, who played Sara Tansey in *The Playboy*, and 'we chatted about last night's fiasco'. 'The players had expected the piece's downfall sooner,' Willie told him. Holloway praised the acting 'and said it was a fine audience to play to. It frankly did not like the play and frankly expressed itself on the matter, having patiently listened to it until the fatal phrase came and proved the last straw.'[8] Yeats arrived back in Dublin the following day, Monday, just in time to see a tiny audience take their seats, with fewer than eighty people sitting in a theatre capable of holding more than five hundred. If Saturday evening had been a case of an audience honestly protesting against a play they did not like, Monday was a completely different affair. After listening politely and patiently to *Riders to the Sea*, about forty members of the audience sitting in the pit, quickly identified by Yeats as supporters of Arthur Griffith's Sinn Féin, began stomping their feet, booing and hissing as soon as the curtain rose on *The Playboy of the Western World*. The actors trudged through the sea of abuse for a while, until Willie Fay stopped the performance, announcing that he was a Mayo man himself, and telling the audience to listen to the play in silence or else the police would be called. This only incensed the audience further, as did the arrival of half a dozen police officers, who stood around stolidly but ineffectually until Lady Gregory and Synge asked them to leave. From the stalls, Lord Walter Fitzgerald made a short speech pleading for the actors' right to be heard, but he too was hooted down. And so the performance continued, for the most part completely inaudible, and even when the players had made their final, merciful exit the rumpus continued until both the house and stage lights were put out, finally silencing the remaining protesters with darkness.

'With the coming of Yeats', the newspaper editor W.P. Ryan commented to the Abbey's business manager, W.A. Henderson, 'I knew that the trouble would be aggravated.'[9] He was, of course, absolutely right. 'The position of attack is far stronger than the position of defence,'[10] Yeats had told Frank Fay a couple of years earlier, and true to his own advice, he went on the attack. He began the day on Tuesday by accompanying Synge, who was miserable with influenza, to the Metropole Hotel, where he gave an interview to the *Freeman's Journal*, in which he declared the autonomy of art, and the need for exaggeration in great art. Of course, Yeats did not expect those who had protested the previous night to understand this, he said, because he could see 'the people who formed the opposition had no books in their houses' – a sentence the *Freeman's* helpfully set in large type when it printed the interview the next day. He went on to say that such 'commonplace and ignorant people' were incapable of following a great leader because they had wrapped themselves up in 'societies, clubs, and leagues', and 'they have been so long in mental servitude that they cannot understand life if their head is not in some bag'.[11] Synge volunteered that the offensive word 'shift' was used in Douglas Hyde's *Love Songs of Connacht* (albeit in Irish), but Yeats was providing much more interesting copy, and Synge's remarks were ignored in the ensuing battle. Meanwhile, back in the theatre, Lady Gregory was doing her bit by suggesting to a nephew that it would be useful if he could bring along to the theatre that night 'a few fellow athletes' from Trinity College, 'that we might be sure of some able-bodied helpers in case of an attack on the stage',[12] not realizing that since the eighteenth century

mobs of drunken Trinity students had been used in Dublin to provoke
– not prevent – theatre riots.

Shortly after seven o'clock that evening, a crowd began to gather
around the pit-door of the Abbey on Marlborough Street. By 7.30, the
forty or so young men waiting for the doors to open noticed a posse of
policemen being let in through the stage door. At ten to eight, the
house doors opened, and there was a rush to the sixpenny seats in the
pit. At about eight o'clock, twenty Trinity students entered the building in varying degrees of inebriation, and were given free seats in the
more expensive stalls. They were accompanied by a Galwayman in a
large overcoat (a later satire refers to him as 'Napoleon'), who decided
to get things moving by offering to fight anyone in the pit on the spot,
before standing up on a chair to make a speech which came to the
resounding conclusion: 'I am a little bit drunk and don't know what I
am saying' – words duly reported in the next morning's papers. Most
of the audience, including the pit he had offered to fight, enjoyed his
performance, and so he obliged their interest by weaving his way up to
the side of the stage, and playing an unsteady waltz on the theatre's
piano, before being escorted back to his seat by some of the theatre's
house staff, protesting 'they won't allow me to speak although I am a
Labour member' (general laughter). Yeats and Gregory were by now
in the theatre, and at 8.15 precisely the curtain went up on *Riders to
the Sea* to an auditorium that was about half full. As had been the case
on previous nights, and as would be the case for the rest of the week,
it was listened to in respectful silence, and enthusiastically applauded
when it was over.

At that point Yeats stood up to pour some oil on the hot coals by
announcing that there would be a public debate on *The Playboy* and
'the freedom of the theatre' the following Monday, at the same time
warning the audience that 'no man has the right to interfere with
another man who wants to hear the play'. The play would be performed until it was heard, he told them, 'and our patience will last
longer than your patience'. Then, at 9.03, after a few Irish airs from the
orchestra, the curtain went up for the third time on *The Playboy of the
Western World*. The opening scene was listened to politely, but when
Christy made his entrance the audience in the pit started to stomp their
feet and make as much noise as possible, while those in the stalls
cheered and clapped with equal vigour, forcing the management to
turn up the house lights.

The Galwayman took this as the cue for some fisticuffs. Yeats at first tried to restrain him, then returned to the stage, which the actors had abandoned. Yeats pleaded with the audience to listen to a play by 'a distinguished fellow-countryman of theirs', telling them they would impair the Irish reputation for 'courtesy and intelligence', at which point someone in the audience began to blow on a bugle. Meanwhile, the Galwayman was calling out to him, 'Woa, woa, you chap there. Woa, be a sportsman', while trying to shake free from the friends who were holding him, in the process upending some of the chairs in the stalls. When he was finally evicted by Synge and Ambrose Power, the burly actor playing Old Mahon, Yeats announced that 'we have persuaded one man who was, I regret to say, intoxicated, to leave the meeting. I appeal to all of you who are sober to listen.'

A Voice from the Pit: 'We are all sober here' (loud applause).

After a short conference, Yeats, Lady Gregory and Synge called in the police, who had been backstage throughout, and, with the help of another of Gregory's nephews, Hugh Lane, began pointing out particularly noisy members of the pit to be evicted. More police arrived, and the orchestra added an extra level of unreality to proceedings by striking up a few jaunty tunes to accompany the arrests. An uneasy calm descended, but as soon as the houselights went down and the play recommenced, the uproar started up again under the cover of darkness, with the stalls and the pit stopping just short of open warfare with one another as cries of 'That's not the West' were repeated again and again. One member of the audience suggested that the police arrest Christy Mahon for the murder of his father, at which the whole house laughed. The police, aided by the managers, continued to pick out members of the audience, some of whom were simply evicted, while others were taken into custody and later charged. In the course of the next hour, things continued more or less like this, with the curtain lowered from time to time when the performance became more than usually inaudible. The Galwayman reappeared, like Old Mahon, at around 10.20, his head reeling from more drink rather than from the blow of a loy, and repeated his offer to fight anyone in the pit. He was forestalled, however, by his friends in the stalls launching into a rousing chorus of 'God Save the King', which was matched by an equally energetic version of 'God Save Ireland' from the pit, by which time it was 10.30 pm, and the final curtain fell on the poor shell-shocked actors.

Once they were finally outside the theatre, the groups in the pit and stalls continued taunting each other as they crossed the Liffey on the students' way home to Trinity, picking up supporters in the street. The name-calling finally erupted into a violent brawl in Westmoreland Street, just outside the walls of the College (and a police station), where there were further arrests. By the next evening, Wednesday, the house had picked up, with about 420 in attendance, and, in spite of the publication earlier that day of Yeats's provocative interview with the *Freeman's Journal*, the night was less rowdy, although it was still diffi-cult to hear much of the play, and the police continued to arrest pro-testers in the audience. Once again, there were fights in the street afterwards. The worst was over, however, and as the week went on, the protests gradually lost some of their energy. Indeed, they were becom-ing self-parodic, so that when on Thursday night Old Mahon described Christy as 'a poor fellow would get drunk on the smell of a pint', some-one in the pit called out 'That's not Western life', to the general amuse-ment of the whole house. The Saturday matinee, although thinly attended, was relatively quiet, and by the final performance on Saturday evening Abbey decorum had re-established itself. 'If we can hold our audiences now for a few weeks', Synge wrote to Lady Gregory a week later, 'we shall be in a better position than ever.'[13]

Throughout the affair, it is possible to trace a thread of drunken hilarity weaving its way through the more serious strands, and by the time of the great debate on the freedom of the theatre on Monday 4 February, this had worked its way to the surface. Contributions ranged from a long, and much interrupted, account of the Covent Garden riots by the theatre historian W.J. Lawrence, to a medical disquisition on sexual melancholia at which 'many ladies, whose countenances plainly indicated intense feelings of astonishment and pain, rose and left the place'.[14] John Butler Yeats made a sly speech about Irish piety, pro-voking the audience to call on W.B. Yeats to 'kill your father'. 'Where's the loy?' someone called from the back of the hall. W.B. Yeats, in full evening dress, stood up to speak several times, and, in the words of Roy Foster, made a speech more 'deliberately offensive to a Dublin audi-ence'[15] than any he had ever made in his life, perhaps trying to shock them into seriousness. He claimed that he would not be swayed by intimidation, and that 'we' – the Protestant directors of the Abbey – 'have not such pliant bones, and did not learn in the houses that bred us a so suppliant knee ("Oh", groans and hisses)'.[16] Much of what was said, however, was inaudible, and although there were some considered speeches from the stage, the real performers were, once again, the audience, who kept up a barrage of heckling throughout the evening. 'I was sorry while there that we had ever let such a set inside the theatre,' Gregory wrote to Synge the next morning, no doubt regretting the introduction of sixpenny seats, 'but I am glad today, and think it was spirited and showed we were not repenting or apologising.'[17]

The Monday debate was by no means the last post-mortem on the week's events, and since 1907 there have been numerous explanations for the riots. The trigger-effect of the word 'shift' suggests that Synge himself was close to the mark when he had observed a few years earlier that he had 'restored sex [to the Irish stage] and the people were so surprised they saw the sex only' (*CL* I 74), and it is certainly the case that the play upset already unstable dogmas of gender and sexuality. The most frequently heard protest – 'that's not the West' – also indicates that Synge had offended an imaginative geography underpinned by fashionable notions of racial purity, in which the West of Ireland, as the part of the country most removed from English influence, was considered to be the last bastion of pure Irish virtues, uncorrupted by foreign modernity. And, of course, there were bound to be politically motivated objections to a play which so consciously mocks heroism, teaching Pegeen Mike that 'there's a great gap between a gallous story and a dirty deed' at a time when so many cultural nationalists were nurturing images of what Synge had called 'Cuchulainoid' heroics. Each of these factors on their own undoubtedly played their part in the audience's reaction, and when unorthodox attitudes to sex, race, identity and violence were mixed they made a dangerously potent brew. This was particularly true on the opening night, when the protests were at their most spontaneous; however, as the disturbances proceeded, it became evident that other issues were at stake as well.

The architecture and seat-pricing policy of the Abbey meant that the *Playboy* riots were unlike any previous Irish theatre protests. In the Abbey, the cheapest seats were those nearest the stage; in all other Irish theatres, the cheapest seats were those farthest from the stage, in the upper galleries. Hence, while the pit had always been a volatile part of the house, the frontline troops in Irish theatre riots had always been the upper gallery. Not only did those who could afford only sixpence (or less) to attend a play usually have good reasons to protest, but post-Restoration theatre design gave them a strategic height advantage when it came to throwing things, and most galleries were reached by a maze of dimly lit corridors in which it was possible to elude the police, or at least to cut down the odds during hand-to-hand combat. Anyone who has spent time in the upper gallery of either the Gaiety or the Olympia Theatre in Dublin will see immediately the advantage of height in planning a disruption. In these theatres today, while there is not much in the way of hand-to-hand combat with the police, certain types of performance, such as popular music or stand-up comedy, open up a space for interaction with the audience, and when this occurs it almost always originates from the top of the house.

By contrast, the 1904 Abbey had no gallery, and apart from a couple of attempts to make speeches from the two-shilling seats in the balcony, the audience in the upper part of the house appear to have been comparatively well behaved, some determined pounding on the balcony rail aside. Indeed, there are no reports of anything being thrown in the theatre on any night of the disturbances, and in this, as in so much else, the *Playboy* riot was a respectable middle-class affair, shot through with an element of restraint in spite of its volatile mixture of serious intentions and giddiness. No seats were broken up, no one was attacked (at least inside the theatre), the temptingly large mirrors, stained glass and portraits of the directors in the lobby remained undefaced, and, in spite of Lady Gregory's fears, no attempt was made to rush the stage, as was to happen two decades later during the *Plough and the Stars* riots. Synge, while vilified in the press, wandered freely around the theatre throughout the week, sweating with influenza, and his *Riders to the Sea* was given a respectful hearing and heartily applauded on even the noisiest nights.

The real confrontation, which became most apparent on the Tuesday night, was not between the audience and the stage, but between the lower-middle-class, predominantly Catholic nationalist, audience who sat in the sixpenny seats in the pit, and the upper-middle-class, predominantly unionist, audience who sat in the three-shilling stalls. 'There was a kind of opposition', as one policemen on duty put it, 'between the occupants of the stalls and the pit.'[18] In spite of Yeats's attempts to rewrite the episode as a philistine mob howling at the independent artist, it became clear in the trials which followed that many of those arrested in the pit were regular supporters of the Abbey, including the Irish-language playwright Piaras Béaslaí and (embarrassingly) Pádraic Colum's father. What was being battled over during the *Playboy* riots was not only the image of the Western peasant or the shocking possibility that Irish women wore underwear; it was possession of the Abbey as a 'national' theatre by two different factions of a doubly divided middle class, as became clear when 'God Save the King' and 'God Save Ireland' were sung simultaneously at the end of the Tuesday night performance. 'We have won a complete victory over the organised disturbers – Sinn Fein men to a great extent', wrote Robert Gregory to his mother. 'It was quite necessary that someone should show fight and we are the only people who have done it.'[19]

Indeed, the battle in the auditorium of the Abbey during *The Playboy of the Western World* uncannily echoes the battle on the stage of the Queen's Theatre Royal in the opening moments of Whitbread's *Wolfe Tone*. When the Trinity students in Whitbread's play attack the College Porter, they are acting out a series of class antagonisms very similar to those which erupted between the three-shilling stall seats and the sixpenny pit seats during the *Playboy* riots. In Whitbread's play, it quickly becomes clear that Shane, an unreconstructed stage-Irishman, is the figure with whom the lower-middle-class and working-class audience are meant to identify, as he speaks in Dublin working-class speech patterns, delivers asides to the audience, and orchestrates the action of the play's episodic plot. Moreover, Shane's politics are unambiguously republican; in the play's opening moments, he is rescued from the attacking students by Thomas Russell, an important figure in the United Irish movement who was later hanged for his part in Robert Emmet's rebellion in 1803. Shane spends the rest of the play extricating an impressively noble, but hopelessly guileless, Wolfe Tone from a series of nefarious plots.

While this may sound to us like laughable stuff, *Wolfe Tone* in performance at the Queen's used a simple, but powerful, device to remind its audience that antagonisms between the audience who applauded patriotic melodramas and upper-middle-class Trinity students extended beyond the walls of the theatre. The Queen's was located on Great Brunswick Street (now Pearse Street), adjacent to the north side of the Trinity campus. In the opening moments of *Wolfe Tone* the large double doors at the back of the stage were opened to present a moonlit vista of the College's New Square, even though in winter this 'set many of the audience to coughing', as one critic complained, 'and is downright cruelty to the people on the stage'.[20] Looking out through the back of the stage at the Trinity campus, the occupants of the sixpenny seats in the Queen's were sizing up enemy territory. When, in

1907, these two adversaries found themselves separated by only a few rows of seats, the results were predictable. 'We always had the stalls on our side,' Yeats claimed at the time of the *Playboy* riots, and Lady Gregory would tell the *Irish Independent* that they could have ended the disturbances at any point 'if the prices of admission were raised'[21] – thereby excluding the sixpenny audience, who were used to watching patriotic melodramas at the Queen's, and who were now attending the Abbey.

In the years leading up to the Dublin Lockout of 1913, there would be other battles fought between these classes; however, at the time of the *Playboy* riots, the field of combat was defined by two competing, culturally specific, understandings of what constituted appropriate audience behaviour in a theatre. When the first protesters were brought to trial, the judge, Justice Mahony, while aware of the absurdity of charging one or two individuals out of so many, took no account of the fact that the offences had been committed in a theatre, and fined them all the maximum 40 shillings, as if they had been disturbing the peace by screaming abuse at passers-by in the street. However, those charged later in the week came up before Justice Wall, who had taken the time to look up precedents for theatre rioting, and had come upon Charles Kendal Bushe's instructions to the jury in what had become known as 'The Bottle Riot', which had taken place in the Theatre Royal, on Hawkins Street, on 14 December 1822.[22]

On that night, almost a century before Synge's play opened, Richard, Marquis Wellesley, the Lord Lieutenant of Ireland, had attended a performance of Goldsmith's *She Stoops to Conquer*. The previous month, Wellesley had banned an annual demonstration by local Orange Lodges which involved decorating a statue of William of Orange on College Green every 4th of November, William's birthday. On Friday, 13 December, there had been a meeting of a working-class Orange Lodge, Number 1612, on Dublin's Werburgh Street, at which money was raised to buy twelve tickets, mostly in the upper gallery, for the following evening's performance. Throughout the day on 14 December, members of the Lodge prepared for the evening ahead, gathering whistles and bludgeons, and printing handbills. By late afternoon about thirty Lodge members were drinking, first in their Lodge (ignoring the injunction to temperance in their oath), and later in a small tavern run by James Flanagan in Dame Court. As they left Flanagan's to go to the theatre, one Orangeman, Henry Handwich, told them: 'Boys, be wicked.'

They were. Handbills fluttered down from the lattices (a small group of boxed seats near the top of the proscenium) as soon as Wellesley entered the auditorium, bearing slogans such as 'No Popery', and throughout the performance there were cries of 'No Popish Lord Lieutenant', 'No Eastern tyrants', and 'Baldy-pated Wellesley go home out of that'. Meanwhile, in the upper gallery, where most of the protesters were seated, long wooden cudgels began to appear, and there was soon open fighting. The situation deteriorated until Henry Handwich, sitting three rows from the edge of the gallery just above the Lord Lieutenant, took a final swig from the bottle in his hand before giving it a side-arm toss over the edge of the parapet. It hit the curtain, and bounced down on to the raked stage, where it rolled into the orchestra. The house by this point was in a state of uproar, and George Graham, another Orangeman sitting in the front row just left of centre in the upper gallery, banged a rattle against the railing so hard that it broke in two, whereupon he hurled the pieces downwards. One piece about eight inches long hit the cushion of the box beside the Lord Lieutenant, occupied by Lady Rossmore, who, being more or less deaf and blind, sat placidly unperturbed throughout the uproar. 'I was not in the least alarmed,' she later said.

As was the case with the *Playboy* riots, there were a number of arrests on the night of the disturbance. In the follow-up, however, Dublin Castle badly overplayed its hand, and initially tried to convict the rioters on a charge of attempting to assassinate the Lord Lieutenant. This not only fell flat when brought before a jury stacked by the Dublin Sheriff, Charles Thorpe, who was a senior Orangeman, but it gave Dublin scope to exercise its considerable powers of mockery (a bottle and a broken rattle hardly made convincing murder weapons):

> Have you heard, or who has not,
> Of this dreadful Orange plot,
> Which lately reared its horrid head
> To strike our Lord Lieutenant dead; ...
> That they might not be detected,
> With hellish prudence they selected
> ... implements so unfit,
> A broken rattle and a bit
> Of wood – that some men even still ... (silly elves!)

Have not yet convinced themselves,
That these wretches did intend
His Ex[cellenc]y's life to end.[23]

A second trial ensued, at which the defendants were tried for 'conspiracy to riot and rioting'. It was also unsuccessful when brought before one of Sheriff Thorpe's juries; however, the legal judgements made during the course of the trial were to have an impact on the trials which followed the *Playboy* riots in 1907. In his summation to the jury, Chief Justice Charles Kendal Bushe produced an important legal definition of the rights of Irish theatre audiences. 'An audience may cry down a play, or hiss, or hoot an actor', he told the jurors; 'an audience may be noisy, but not riotous; besides, this must be the feeling of the moment; if not, it becomes criminal.'[24]

Justice Wall was to quote these words in 1907 as the basis of his judgement when the *Playboy* rioters were brought before him. In choosing this legal precedent, Justice Wall confirmed what the 'Bottle Riot' had established: the legal status of the Irish theatre as a place of public protest. 'This is a most extraordinary case', Justice Wall exclaimed in exasperation at the end of one trial, 'to bring up a man for hissing, when he is the only one arrested, the house being in a state of tumult, one side hissing, the other applauding.'[25] Imposing derisory fines on those brought before him, Wall made it abundantly clear that, following the Bushe judgement, protests inside a theatre were not a matter for criminal prosecutions, provided they were conducted within clearly recognized limits, and did not involved actual assault, damage, or conspiracy. As the week of the riots progressed, newspaper comment across the political spectrum drifted towards Justice Wall's position supporting the traditional rights of audiences, praising the protesters who were voicing a genuine dislike of the play, and condemning those who later attended with a premeditated intention to obstruct the performance. Similarly, the press almost uniformly denounced the Abbey's decision to involve the courts in a situation which was governed by clearly understood protocols of audience behaviour.

And this brings us back to the audience at the Queen's Theatre Royal, and their insistence on the right to respond to the action on the stage. Looking back from a theatre culture in which silence in the auditorium is a norm, it is easy to dismiss these audiences as boorish mobs; in fact, they were the inheritors of a theatrical tradition which had a basis in law. The 1907 Abbey, on the other hand, with its stern warnings against latecomers rattling the stall doors, was making a conscious effort to restrict the rights of a theatre audience to something more in line with upper-middle-class notions of decorum. From this point of view, much of the heckling and hissing that Yeats and Gregory found so offensive was in fact the audience attempting to prevent an erosion of its traditional rights. With the benefit of hindsight, we know that those rights were being eroded, and by the 1950s the Irish theatre would be the solidly middle-class edifice that in recent decades companies like Passion Machine have tried to open up. Again, Lady Gregory's comments are telling: 'I was sorry that we had ever let such a set inside the theatre.' Joseph Holloway, on the other hand, who revelled in what he called 'the genuine Queen's audience', praised the audience's 'frankness' on the opening night of the *Playboy*, and the audience's own self-imposed limitations during the protest indicate that they recognized very clearly just how far they were entitled to go. Heckling, making noise, even the occasional brawl, were all part of theatre-going; destroying the theatre or attacking the actors was not. 'The stage became spectators', concluded *The Abbey Row*, a satirical account of the affair, 'And the audience were players. Whether the play was good or bad, / It really didn't matter'.[26] Synge, who, of all the Abbey directors, was most in sympathy with the popular tradition represented by the Queen's, seems to have shared this view. 'It is better any day to have the row we had last night', he wrote to Molly Allgood the morning after the first protest, 'than to have your play fizzling out in half-hearted applause. Now we'll be talked about. We're an event in the history of the Irish stage' (*CL* II 285).

MARTIN HILSKÝ

Re-imagining Synge's Language: The Czech Experience

'In writing *The Playboy of the Western World*, as in my other plays, I have used one or two words only that I have not heard among the country people of Ireland, or spoken in my own nursery before I could read the newspapers' (*CW* IV 53). Synge's well-known words are quoted by Karel Mušek in the first Czech translation of *The Playboy*, published in 1914 in Moravia. From Mušek's comments upon the play and from the translation itself it becomes obvious that Synge's 'Preface' (1907), or rather Mušek's interpretation of it, provided the linguistic and cultural key to Mušek's rendering of *The Playboy*. His approach can be summarized in one sentence: the language of *The Playboy* is the language of Irish peasants, it is the language that Synge learned from 'a chink in the floor of the old Wicklow house' (*CW* IV 53). Mušek therefore decided to use one of the Moravian dialects in his translation of *The Playboy*. The dialect differs from standard Czech in some points of morphology and syntax but there is not one single word in the translation that would not be understood by a Czech reader or spectator. Mušek's strategy was to give a flavour of the peasant language to his translation and to dramatize the difference between the standard Czech and the peasant dialect. It also served an important cultural purpose: it integrated the language of *The Playboy* into the tradition of the Czech rural drama at the turn of the century.

Mušek's translation of *The Playboy* was used three times on the Czech and Moravian stages (Prague 1916, Prague 1928 and Ostrava

151

1940) before being superseded in 1961 by the translation of Vladislav Čejchan (Prague 1962, Brno 1969, Příbram 1970, Šumperk 1977, Ostrava 1978, Karlovy Vary 1978, Cheb 1982). Čejchan modernized the language of *The Playboy*, and instead of the peasant dialect he used colloquial Czech of the variety commonly spoken in Prague. By the 1960s Mušek's language was considered obsolete on the stage and the theatres required a new, modern stage idiom. Čejchan meets this cultural requirement, although, at least in my view, in his attempt to bring the play closer to everyday contemporary Czech usage the strangeness and poetic quality of Synge's language are almost completely lost.

The Playboy has kept an impressively steady presence in the Czech theatre since 1916, but what happened in the mid-nineties had no precedent. Three productions of *The Playboy* appeared almost simultaneously in 1995 and 1996, each of them in a different translation. In 1995 the small, experimental Theatre on the Balustrade (Divadlo Na zábradlí) in Prague produced the play in Mušek's translation, the National Theatre of Moravia and Silesia (Národní divadlo moravskoslezké) in Ostrava used Čejchan's rendering, and in the same year the National Theatre in Prague commissioned a new translation from me. My intention was not simply to provide a new translation of the play but to attempt a new approach to *The Playboy*, in short, to re-imagine and re-invent Synge's language in Czech and achieve the doubleness of effect which is so characteristic for *The Playboy*.

The hostile critics of Synge maintained that *The Playboy of the Western World* was written in a language that no one actually spoke in Ireland and that the diction of the play was unnatural, contrived and extravagant. As St John Ervine once said, Synge was 'a faker of peasant speech'.[1] The debate about Synge's language seems to suggest that both Synge and his opponents were right. The text of *The Playboy* does not contain one word that Synge did not hear in Irish villages or on the Aran Islands: Synge's was indeed a peasant speech racy of the soil. But it is equally true that no one ever spoke the cadenced prose used in *The Playboy of the Western World*. L.A.G. Strong puts it succinctly: 'The language of Synge's plays is *not* the language of the peasants, insomuch that no peasant talks consistently as Synge's characters do: it *is* the language of the peasants, in that it contains no word or phrase a peasant did not actually use.'[2]

The paradox is only apparent since literary or poetic language never is, nor can be, mere transcription of 'real' or 'overheard' language. The language of a poem or a play is always a creative act, an act not of recording but of radical transformation. *The Playboy of the Western World* is not a work of descriptive realism and its language is not a reproduction of the Irish peasants' speech, but rather the distilled soul of that language. In other words, the language of *The Playboy* is both natural and artificial, a literary construct that nonetheless evokes the natural and genuine qualities of the peasants' language. In this sense, Synge did not simply imitate or copy the speech of Irish peasants so much as he invented it.

As Declan Kiberd reminds us, Synge, Yeats and Lady Gregory were all fond of quoting Goethe's famous dictum 'Art is art because it is not nature', and Synge's favourite quotation from Mallarmé sums up his own theory of language: 'The language of the streets, the common spoken language, has nothing to do with literature, it exists only as colours or sound exist for the painter or musician and the writer must use it in a free independent way to form the language of literature.'[3] And Kiberd, who in his *Synge and the Irish Language* usefully made available parts of the unpublished manuscripts and notebooks of Synge, quotes from Synge's comments on the language of Yeats and Maeterlinck: 'Their style is a direct idealisation of their own voices when at their fullest and best. They differ from the ordinary spoken language as Venus de Milo differs from an average woman.'[4]

Synge's language, then, may be described as a heightened use of an authentic speech and its rhythms. But how to translate the peculiar intensification of the common speech, the 'estrangement', the 'foregrounding' of the difference, the deviation from the norm of English which is at the heart of Synge's language? How to achieve the lyrical intensity which is peculiarly Synge's? How to approach the very limit of linguistic extravaganza and stylization, Synge's 'poetry talk', without being artificial, contrived, strained and hyper-aesthetic? These and similar questions gradually gave the direction and shape to my translation of *The Playboy*.

At the beginning of my long search for the semantic gesture of the translation was the decision *not* to translate *The Playboy* into a regional dialect. Although Mušek's antiquated language has acquired a special aesthetic quality with the passage of time, a straightforward anchoring of *The Playboy* in one specific Czech or Moravian, or indeed Central European, locality has obvious dangers. A Moravian village quite simply is not a small rural community of north-west Mayo. (Brittany may be another matter.) Any Czech or Moravian dialect would invite a contemporary spectator or reader to perceive *The Playboy* as a late-nineteenth-century regional play or romantic exercise in local colour. The cultural poetics of the local colour would eliminate that linguistic and cultural duality which is the essence of Synge's idiom.

The actual process of translation gradually developed in three stages. In the first it was necessary to translate as accurately as possible the text and adequately interpret the stage situations of Synge's play, to get the sentence perspective in focus and to deal with such specific problems as 'bona fide travellers', 'himself', etc.[5] Even simple things that are no obstacle to a reader of Synge in the original presented difficult problems in the translation. The phrases 'master of the house' and 'woman of the house', used by Christy immediately after he enters the stage, are good examples. Both the rhythm of the phrases and their cultural connotations are hard to realize in the Czech medium. The literal translation 'paní domu' and 'pán domu', although quite common, would not be used in addressing a person. The problem, in fact, is not linguistic but cultural; moreover, one is bound to lose the special rhythm of the phrase if one opts for other solutions ('pane', 'paní' or 'pane hospodáři', 'paní hospodyně').

Rhythm and meaning were my main concern even before I started working on the translation, when thinking of a suitable title for the play. Its Czech version, established by Karel Mušek in 1914, is *Hrdina Západu*, which translates back into English as *The Hero of the West*. The losses in the meaning and sound structure of the Czech title are apparent at first sight. The beautiful rhythmic wave of the English (or Anglo-Irish) word 'playboy', consisting in the diphthongs 'ei' and 'oi' and the alliterative interplay of 'p' and 'b', is lost in the harsh sound of the rolled 'r' in the Czech word 'hrdina', and the alliterative phrase of the original 'Western World' is reduced to the Czech 'Západ' (West). Even more significant are the semantic losses of the Czech title. The rich ambiguity of the word 'playboy' is reduced to the apparently unambiguous word 'hero' (hrdina). Karel Mušek, who came to Ireland in 1906, met Synge and discussed with him the play which was then in progress, comments upon the title in a preface to his translation: 'The word "playboy", literally "boy of the game", refers to an Irish game of "throwing stones" and is, in fact, an Hibernian jargon. It denotes firstly a person who "plays", either an athlete or an actor or watcher of games, secondly a person that takes much pleasure in games and playing, and thirdly a person that boasts, a braggart, a deceiver.'[6] It is obvious that Mušek's title fails to carry those meanings – if indeed the title does carry such a range of significance – but that is not Mušek's fault. The first French translator, Maurice Bourgeois, decided for *Le Baladin du Monde Occidental*, arguably a more beautiful title, yet also lacking the ambiguity of the original (contemporary French translators keep Bourgeois's title, by now traditional, but modify it with interesting subtitles – *Le Beau-parleur des Terres de l'Ouest* or *L'Enjôleur des Terres de l'Ouest*).

Both the sound structure and meaning of the original title contain an element of duality: the word 'playboy' consists of two words and its meaning connotes a duality that anticipate the drama of Christy Mahon, his truth but also his lie, his glory and his folly. Christy Mahon is both a marvellous hero and a pathetic fool, a poet and an impostor, a 'mighty' hero and a 'wonder'. The duality and triumph of Christy Mahon (and of the whole play), however, lies in the fact that it is through his lies and delusions that Christy Mahon finally arrives at genuine self-knowledge.

The titles of classics or modern classics present a specific textual problem for the translators since they are likely to be recycled in the cultural discourse (in the press, encyclopedias, histories of literature.) much more frequently than any other part of the text of the work in question. To some extent they have a cultural life independent of the plays, poems or novels to which they were originally attached. Once a title is established, it is immensely difficult, often unwise, to change it.

I decided to respect the established title which, however imperfect and reductive, has one advantage: it suggests not only the heroic dimension of Christy Mahon that can be traced back to Cuchulain, but also its ironical reversal. The word 'hero' has not had an untroubled life in the Czech cultural environment. The First World War and the publication of *The Good Soldier Schweik* problematized the figure of a hero, whereas in the political atmosphere of Communism after the Second World War, especially in the 1950s, when the words 'hero' and 'heroism' were much recyled in the cultural discourse, the title *The Hero of the West* could easily be misunderstood as part of the politicized geography of the Cold War. *The Hero of the East* would obviously be much more desirable in the political mythology of the 1950s. The outcome of these changes in the political semantics of the word was a certain devaluation of the very concept of heroism. Nowadays the ironical meaning of the word is very widespread, e.g. in the phrase 'ty jsi ale hrdina' ('what a hero you are', meaning 'what a coward you are'). The word 'hero' thus ironically reflects upon itself, mirrors itself and in this self-reflexive energy some of the ambiguity of the word 'playboy' may be restored.

In the Czech text of the play the word 'hrdina' (hero) is for the first time used by Pegeen after Shawn Keogh tells her of the man groaning outside in the darkness. 'Well, you're a daring fellow,' says Pegeen to him ironically, and the Czech word 'náramnej hrdina' not only echoes the title but also establishes a verbal bond between Shawn and Christy. Christy is, at the beginning of the play, as timid, self-deprecating, shy, cowardly and fearful of father figures, the law and women as Shawn. In the semiosis of the play this verbal link between Shawn and Christy is supported by a specific kind of cross-dressing: Christy dons Shawn's new hat, his breeches with the double seat and his new coat and achieves his triumph in the borrowed dress. After Old Mahon has pub-licly denounced him and the second 'murder' has been committed, the motif of cross-dressing is repeated (Sara and the Widow Quin fasten a petticoat round him). Like almost any other motif, image or situation of the play, the stage metaphor of the dress is repeated, with variations, several times. Its importance is emphasized by the simple fact that the play opens with Pegeen speaking about her wedding garment: 'Six yards of stuff for to make a yellow gown. A pair of lace boots with lengthy heels on them and brass eyes. A hat is suited for a wedding day.' Then Michael Flaherty holds up Shawn's coat and jeers: 'Well, there's the coat of a Christian man.' Then Shawn offers his fancy coat to Christy and almost simultaneously promises to give a wedding outfit to the Widow Quin if she marries Christy: 'I would, surely, and I'd give you the wedding ring I have, and the loan of a new suit, the way you'd have him decent on the wedding day.' And then Christy is forced to wear a petticoat. A hero in a woman's dress! The dress image was much used in the Prague production and its grotesqueness contributed to the perverted cruelty of the concluding scene, in which Christy is almost lynched by the bloodthirsty mob.

I became interested in the possibilities of the verbal mirroring that would reflect semiotically upon the material stage images. Translation is interpretation, as everyone knows, and in translating *The Playboy* it was not essential for me whether or not Christy is a Christ figure or a parody of Cuchulain or *Oedipus Rex*. I was much more interested in the theatre situations through which Christy's progress was presented on the stage. Was it possible to find the verbal parallels for Christy's development charted, for example, by the changes of his dress? Christy is no hero at the beginning of the play, but gradually, as his behaviour and his language change, he becomes more and more self-assured, even triumphant. He borrows an elevated rhetoric in this process of becoming a hero. When the truth about his 'heroic' act is revealed, his status is demolished, only to be born again at the very end of the play: Christy becomes a hero in the sense that he successfully undergoes these rites of passage. The conviction of Pegeen's last words in the play 'Oh, my grief, I've lost him surely. I've lost the only playboy of the western world' is the test of any performance of *The Playboy*. In the Prague production a slightly changed sentence perspective and rhythm, together with the renewed value of the word 'hrdina', dramatized the sense of loss (for Pegeen) and triumph (for Christy): 'Panebože! Ztratila jsem ho! Jedinej hrdina Západu! A já ho ztratila!' Thus the changes of the Czech word 'hrdina' in its ironic and non-ironic meanings could provide a verbal parallel for the metamorphoses of Christy Mahon in the play.

When working on the translation I increasingly recognized the immense difficulty of translating Synge's Hiberno-Irish idiolect in which the English surface structure is constantly undermined by the deep structure of the Irish syntax. It is not an exaggeration to say that Synge's idiolect is a translation from the Irish of Aran into English, rather than a representation of the English spoken by the peasants, and that translating Synge is, in a very special sense, translating a translation.

Synge's Anglo-Irish idiolect has been analyzed by Declan Kiberd, and his comments and insights are invaluable for any translator of Synge. It is good to keep in one's mind that 'the Irish language is a concrete, noun-centred medium, with a marked preference for the specific mode of expression'; that in Synge's idiolect the relative pronouns 'that', 'which' and 'where' are often suppressed; that subordinate clauses are very infrequent in Synge's play; that adverbial clauses are introduced with 'and' rather than with 'where' or 'when'; and that 'it is' is used to emphasize the word immediately following ('Isn't it long the nights are now, Shawn Keogh?' says Pegeen at the beginning of the play). Some of these patterns are hard to realize in Czech but the concreteness of expression can be achieved in many ways and the avoidance of subordinate clauses is almost natural to colloquial Czech. I tried to stick to these principles as consistently as possible and to respect the repetitive, waving, groping, circular movement of Synge's language. The Czech translation was gradually taking shape but there was still something lacking. I thought that Synge's text had a stronger rhythmic impulse than my translation.

This impression became even stronger after I saw a film version of *The Playboy* in which Synge's Anglo-Irish was rendered in a kind of chant or recitative. This experience of the heightened music of Synge's language was immensely important to me and it led me to a closer examination of the play's rhythmic patterns.

I soon found out that all the characters in *The Playboy* speak more or less in the same way and that there was no substantial difference between the language of Irish peasants and the language of legendary heroes and heroines in *Deirdre of the Sorrows*. Synge had no need to distinguish between 'high' and 'low' language; his tinkers, beggars, vagabonds, fishermen and peasants use the same kind of stylized and half-artificial Anglo-Irish that is spoken by the legendary heroes inspired by the Irish romances and myths. There is a touch of the Irish legendary hero in Christy Mahon and there is something of an Irish peasant woman in Deirdre.

Synge's theatrical language thus differs radically from the language of Shakespeare, who uses prose, blank verse and rhymed verse for his complex and richly varied characterization. Whereas Shakespeare's use of language is based upon contrasts and tends to variety and differentiation, Synge's language tends to unification. Synge's effort is not to provide a fully individualized and differentiated language for each of his characters, but rather to invent one language for all the characters. Christy Mahon, Pegeen, Widow Quin and Old Mahon are entirely different human types, but their sentences have a similar structure and the same words are repeated in them. The word 'maybe', for example, one of the stylistic dominants of the play, does not serve the purposes of psychological realism but modifies the cadences of the whole of the play.

One of the most interesting general features of Synge's aesthetic or 'literary' use of language lies in the rhythmical patterns of the play. These patterns vary in intensity. At some moments they have the form of regular metre, often strengthened by alliteration. *The Playboy* is written in prose, but its language, due mainly to its rhythm and its irregular but strongly pronounced metrical impulse, acquires a very distinctive poetic quality. The rhythm and metre of Synge's language can be perceived in the very first speech in the play. 'A hat is suited for a wedding-day', says Pegeen. The strangeness and simple beauty of this short sentence lies not only in the elliptical 'A hat is suited' but also in its rhythm and meter: Pegeen's line is a perfect iambic pentameter. As P.L. Henry says, 'the rhythm of this phrase and particularly its cadence might be said to haunt the whole play'.[7]

Throughout the play there is a repeated speech pattern consisting of five syllables, the first and last of which is accented, so that the speech unit corresponds to the second half of the iambic pentameter. Its rising metre gives a peculiar chanting quality to Synge's language. Dozens and dozens of examples could be quoted. Most frequently this rhythmical and metrical pattern appears in simple colloquial phrases referring to space or time: 'in the dead of night', 'in the fogs of dawn', 'in the heat of noon', 'in an August fair', 'in the heart of man', 'in the sight of all', 'in a sweat of fear', 'from the dusk to dawn', 'from the dawn to dusk'.

In the second stage of my work on the translation I concentrated upon this underlying rhythmical and metrical impulse of Synge's play. I wanted to follow Synge and use authentic and perfectly natural Czech, yet heightened by means of its changing rhythm and metre. The Czech text of the play gradually became a poem in prose, a recitative, a musical structure. Each syllable was important and my efforts concentrated upon the accurate rendering of the five-syllable speech units I have just mentioned. Often it was possible to be literally faithful to both rhythm and meaning: 'in the dead of night' became 'černočerná noc', 'in the west or south' turned into 'na západ či jih'.

It was a joy to work on this rhythmical and metrical pattern because Synge's Anglo-Irish idiolect almost miraculously gave itself to the Czech rhythmic pattern. The regular iambic pentameter (beginning with unaccented syllable and ending with the accented one) is hard to achieve in Czech since the language has a natural inclination to falling, not rising metre, but Synge's half-lines with their accents on the first and last syllable lend themselves perfectly to the Czech medium, as the following examples may show: 'jeden lidskej krok', 'držet noční stráž', 'celej tenhle kraj', 'kdo to vlastně byl', 'možná taky ne', 'budeš mlčet, vii', 'kéž by ji vzal čert', 'nebezpečnej chlap', 'ušlej k smrti jsem', 'každej slušnej chlap', 'proto po vás jdou', 'ať pán nebo kmán', 'důvod jako hrom', 'takže nemám strach', 'holky jako lusk', 'spal a jed a pil', 'dřel a dřel a dřel', 'jako norskej král', 'celý tejdny pil', 'co to je bejt sám'. These phrases are natural, even colloquial, yet their rhythm and metre have the cogency that accurately reflects Synge's original.

Finally, in the third stage of my work on the translation I concentrated my attention on those situations in which Synge breaks the regular rhythm and metre of his phrases. I wanted to be faithful to Synge even in this respect and syncopate his language wherever the original required it. But the rhythmical underlayer of the play was preserved and individual replicas were woven into it.

It was my desire that the text of the translation have two layers: the colloquial surface structure and the rhythmical and metrical deep structure. In certain situations of high emotional intensity the deep structure 'surfaced', so to speak, to recede again in other situations; and this ebb and flow provided the larger rhythmical pattern of the play. The rhythmical pattern became the vehicle of diverse kinds of discourse, such as folkloric language, biblical language, or the language of sermons and prayers, and it indirectly realized the primitive, mythical substratum of *The Playboy* and the oral tradition from which Synge's language grew.

Ultimately, it was my desire not to use one spent image or cliché, one joyless or pallid word, in the text of the translation. I wanted the language of the Czech *Playboy* to be rare, full-bodied, fresh and beautiful, in short as fully flavoured as a nut or apple.

GERALD DAWE

Distraction
after Synge

I wander around the last place I had –
the private gardens I could look out on,

awaiting proofs, a letter from one or the other;
my poor mother who misunderstood it all.

Paris was fun. I knocked about a bit
but deep in my heart of hearts

I knew all along I had to answer
to the valleys of an imagined people;

the twists and turns of their language,
the girl whose shoulder brushed mine

and whose undisclosed body drove me
to distraction when I sat on the rocks,

the black edge of the north island
in front, the Bay almost too blue.

In the early hours now I walk by
the quayside and yards of the Steamship Co.

A dog ferrets through the hotel's rubbish
the local lad, pale as a ghost, dumped

last night out of sight, betwixt and
between my leaving and my return.

ANTHONY ROCHE

J.M. Synge and Molly Allgood: The Woman and the Tramp

J.M. Synge wrote in his preface to *The Playboy of the Western World* that 'All art is a collaboration' (*CW* IV 53). The most significant collaboration between the playwright and an Abbey Theatre actor, and the one which this essay wishes to explore, was that with the actress Molly Allgood. It was she for whom he wrote his two final, and arguably greatest, female roles, Pegeen Mike in *The Playboy of the Western World* and the eponymous heroine of *Deirdre of the Sorrows*. But they were also intimately involved offstage, their romance leading to a formal engagement and a deferred plan to marry. This close relationship between a Protestant and a Catholic, between a director of the Irish National Theatre and one of the employees, sent shock waves through Synge's strict evangelical family and his fellow directors. The inner drama is laid bare in the almost daily letters they exchanged over a period of several years. As one might expect from a couple who both sought their profession in the theatre, there was a strong degree of role-playing, most manifestly evidenced by the personae they chose to adopt in their correspondence. Synge's letters to Molly were addressed to his 'changling' (*sic*) and were signed 'Your old Tramp'; hers have not survived. These key terms were also deployed in his plays and suggest that the letters may be read as further textual evidence of the complex interchange in Synge between life and art, with both clearly undergoing a substantial degree of self-fashioning.

Synge's identification with the figure of the tramp was deep-rooted and of long standing. It preceded his first meeting with Molly Allgood. In his essay 'The Vagrants of Wicklow', which the editor of his *Prose* surmises was probably written in 1901–2, Synge in an oft-quoted passage makes a parallel between 'the gifted son of a family' and 'a tramp on the roadside':

In the middle classes the gifted son of a family is always the poorest – usually a writer or artist with no sense for speculation – and in a family of peasants, where the average comfort is just over penury, the gifted son sinks also, and is soon a tramp on the roadside. (*CW* II 202)

This passage conveys the sense of alienation Synge experienced as a writer/artist from a middle-class family. What interests me is the elision, the sleight of hand, by which his self-identification finds its way to the desired objective of a tramp on the roadside. This transformation is achieved not by means of anything resembling rational argument, but through verbal parallelism and the introduction of a middle term, a peasant family. The passage does not literally claim that a son of the middle classes is ineluctably or indeed ever going to end up as a tramp on the roadside. But the careful verbal orchestration enables that end to be arrived at syntactically by its parallel and by a consequent blurring into near oneness of the two gifted sons. The passage, for all of its romanticism, also exudes a sense of financial insecurity, of a downward mobility which has obscured the first term, the landowning classes to which the Synges had belonged a generation or two earlier.

A less often quoted passage occurs later in 'The Vagrants of Wicklow', where Synge writes that 'some incident of tramp life gives a local human intensity to the shadow of one's own mood' (*CW* II 204). This passage has a direct bearing on one of the two one-act plays completed by Synge in the summer of 1902, *The Shadow of the Glen*, in which the figure of the Tramp makes a memorable appearance. The story which was to form the basis for *Shadow* was first told to Synge on the Aran Islands, but it had a mainland setting and was to be carefully translated by Synge into the Wicklow landscape he knew so well. The other two aspects he developed in his play were the role of the wife, considerably expanded from the original in terms of what she says and does, and the replacement of the anonymous narration of the storyteller by the figure of the Tramp. In the Aran original, the narrator says very little and largely acquiesces in the punishment of the unfaithful wife by her jealous husband.

In the light of Synge's comment, what is so striking is the extent to which the presence and dramatic deployment of the Tramp in the scenario greatly increases the 'human intensity' of the piece, deflecting it away from farce or melodrama. In part, this is achieved through the Tramp's sympathy towards the young wife Nora as she unfolds her tale of loneliness in a barren marriage. The sympathy is made manifest in his crucial decision to intervene when Nora's husband threatens to throw her out: 'It's a hard thing you're saying, for an old man, master of the house; and what would the like of her do if you put her out on the roads?' (*CW* III 53). The Tramp and Nora have found common ground in their mutual admiration for the recently deceased Patch Darcy, a social renegade from the 'back hills'. When Dan Burke revives, he specifically rebukes the 'blathering' between his wife and the Tramp about 'Darcy (*bitterly*) – the devil choke him' (*CW* III 43) as indicating the growing bond he detects between them. The play maintains a deliberate oscillation between the romance and realism of life on the roads. On the negative side, there is the fate of Patch Darcy, his decomposing body eaten by the crows; and the woman whom Nora has identified as a negative emblem of her possible fate, 'Peggy Cavanagh, who had the lightest hand at milking a cow that wouldn't be easy, or turning a cake, and there she is now walking round on the roads ... with no teeth in her mouth, and no sense' (*CW* III 51). When Dan banishes his wife from the household to a life on the roadside, he again invokes the figure of Peggy Cavanagh: 'Let her walk round the like of Peggy Cavanagh below, and be begging money at the cross roads, or selling songs to the men' (*CW* III 53). Nora is quick to point out that there is no escape from dying or decay in any locale, and that her husband's masquerade is only a rehearsal for the death he will one day undergo. It is the Tramp who verbally undertakes to transform the material conditions of the natural enivironment into a fine imaginative prospect, as Nora was only the first of many critics to recognize.

But this final reworking of the play's material conditions does not come from nowhere, as it may appear to do. For the dramatic function of the Tramp resides in part in his primary activity throughout the play, subjecting everything he sees and hears to enquiry. Rather than neutrally entering his environment and receiving his shelter and drink, the Tramp comments repeatedly on the oddity of what he sees: of the elaborate preparations for a wake which no one is attending; of the 'queer' look on the face of a man reputedly dead (*CW* III 33). In so doing, he isolates and renders self-conscious the folkloric elements so seamlessly presented in the folktale Synge originally heard, facilitating the process by which his creator will send them in a different direction from the original. The Tramp's most brazen efforts in this regard *vis-à-vis* Nora Burke occur when he comments on his own strangeness, and notes how she has not flinched from admitting a strange man into her house. The Tramp is more than the vehicle by which the psychological and social truths underlying the folktale are laid bare; he plays an active part in their deconstruction.

Although Molly Allgood did not originate the part of Nora Burke in *Shadow*, Synge cast her in the play when he conducted rehearsals himself for an English tour in early 1906. As he reminds her in a later letter: 'Don't you remember how clear I was when I was teaching you Nora B[urke]?' (*CL* I 217). The nineteen-year-old actress had followed her elder sister, Sara Allgood, into the Abbey Theatre in late 1905, taking the stage name Maire O'Neill to avoid confusion and establish her independence. Her first stage role was a walk-on part in Synge's *The Well of the Saints*. But it was Molly's being cast as Nora some months later that brought her acting to wider attention and inaugurated her romance with the playwright. As Ann Saddlemyer puts it in her edition of the *Letters*, 'through the speeches of the Tramp, [Synge] courted her ... [and] when [he] accompanied the players to Wexford on 26 February [1906], his relationship with Molly was apparent to all' (*CL* I 146).[1] There is a strong vein of romantic nature imagery in the letters that Synge and Molly soon exchanged which recalls the final lengthy speech by the Tramp in Synge's play: 'Remember in three little weeks there'll be another new moon, and then with the help of God, we'll have great walking and talking at the fall of night' (*CL* I 200). But the letters reveal a great deal else besides and frequently adopt a querulous, carping tone that resembles less the romantic outsider than the aged, possessive, jealous husband, as Synge himself appears to half-recognize when he signs an early letter to Molly 'Your old Tramp alias Dan Burke!' (*CL* I 178).

The letter in question has to do with the prospect of Molly stepping out into the natural world, not with the playwright, but with her fellow Abbey Theatre actors, and with one in particular: 'I heard accidentaly [*sic*] of your walking arm in arm with Wright [Udolphus 'Dossie' Wright, also nineteen] at Longford. Is that true?' (*CL* I 176). It is in this context, and on this occasion, that Synge changes the way he addresses her in the letters, switching from 'Molly' to 'changling'. The latter term, with its fairy associations, underlines the extent to which the relationship with Molly has transported Synge from everyday cares and a lonely existence into the heightened possibility of otherness with which all romantic affairs in his plays and poems are infused. It is also a tribute to her art, to her ability as an actress which he consistently praises, not least when she is performing in his plays. As he writes to her at the height of the riots over *The Playboy of the Western World*: 'You don't know how much I admire the way you are playing P. Mike in spite of all the row' (*CL* I 288). But Synge's attitude towards Molly's acting remains consistently positive only so long as she is on the stage. When she is off it, other realities intrude, social, sexual and cultural. His letters on their backstage meetings at the Abbey register degrees of distance, in particular an inhibition on the talk which is so much cherished and sought after in the letters. In their social relations at the theatre one is more aware of the Synge who is on the Board of Directors and the Molly who is a paid employee:

You must not mind if I seem a little distant at the Theatre, every one is watching us, and even when we are publicly engaged I do not care to let outsiders see anything ... Last spring we had to do our talking in the Theatre as we did not see each other elsewhere but now, thank God, we can have our talk on green hills, that are better than all the green rooms in the world. (*CL* I 211)

The uneasiness Synge expresses in the letters with regard to Molly's temperament and behaviour most often locates itself in the term 'actress'. When he speaks of their imagined future and of 'the sort of life you'll have with me', he frames and expresses it in terms of nature and art – 'the life I mean that we have out on the hills, and by the sea on Bray head and in the art we both live for' – and yet what threatens to 'ruin' that happiness forever is that Molly is 'so young and so quick and an actress' (*CL* I 208–9). Part of the paradox involved here is that acting is something that requires his beloved to remain true to herself and to her instincts – 'I think you may turn out a very fine actress – if you can only preserve your sincerity' – and yet also to change, to undergo conscious training and development: 'you will never reach the very top ... unless you read plenty of what is best and train your natural instincts. There is a sermon!!' (*CL* I 249, 303). Synge's letters to Molly are full of advice on what to read if she is to 'improve' herself, and it is often difficult to determine whether he means professionally or socially. The strain of the 'actress' paradox continues to exercise itself through repeated statements that he loves her just as she is, mingled with complaints that she is not other than she is.

Synge and Molly cemented their relations when they were on tour in Scotland in early 1906; fellow actors spoke of their surprise when they saw the normally reserved Synge with his arm around her, and Annie Horniman was appalled at their visible intimacy. It was not unheard of, in the theatre or elsewhere, for male members of a wealthier class or in a more privileged position to take sexual advantage of beautiful young women. As Vivian Mercier remarks: 'Synge was consciously a gentleman by birth and upbringing. At 35, when he first met Miss Mary Allgood, he might have allowed himself liberties with a woman of his own age and class who happened to love him, but with a girl still in her teens he had too much integrity to play the role of "seducer".'[2] Others might not show the same restraint and, as Synge's illness increased the physical separation between them, he frequently thinks of Molly in the company of 'men who dangle after actresses', those for whom the lady is a tramp, and warns her accordingly: 'you must know as well as I do the low scurilous [sic] thoughts medical students and their like have when they dangle after actresses! ... I know too well how medicals and their like think and speak of the women they run after in Theatres, and it wrings my heart when I think what that man may be saying and thinking of my little changling, who is so sweet and so innocent and whom I love so utterly' (CL I 245, 249). When he thinks of her in this light, the term 'actress' takes on the sexually ambiguous connotations it would have had for members of his own class, the same puritanical dread that kept his own immediate family from ever entering a theatre.

Synge in this letter strives to hold separate and to contrast the urban world of theatres as the world of (fallen) experience with the rural world of the Wicklow hills, with its magical associations of innocence. But the word Synge adopted as his pet name for Molly is the most slippery and uncertain of those in the fairy lexicon. Angela Bourke has written of an Irish woman, Bridget Cleary, who was burned to death by her husband in 1895 because, it was claimed, she was a changeling. The term 'changeling', according to Bourke, gives ambivalence 'a stage on which to perform';[3] where most of those who are taken by the fairies can be deemed absent, in the case of a changeling the young woman has, and has not, gone away to fairyland, since her place has been taken by one of the 'others' (the fairy people) magicked into her likeness: 'she did not wholly disappear into fairyland, therefore what was left in her place was a changeling'.[4] The changeling is not fully absent, because visually present, while appearing curiously removed. The term can also be used to 'explain' behaviour that is aberrant, intolerable or somehow threatening to the social order. Synge longs to be with his changeling in the hills of Wicklow, the location where she can be most fully herself; but more often they find themselves in the daylight urban world where Molly both is and is not herself.

The different strains that the letters between Synge and Molly reveal can be mapped symbolically on a geographic continuum. Between the refuge of the Wicklow hills and the ambivalent space of the Abbey Theatre falls the suburbs, that zone in which Synge lived, from which he forayed but to which he always returned. Vivian Mercier has written of Synge as a suburban writer as follows: 'The flight to the suburbs in the second half of the nineteenth century, with its concomitant building of Evangelical Protestant churches ..., was principally a Protestant one. Hence the middle-class constrictions of suburban life, notoriously galling to the artistic temperament, were intensified by the rigours of a voluntary ghetto.'[5] Mercier views Synge's suburbanness as informing the 'cult' of tramps, tinkers and beggars in his plays – the temporary refuge from his real environment which the summer sojourns with his mother in various Wicklow houses also provided. But it is in the first year of Synge's relationship with Molly that it becomes clear how 'his suburban roots went much deeper than he had imagined'.[6] These suburbs, as Mercier points out, were made possible by new developments in technology – railways, trams, etc. The different psychic strata of Synge's identity which I have outlined above had a peculiar reliance on the railway. The meetings with Molly were invariably arranged as follows: she would take the train from the centre of Dublin, southwards towards Bray; Synge would board the train at either Sandycove or Glenageary, and both would get off at Bray. If he did not spy her on the platform, he would assume she had not come and would return home. From Bray the couple were free to indulge in long walks further into County Wicklow.

But the clandestine, anonymous cover (or 'privacy') given to burgeoning sexual relationships by the railway system could not last for ever. As the relationship between Synge and Molly continued, it became natural that she should wish to come and visit him at his 'home' – the house at Glenageary where he and his mother most often resided, with its name ('Glendalough House') transported from County Wicklow to the Dublin suburbs. Synge agonizes and frets over Molly's being invited to the house, postponing it until he can do so no longer. The inhibitions that prevailed at Molly's first entrance across the Synge family threshold are described in the letter he wrote to her immediately after that visit: 'It is curious what a little thing checks the flow of the emotions. Last evening because there was a sort of vague difficulty or uncertainty about our positions in this house we were as stiff as strangers.' The paralysis only eases when Molly has departed and Synge is free to imagine: 'As soon as you were gone I began imagining that you would get into the wrong train and be carried off to Bray and then have no money to take you home. I saw you as plainly as possible standing in your long coat on the platform in Bray explaining your case to the station master and porters! It looked very funny. Dear heart I wish I had you here every day what a difference it would make' (*CL* I 239–40). The final wish is poignant but unconvincing; one cannot imagine any suburban dwelling comfortably housing the pair of them. Synge sees his fiancée plain only when he is free to imagine her in scenarios which she has inspired.

When it comes to assessing Molly Allgood's side of the relationship, and her contribution to the collaboration, it is to the dramatic scenarios of *The Playboy of the Western World* and *Deirdre of the Sorrows* that one must turn. We do not have Molly's side of the correspondence: Synge appears to have destroyed her letters just before he entered the Elpis Nursing Home for the last time early in 1909. But there are a few surviving indications of her side of the exchange, notably the one-word comments she has written over several of his letters: 'idiotic', 'appalling', 'peculiar' and 'reconcile' give the flavour. And this one surviving handwritten letter from her, scribbled across the top of one of his, suggests that she may have given as good as she got:

you may stop your letters if you like, I dont care if I never heard from you or saw you again so there! & please dont let thoughts of me come into you your head when you are writing your play. It would be dreadful if your speeches were upset. I dont care a 'rap' for the theatre or anyone in it the pantomime season is coming on & I can easily get a shop; in fact I shall go out this afternoon & apply for one. (*CL* I 218n1)

The context of the letter from Synge which provoked this angry response is revealing. For he was in the toils of writing *The Playboy of the Western World* and had used his absorption in the act of composition as the reason for not going to see Mrs Allgood (presumably to win her around to the idea of his marrying her younger daughter) and for putting off a walk with Molly herself:

I am very bothered with my play again now, the Second Act has got out of joint in some way, and now its all in a mess. Dont be uneasy changling, everything is going on all right I think, I will go and see your mother soon, I dont much like the job so I keep putting it off ... I half thought of going in to town to take you for a walk but I thought it better to stick to my work. (*CL* I 217; letter of 16 October 1906)

The conflict between life and art evident here also has the personal dimension of a spirited exchange between two argumentative individuals with strong personalities. This quality is no less apparent in many of the speeches between Christy Mahon and Pegeen Mike in the play on which Synge was working. The verbal snap of the fingers which Molly delivers in her line 'I dont care a "rap" for the theatre or anyone in it' is reproduced in the lines with which Pegeen concludes her longest and bitterest row with Christy: 'if you vexed me a while since with your leaguing with the girls, I wouldn't give a thraneen for a lad hadn't a mighty spirit in him and a gamey heart' (*CW* IV 113).

In the letter from Synge which Molly objected to, part of the conflict centres on the single greatest recurring motif in their letters: the deferral of their plans to marry. External reasons are not far to seek: the opposition of both families; the straitened financial circumstances the couple would inherit (both were living at home); the uncertainty surrounding Synge's health. But throughout the letters, even before the operation in Easter 1908 when it became fatally clear how ill he was, there is the sense of their marriage as an ever-receding goal. Synge finally gets around to telling his mother – doing so from England, since he fears his own violence in the face of her reaction – only to have Molly ask him to hold off from telling Lady Gregory. On the surface, his letters during the composition of *The Playboy* never break with a positive and forward-looking view of their marriage; it is only in the composition of *Deirdre* that they take a more pessimistic turn. But in the numerous drafts of *The Playboy of the Western World* and all the different options he tried out in relation to the scenario – including, in the earliest draft, directly representing the argument between father and son – the one possibility that was never canvassed was that the play should conclude with the marriage of Christy and Pegeen. There was always to be a sundering.

I wish to consider this artistic decision to avoid a Christy–Pegeen marriage in the light of the *Playboy*'s development of the woman-and-the-tramp scenario. The row which broke around the first production of *The Shadow of the Glen* had to do with the behaviour of the young woman at its close. As Arthur Griffith wrote in *The United Irishman*:

> Man and woman in rural Ireland, according to Mr. Synge, marry lacking love, and, as a consequence, the woman proves unfaithful. Mr. Synge never found that in Irish life. Men and women in Ireland marry lacking love, and live mostly in a dull level of amity. Sometimes they do not – sometimes the woman lives in bitterness – sometimes she dies of a broken heart – but she does not go away with the Tramp.[7]

I have always felt that *The Playboy of the Western World* is among other things a variation upon the material and core situation of his 1902 play, testing the hypothesis of what happens when the woman does *not* go away with the Tramp. The adulterous side has been lost, since Pegeen is still single, though in many ways bound to her widowed father in the role of carer. The dramatized departure of the woman from a situation carrying with it a good deal of internal colonization and thwarted opportunities is no longer advanced as an uncomplicated possibility and cannot be realized through the figure of the play's Tramp character, Christy Mahon. In the light of what I have so far considered in this essay, the promise that the wanderer holds out of a refuge through an imaginative interaction with nature can no longer be so readily sustained. When Christy indulges in descriptions of his earlier solitary forays into the natural world, where 'I'd be as happy as the sunshine of St. Martin's Day, watching the light passing the north or the patches of fog', Pegeen in Act III advances the possibility that 'If I was your wife, I'd be along with you those nights, Christy Mahon', not taking her death but 'shelter[ing] easy in a narrow bush' (*CW* IV 83, 149). But the romantic vision cannot embrace the shared possibility of marriage, and Pegeen immediately withdraws and cancels her marital hypothesis with the qualification that 'we're only talking maybe, for this would be a poor thatched place to hold a fine lad is the like of you'. Their shared existence in the natural world is denied because, paradoxically, they cannot continue to cohabit in their present environment. The prospect Christy holds out is only verbal, and cannot be translated fully or successfully into their present material conditions. The woman in this dramatic instance will *not* go away with the Tramp because, in a reversal of the earlier play, all he has to offer is a fine bit of talk.

It would be wrong, of course, to identify Synge and Molly too absolutely with Christy and Pegeen. For one thing, Synge has given his own 'Christian' name, John, to the most craven character in the play, Shawneen (little John or Johnnie) Keogh. For another, Pegeen has to share space with the Widow Quin, who makes a determined set for Christy, despite being characterized as a woman who has not only killed her husband but buried her children. Is there a shadow here of the closeness between 'Johnnie' Synge and his widowed mother which persisted up until her death, less than six months before his own? Certain it is that, in Synge's last two plays, the natural world no longer offers the positive and uncomplicated alternative to the household community it did in his earlier work and that this alteration has profound bearings on relations between hero and heroine and the life they seek to lead together.

A study of the letters between J.M. Synge and Molly Allgood suggests strongly the extent to which he wrote his last play as a vehicle for his fiancée. Here at last was a role that would crown her rising through the ranks of the Abbey Theatre. The kind of play and choice of part could be seen as of a piece with Synge's efforts to 'improve' Molly, urging her away from trashy romantic novels and towards the world of poetry and art. It would also impress Yeats, a concern that emerges in the letters when Synge reports back to Molly on any positive remarks made about her acting by the great man, who was initially unimpressed by her performance as Nora Burke. Yeats had also denied that anyone in the Abbey company was up to the demands of playing the title role when he came to cast his version of *Deirdre* some years earlier, and went to great lengths to import a Miss Darragh to play the tragic heroine. Synge was also answering Yeats's conception of the role by writing in an earthier, more vigorous style and by trying to imagine how these 'Saga' people lived, moved, thought and managed their day-to-day existence; these were qualities that he thought Molly would bring out in the role.

The parallel between the letters exchanged between Synge and Molly and the writing of the scenario of *Deirdre of the Sorrows* is much more exact than was the case with *Playboy*. In one of those letters, he chides her that she must not be 'jealous' of the time and energy he is devoting to *Deirdre* because he is writing 'a part for YOU' (*CL* II 75).

The same conflict between writing the play and advancing the marriage with Molly re-emerges; but now the writing of the play is expressed in explicitly sexual terms which indicate the degree of displacement at work: 'I am squirming and thrilling and quivering with the excitement of writing Deirdre and I *daren't* break the thread of composition by going out to look for digs and moving into them at this moment ... Let me get Deirdre out of danger – she may be safe in a week – then Marriage in God's name. Would you mind a *registry office* if that saves time?' (*CL* II 92; letter of 29 November 1907). The composition of *Deirdre* was not completed in a week; it continued through the sixteen months of life remaining and was left unfinished. Nor were Synge and Molly ever to be married. In the play itself, Synge found a means of articulating the great divide which lay between himself and Molly which he could not admit in the letters. The parallel between his life and his art rather leads him to distort the scenario's development, stressing the role of King Conchubor at the expense of the young lover, Naisi; the latter lacks all dramatic conviction, and is admitted by Synge to be the weakest part, while the former is full of passionate intensity. Naisi is the wanderer who enters Deirdre's cottage from the woods and who brings her away to an enchanted sojourn in Scotland/Alba; but Synge can now find little identification with this tramp-like figure from the outdoors, and the promise of nature is an empty one; the two lovers are soon on their way back to Ireland for Deirdre's final encounter with the aged High King.

In the play, the old woman Lavarcham points out to the King the inappropriateness of his proposal to marry Deirdre: 'it's a poor thing, Conchubor, to see a High King the way you are this day, prying after her needles and numbering her lines of thread' (*CL* II 189). Lavarcham has already spoken of the King's jealousy and of the quarrels that repeatedly blow up between Deirdre and himself. But what emerges most strikingly in the play is a factor never explicitly mentioned in the letters between Synge and Molly: the great age difference between the two lovers. The High King admits her youth as a major source of his attraction to Deirdre; and in their final scene together Deirdre declares that away from the councils of state, face to face with her, 'in this place you are an old man and a fool only' (*CL* II 265). The most painful letter in the Synge–Molly correspondence is one of the last, just before Christmas 1908. Synge had spoken to her earlier, when she was meet-ing Annie Horniman, of the importance of wearing masks, but one feels in the following that there are no more masks as he tells her how serious his condition is:

I feel humiliated that I showed you so much of my weakness and emotion yesterday. I will not trouble you any more with complaints about my health ... but I think I owe it to myself to let you know that if I am so 'selfpitiful' I have some reason to be so ... as Dr Parsons report of my health, though uncertain, was much more unsatisfactory than I thought it well to tell you. I only tell you now because I am unable to bare [sic] the thought that you should think of me with the contempt I saw in your face yesterday. (CL II 236–7)

In his next letter to her the mask is back in place, as he concentrates on the writing of *Deirdre* and on the new parts he has added, principally a character, Owen, who is driven crazy for the love of Deirdre. But it is in the direction of the grave that both the letters and the play are moving, and Deirdre's reply may also speak for Molly: 'I'll say so near that grave we ... seem lonesome people, and by a new made grave there's no man will keep brooding on a woman's lips' (*CW* IV 253).

The last collaborative exchange between Synge and Molly was a poem he completed in October 1908. As he writes to her: 'I did one new poem – that is partly your work – that he [Yeats] says is *Magnificent*':

> I asked if I got sick and died would you
> With my black funeral go walking too,
> If you'd stand close to hear them talk and pray
> While I'm let down in that steep bank of clay.
> And, No, you said, for if you saw a crew
> Of living idiots, pressing round that new
> Oak-Coffin – they alive, I dead beneath
> That board – you'd rave and rend them with your teeth.
>
> (*CL* II 204–5)

Synge's poem has added violence to Molly's original reply: 'No, for I could not bear you dead and others living on' (*CL* II 205n2). But the same sentiment she uttered remains at the core of the poem, emerging from this dialogue between the two lovers, with the frank admission that one of them is not going to survive. *Deirdre of the Sorrows* was staged at the Abbey Theatre on 13 January 1910, with Synge's death having provoked a most extensive and unusual collaboration. The play had been assembled and edited by Yeats, Lady Gregory and Molly Allgood; the production was co-directed by the two women; and, as

Synge had always intended, Molly played Deirdre. In the play's final moments, it is the woman who has the last word in some of the greatest lines Synge had ever written, the speeches beginning 'Draw a little back with the squabbling of fools when I am broken up with misery' and 'I have put away sorrow like a shoe that is worn out and muddy' (*CW* IV 267). In the place of the Tramp and his swaggering speeches is the enfeebled, aged figure of Conchubar, 'hard set to see the way before' him and led off stage at the close by Lavarcham (*CW* IV 269).

No letters were needed for Synge's final five weeks in the Elpis Nursing Home. Molly attended him every day except for a week's touring in Edinburgh. This enabled a degree of intimacy and access which they had never formerly enjoyed, and made her an invaluable oral resource for Yeats as he began the mythologising of Synge, who 'dying chose the living world for text'.[8] But the most important difference between the two writers had emerged in a letter written by Synge to Molly on the death of his mother which gave what might well be his most considered view on the life-art debate which this essay has considered:

As you are not here I feel as if I ought to keep writting [*sic*] to you all the time although tonight I cannot write all that I am feeling. People like Yeats who sneer at old fashioned goodness and steadiness in women seem to want to rob the world of what is most sacred in it ... I am afraid to think how terrible my loneliness would be tonight if I had not found you. It makes me rage when I think of the people who go on as if art and literature and writing were the first thing in the world. There is nothing so great and sacred as what is most simple in life. (*CL* II 221; letter of 9 November 1908)

ANN SADDLEMYER

Synge's Soundscape

L isten!
  Listen again!
    Listen harder!

MARY   There's the sound of one of them twittering yellow birds do be coming in the spring-time from beyond the sea, and there'll be a fine warmth now in the sun, and a sweetness in the air, the way it'll be a grand thing to be sitting here quiet and easy, smelling the things growing up, and budding from the earth.

MARTIN   I'm smelling the furze a while back sprouting on the hill, and if you'd hold your tongue you'd hear the lambs of Grianan, though it's near drowned their crying is with the full river making noises in the glen.

MARY   [*listens*]. The lambs is bleating, surely, and there's cocks and laying hens making a fine stir a mile off on the face of the hill. (*CW* III 131–3)

Perhaps more than any other passage in his plays, this exultant exchange from Act II of *The Well of the Saints* reflects the intensity with which Synge's own senses were attuned to the sounds and sights of nature. But there is a special relevance to this celebration in a play about two blind beggars who prefer a world shaped by their own needs and desires to the mundane working existence of (in Lady Gregory's phrase) 'roast and boiled and all the comforts of the day'. The very setting, close to the Valley of Saints and Seven Churches in County Wicklow, is appropriate for Synge's own version of the great debate between Oisín and St Patrick, which takes place later in the play:

MARTIN: I'll say it's ourselves have finer sight than the lot of you, and we sitting abroad in the sweetness of the warmth of night [SAINT *draws back from him*] hearing a late thrush, maybe, and the swift flying things do be racing in the air till we do be looking up in our own minds into a grand sky, and seeing lakes and broadening rivers and hills are waiting for the spade and plough ... What call have the like of you to be coming in where you're not wanted at all, and making a great mess with the holy water you have and the length of your prayers? [*Defiantly*] Go on, I'm saying, and leave us this place on the road. (*CW* III 140–5)

In *Ulysses* James Joyce recalls a picnic in Clamart woods when he and Synge were both in Paris in 1903, casting Synge, 'Faunman', as Jaques/Oisín to Joyce's Touchstone/Patrick.[1] When the two expatriates held their famous picnic, Synge showed his fellow Dubliner the manuscript of *Riders to the Sea* and they argued about the nature of tragedy. During that period, Synge was once again revising his first Wicklow play, *When the Moon Has Set*, and formulating his own aesthetic, much of which went undigested into this unsatisfactory work. Did he announce to Joyce the statement recorded in his notebook, 'a pantheistic emotion ... seems the inevitable and ultimate mood of all art'?[2] Or this passage from *Etude Morbide*, another work of his Parisian years: 'All art that is not conceived by a soul in harmony with some mood of the earth is without value' (*CW* II 35)? Even as a young child he had been a worshipper of nature. He relates in some early autobiographical notes: 'I remember that I would not allow my nurses to sit down on the seats by the Dodder because they were made. If they wished to sit down they had to find a low branch of a tree or a bit of rock or bank' (*CW* II 5). Joyce's image of him as latter-day Oisín, 'the little faun', held a great deal of truth.

But how did Synge see himself? An exile from the faith of his mothers and the constricting middle-class community of Kingstown, certainly. An artist, definitely. A solitary, romantic brother to the wandering tramp or vagrant seeking a hint of 'the manifold and beautiful life' of an earlier Europe; yet at the same time a detached, ironic observer of 'the tragedy and humour' which swing between what he defined as 'the two poles of art'. Above all, a *listener*: 'When I was writing *The Shadow of the Glen*, some years ago,' he wrote in his preface to *The Playboy*, 'I got more aid than any learning could have given me, from a chink in the floor of the old Wicklow house where I was staying, that let me hear what was being said by the servant girls in the kitchen' (*CW* IV 53). Synge might have lived to regret that simple description of his methodology, as have some of his more defensive supporters, but the image is as truthful as it is courageous. Jack Yeats caught that watchful alertness in the casual drawings he made of his friend.[3]

In his prose essays, Synge records his sensitivity to the 'peculiar climate' he found on his travels through Ireland; 'peculiar', 'intense', 'queer' and 'singular' are favourite words to evoke the experiences Joyce would later call 'epiphanies'. He describes in his autobiography his early adventures as a young naturalist:

> To wander as I did for years through the dawn of night with every nerve stiff and strained with expectation gives one a singular acquaintance with the essences of the world. The obscure noises of the owls and rabbits, the heavy scent of the hemlock and the flowers of the elder, the silent flight of the moths I was in search of gave me a passionate and receptive mood like that of early [man]. (*CW* II 9–10)

Elsewhere, in his Wicklow essays, he listens intently to the sounds rising out of the mists and fog: 'Above everything my ears were haunted by the dead heavy swish of the rain' (*CW* II 192). Sometimes the very silence is so great that 'three or four wrens that are singing near the lake seem to fill the valley with sound' (*CW* II 234). At other times 'flocks of golden or green plover fly round and round [in an] infinity of crying' (*CW* II 194–5). On Aran he finds the language of the birds 'easier than Gaelic, and I seem to understand the greater part of their cries, though I am not able to answer' (*CW* II 73–4).

On his way to the Blasket Islands his first impression is of unfamiliar sounds:

> We passed Dunmore Head, and then stood out nearly due west towards the Great Blasket itself, the height of the mountains round the bay and the sharpness of the rocks making the place singularly different from the sounds about Aran, where I had last travelled in a curagh. (*CW* II 247)

Once there, he captures the spirit of the islanders first through the sound of their dancing:

> The women, as usual, were in their naked feet, and whenever there was a figure for women only there was a curious hush and patter of bare feet, till the heavy pounding and shuffling of the men's boots broke in again. The whirl of music and dancing in this little kitchen stirred me with an extraordinary effect. The kindliness and merrymaking of these islanders, who, one knows, are full of riot and severity and daring, has a quality and attractiveness that is absent altogether from the life of towns, and makes one think of the life that is shown in the ballads of Scotland. (*CW* II 256)

While on Inishmaan he explores the psychic quality of the neighbour-
hood by describing a dream of excruciating intensity beginning with 'a
faint rhythm of music' 'far away on some stringed instrument', which
as it comes closer gradually increases 'in quickness and volume with an
irresistibly definite progression':

When it was quite near the sound began to move in my nerves and blood, and to
urge me to dance with them.

I knew that if I yielded I would be carried away to some moment of terrible
agony, so I struggled to remain quiet, holding my knees together with my hands.

The music increased continually, sounding like the strings of harps, tuned to a
forgotten scale, and having a resonance as searching as the strings of the 'cello.

Then the luring excitement became more powerful than my will, and my limbs
moved in spite of me.

In a moment I was swept away in a whirlwind of notes. My breath and my
thoughts and every impulse of my body, became a form of the dance, till I could
not distinguish between the instruments and the rhythm and my own person or
consciousness.

For a while it seemed an excitement that was filled with joy, then it grew into
an ecstasy where all existence was lost in a vortex of movement. I could not think
there had ever been a life beyond the whirling of the dance.

Then with a shock the ecstasy turned to an agony and rage. I struggled to free
myself, but seemed only to increase the passion of the steps I moved to. When I
shrieked I could only echo the notes of the rhythm.

At last with a moment of uncontrollable frenzy I broke back to consciousness
and awoke.

I dragged myself trembling to the window of the cottage and looked out. The
moon was glittering across the bay, and there was no sound anywhere on the island.
(*CW* II 99–100)

This is powerful writing, but it is also dangerous – both in what it
gives away of the man and in how easily it seduces both author and
reader into a 'land of fancy'. For just as poetry requires 'the strong
things of life' – even brutality – to give it strong roots (as Synge put it
in his famous preface), so do prose and drama. For Synge the greatest
of all artists have both qualities: 'they are supremely engrossed with life
and yet with the wildness of their fancy they are always passing out of
what is simple and plain' (*CW* I xxxvi). And so, even in his (apparently)
simple nature essays, he is careful to move from one pole to the other:

I lay in the grass in a sort of dream with a near feeling of a number of scenes that I
have been in. I saw the wet roads in Wicklow with sky and sunshine in the ruts, and
corners of old woods, and the moving seaweeds that are round Aran; I saw Kerry
with bright bays and many scattered people cutting patches of oats or driving their
donkeys. Then I came back to the cottage with my throat dry thinking in what a

little while I would be in my grave with the whole world lost to me.

In the laneway as I was turning in there were a number of tinkers yoking up for a journey. One of them took a nose bag from a pony he had been feeding and threw it to a man with a red mare across the road.

'There', he said, 'put her nose into that.'

'I will surely,' said the man, 'what would I want putting her [arse] into it. I ask you in the name of God?' (*CW* II 201)

Synge's delight in the richness of language, the joyful shock to the ear of newly-coined phrases, is well known. Alan Bliss, Nicholas Grene and Declan Kiberd have written comprehensively of his adoptions, translations and mistranslations from the Irish, his distillation and selection of the language and rhythm of the Anglo-Irish idiom, his debt to Douglas Hyde and Lady Gregory, his verbal and syntactical inventions. I would like to suggest some of the impulses that led him to experiment so uniquely with language, creating his own Syngesong, and the soundscape of his plays. As a linguist familiar with six languages – although he managed to misspell consistently in all of them – he had a quick ear for nuances and intonation, even when he could not fully comprehend their meaning. Many of these experiences are recorded in *The Aran Islands*:

Then [old Mourteen, his Irish teacher] sat down in the middle of the floor and began to recite old Irish poetry, with an exquisite purity of intonation that brought tears to my eyes though I understood but little of the meaning.

... several times when the young man finished a poem [from *The Love Songs of Connacht*] [the old woman of the house] took it up again and recited the verses with exquisite musical intonation, putting a wistfulness and passion into her voice that seemed to give it all the cadences that are sought in the profoundest poetry.

... a wonderfully humorous girl ... has been spinning in the kitchen ... . The morning she began I heard her exquisite intonation almost before I awoke, brooding and cooing over every syllable she uttered ... (*CW* II 56, 112, 143)

Not all such experiences gave pleasure. On the south island he fell in 'with a curious man' who 'began singing to show what he could do. The music was much like what I have heard before on the islands – a monotonous chant with pauses on the high and low notes to mark the rhythm; but the harsh nasal tone in which he sang was almost intolerable' (*CW* II 140–1).

For almost ten years Synge attempted to identify and codify the process by which the human voice might capture the intrinsic melody of poetry. An unpublished but frequently revised essay called 'The Duality of Literature' recalls his emotion on hearing old Mourteen recite, and concludes that poetry, being a form of music, has 'a double existence', 'one given by the composer and the other by the interpreter or performer'. Folk melodies 'contain their own signature in a way complex art cannot do. They require no notes of expression or crescendos to lead the performer ... The emotions that they contain are so simple and so universal that no one with any [understanding] of art can mistake the significance.' Folk poetry was originally recited by the poet himself 'with the music that he conceived with the words in his moment of excitement'. His hearers, Synge surmises, repeated the work they admired with the exact music of the poet, and so passed on with the words the intonation still faithfully followed by the Aran Islanders. For him, meaning is inherent not only in the words, but in 'a tissue of the subtlest intonations'. 'The finest melody if tapped on the piano without expression has no meaning and it is thus English readers treat their poets.'

How can one devise a science which will once again 'render the poet's voice immortal'? Like Yeats, who with Florence Farr at the same time was experimenting with the psaltery to develop his own method of recitation or 'cantilating', and like Hopkins before them, Synge first contemplated a system of musical annotation. However, his protagonist in 'The Duality of Literature' (a violinist and poet named Costello) says, 'Sometimes in my M.S. I have marked all the intonation ff. rall. etc. but it has a certain affectation and what is worse would become mechanical with the reader.'[4] So much for Yeats and Florence Farr! For Synge, another method would have to be found.

As late as 1904 Yeats was still trying unsuccessfully to persuade Synge to accept his 'musical theories'. But unlike Yeats, who was notorious for his tone-deafness, Synge (like James Joyce) was an accomplished musician, and had, in fact, contemplated a career as a performer and composer. And so he brought to his experiments with prosody a technical awareness evident not only in his theorizing but later, as we shall see, in his plays. It could be said with some truth, in fact, that his fascination with literature grew as much out of his musicianship as from his boyhood studies of nature. Very early the family observed that his ear was keen enough to detect an instrument out of tune. His brother Sam taught him to play the concertina. Then at the age of sixteen he began to study the violin. While observing family tradition by enrolling in Trinity College, where he did his best work in languages (other than English), he simultaneously (and with a great deal more enthusiasm) took classes in violin, theory and composition at the Royal Irish Academy of Music. He also joined the student orchestra, and later, in sensuous and typically revealing prose, recalled the 'unusual pleasure' of that experience:

> The collective passion produced by a band working together with one will and ideal is unlike any other exaltation ... We played the *Jupiter Symphony* of Mozart ... and a Jewess was playing at the desk before me. No other emotion that I have received was quite so puissant or complete. A slight and altogether subconscious avidity of sex wound and wreathed itself in the extraordinary beauty of the movement ... One is lost in a blind tempest [of music] that wails round one with always beautiful passion, the identity is merged in a ... symmetrical joy, cathedrals build themselves about one with the waves of purple storm, yet one remains sane and a man. (*CW* II 14).

From 1892 he kept a notebook in which he jotted down the titles of many of the pieces he was working on or painstakingly analyzing, by such a wide range of composers as Hans Sitt, Spohr, Paganini, Viotti, Schubert, Haydn, Bach, Beethoven and Mozart. He also kept many of his exercises in counterpoint (from two to twelve parts) and musical form, and was particularly proud of his studies in the fugue. When he was nineteen he won a prize in counterpoint, and two years later a scholarship in harmony and counterpoint. Among his own compositions are a scherzo for string quartet; sonata movements for violin and piano; and a theme and variations for violin and piano (which he considered his best). He contemplated a string symphony, a clarinet quartet, and an opera (appropriately – for he was becoming increasingly nationalist in sympathy – entitled *Eileen Aroon*). He describes his youthful ambitions in a fragment of autobiography: 'Often ... I worked myself into a sort of mystical ecstasy with music and the works of Carlyle and Wordsworth which usually ended by throwing me back into all manner of forebodings. I began to write verses and compose. I wished to be at once Shakespeare, Beethoven and Darwin; my ambition was boundless and amounted to a real torture in my life. I would go down on my knees at times with my music paper on a chair before me and cry to God for a melody' (*CW* II 12).[5] Fortunately his love of the countryside kept Synge sane and healthy: he could cycle up to sixty miles through the Dublin mountains without any strain. And his diary records for one May morning in 1893, 'Walked to Carrickmines. Practised on a dandelion stalk till I mastered the reed sound – and brought three corncrakes across a field by it.'

Alarmed by her youngest son's obsessions, Mrs Synge confided her concerns to his older brother:

Johnnie is so bewitched with music that I fear he will not give it up. I never knew till lately that he was thinking of making his living by it seriously; he spares no pains or trouble and practises from morning till night, if he can. Harry [her son-in-law] had a talk with him the other day, advising him very strongly not to think of making it a profession. Harry told him that all men who do take to drink. And they are not a nice set of men either, but I dont think his advice has had the least effect … the sound of the fiddle makes me quite sad now. I used to think it was only a harmless amusement and it kept him out of mischief, but it seems now likely to lead to mischief.[6]

However, his mother continued to accompany him on the piano, and finally, when an elderly religious cousin – who was also a professional pianist and teacher – persuaded her that not all musicians were sinful, Synge was granted permission to continue his music studies in Germany. He continued his study of the violin and took up the piano. But within a year, he had once again turned course, and abandoned all plans to make music his career.

We will never know for certain what made him change his mind. In a letter to his German translator he states simply, 'I saw that the Germans were so much more innately gifted with the musical faculties than I was that I decided to give up music and take to literature instead' (*CL* I 127). The hero of *Etude Morbide*, which Synge later described as 'a morbid thing about a mad fiddler in Paris' and grew to hate, has a breakdown after collapsing at a concert through failure of nerve. In the same work the hero writes, 'Music is the finest art, for it alone can express directly what is not utterable, but I am not fitted to be a composer' (*CW* II 35). Probably all these reasons are true. Certainly those compositions that survive among his papers are undistinguished, although technically accurate; and Synge's nervous, excitable temperament would make performance in public highly unreliable. And so, strengthened by his technical knowledge of music, trained ear, and naturalist background, he turned to those other 'arts of Time', prose and poetry. Ever the theorist, about this time he sketched in his notebook the relationship of the arts to form and subject matter: the *caoineadh* and ballad poetry, he argued, were 'form without ulterior ideas'; music, architecture and painting were 'form with ideas'; higher poetry and drama, 'ideas with form'. He would aspire to the last.[7]

Concern with form was a constant. So too was concern with harmony and rhythm. He found all three in nature: 'Every life is a symphony, and the translation of this life into music, and from music back to literature or sculpture or painting is the real effort of the artist,' he wrote in his autobiography (*CW* II 3). And in his Aran notebook he elaborated on this condition of music:

When the sun is covered six distinct and beautiful shades still blend in one another – the limestone, the sea leaden at my feet and with a steel tinge far away, the mountains on the coast of Clare and then the clouds transparent and opaque. There is not any affectation in borrowing a term from music, no pictorial wording can express these movements ... – today three delicious movements differ only from a symphony in that the finale is always the opening of a new design. There are these – the dim adagio in six tones, the presto of the quick colourless rain followed by a glorious allegro con brio where sun and clouds unite in brilliant joy.[8]

So Synge set out conscientiously to achieve 'perfect form ... with a mature philosophy', mindful also of the need to find some method of conveying the artist's personal style. How to make both performer and audience listen to the rhythm and intonation, and grasp the overall form? Not surprisingly, he turned first to his formal study of music. His first completed play, *Riders to the Sea*, so nearly approaches the operatic form that when Ralph Vaughan Williams chose it for libretto, he was able to take over the text completely, barely adding one line; kept instrumentation to the barest essentials; employed folk songs for colour and immediacy; made effective use of the chorus of keening women; and made the sound of wind its only conclusion. A few years later Joyce's friend Carlo Linati adapted *The Shadow of the Glen* as *La Veglia* (*The Watch*), which was set to music by his fellow Italian Arrigo Pedrolo. Later Synge would write with an awareness of the voices and appearance of his actors; but *Riders to the Sea*, like *The Shadow of the Glen*, was completed even before he had seen Willie Fay's small Irish Dramatic Company perform. Nor had he been a regular theatre-goer in Paris or Dublin. For subject matter and characters he drew upon his experiences in Aran and Wicklow; for dialogue his keen ear for the tricks and nuances of speech and languages; for form and sound his training as a musician. Most of all, in this first finished play, he drew upon his knowledge of music as one of the arts of Time.

The sea broods over *Riders to the Sea* from the opening speech of the young girls. There is no synonym, no adjective, no personification for 'the sea'; the words appear on every page, the rhythm takes on the relentless beating of waves. The sea provides signature (a musical term for both key *and* time) and leitmotif for the entire work, while the insistent voice and presence of Maurya offer the only counterpoint. Throughout, in one resounding harmonic chord, the past is imposed upon the present, the supranatural blends with the natural, the Christian is submerged in the pagan, as the inevitable ritual renews itself and the constant beating of water on rock is reflected in the erosion of Maurya's past and future. As we watch and listen, for each past loss is relived in the present, the sea's blows crashing in upon her, Maurya becomes a rock herself, Mother Island. Against this eternal rhythm of nature the characters move in deliberate dreamlike measures towards their destiny.

This prevailing atmosphere produces the quality of the symphonic or – to use Richard Strauss's term – tone poem, one unbroken great movement rising to the *caoineadh* of the chorus of women and Maurya's paean of grief and resignation. Yet within that overarching movement we can observe the carefully worked smaller phrases of action, punctuated by silences as deliberately counted as bars of music. For Synge wrote and rewrote each passage of his plays until they were so seamless that not a word or gesture could be displaced without wrenching the whole.

Take the opening scene as example: observe the quietness of the first moments, each dictated action so deliberate and unhurried, carefully and clearly establishing the relentless pace of nature and 'the sea'. Even the rhythm of Cathleen's spinning wheel (a visual reminder also of fate) is incorporated in this pattern of inexorability. With Nora's entrance we have the counter-movement, anxious hurried questions punctuating her older sister's slower, intuitive actions. Urgency and inevitability play against each other, the unanswered questions winding us in until Maurya's grave and querulous entrance halts the forward action as abruptly as Nora's parcel caused Cathleen to 'stop her wheel with a sudden movement, and lean out to listen' (*CW* III 5).

With Bartley's quiet and sad entrance the tempo slows further until it meets Maurya's prevailing key. Too lost in grief, Maurya allows him to depart without a blessing. Once again the tempo picks up as the ever-practical Cathleen realizes they have forgotten to give Bartley the freshly baked bread, and the girls persuade their mother to go out to meet him. Laboriously, she leaves the cottage, the stick left by her drowned son beating the time of her exit.

In this next scene, the mood changes once more. The urgency of the girls' speeches – which have grown longer under Maurya's influence – is intensified by the struggle with the salt-hardened knot. But even grief itself is cut short by the exigencies of the moment: the young girls' almost formal lament is not yet allowed completion. That cannot occur until we (and they) comprehend the full extent of Maurya's loss, and the dreaded death of yet another son is fulfilled. The theme swings back and forth between anxious doubt and definite admission, then certain knowledge and concern to protect Maurya. Carefully, Synge builds up to grief, without allowing it to swell into the final *caoineadh*; the two young girls retain individual voices while being drawn into the resounding climax. But that too is led up to, then drawn back, reflecting the progress of the fugue. When the chorus of women appears at the door – beckoned by Maurya's silent gesture – they enter soundlessly, picking up the *caoineadh* Maurya has already sounded only after Bartley's body joins her litany of loss, and present confirms and reinforces past. Their formal grieving continues under and about Maurya's speech, swelling to the end, punctuating her final statements and finally carrying her personal grief into a fulfilling final phase. I would suggest that in the ongoing debate – first introduced by Joyce – over the tragic quality of *Riders to the Sea*, there is indeed a sense of catharsis, but it is perhaps more strictly musical than traditionally Aristotelian.

Just as the play begins in watchful silence, so it ends in silence as the *caoineadh* rises and falls, then sinks away to the curtain. Synge would continue to use this framework of silence, forcing his audience to attention by inviting them to lean into the created universe of the play. Recall the opening of *The Shadow of the Glen*, with Nora quietly moving about the room, 'looking now and then at the bed with an uneasy look' (*CW* III 33), until we hear the first sound, which is someone knocking 'softly' at the door. We are stilled into listening. The stillness of an isolated shebeen in Mayo in that noisiest of plays, *The Playboy of the Western World*, is emphasized first as we overhear Pegeen's opening litany, then Shawn Keogh's uneasy entry and evocation of the sounds of nightfall: 'I could hear the cows breathing, and sighing in the stillness of the air, and not a step moving any place from this gate to the bridge' (*CW* IV 67).

Then there is *The Well of the Saints*, apparently a landmark play for both Yeats and Beckett. Beckett was content to drop the title into a pool of unannotated approval: when asked by Cyril Cusack to send a message for the Shaw centenary celebrations in Dublin, he replied:

I wouldn't suggest that G.B.S. is not a great play-wright, whatever that is when it's at home. What I would do is give the whole unupsettable apple-cart for a sup of the Hawk's Well, or the Saints', or a whiff of Juno, to go no further.[9]

Yeats, in one of his last essays, is typically more expansive and self-revealing:

When I follow back my stream to its source I find two dominant desires: I wanted to get rid of irrelevant movement – the stage must become still that words might keep all their vividness – and I wanted vivid words ... perhaps I was Synge's convert. It was certainly a day of triumph when the first act of *The Well of the Saints* held its audience, though the two chief persons sat side by side under a stone cross from start to finish.[10]

Never mind that the first act contains more action than this, beginning with the blind couple groping their way on stage and ending with considerable physical energy on the part of both Martin and Mary Doul; Yeats's private memory is unerringly accurate, for the action of *The Well of the Saints* is conjured up out of the darkness by the two blind beggars who embrace an alternate agenda to the seeing world and are not satisfied until the contrapuntal themes are, however uneasily, inverted.

Perhaps it is the play's formal structure Beckett found sympathetic, for it seems to me that *The Well of the Saints* is crafted with the deliberate design of a double fugue, a polyphonic composition with two themes or subjects presented and developed simultaneously from the start. The blind couple introduce these two themes. To Martin Doul the world is not as it seems or should be: 'For you've a queer cracked voice ... if it's fine to look on you are yourself' is almost his first speech to Mary Doul. For Mary Doul there is always a way of rationalizing oppositions:

Who wouldn't have a cracked voice sitting out all year in the rain falling? It's a bad life for the voice, Martin Doul, though I've heard tell there isn't anything like the wet south wind does be blowing upon us, for keeping a white beautiful skin – the like of my skin – on your neck and on your brows, and there isn't anything at all like a fine skin for putting splendour on a woman. (*CW* III 71)

Still Martin has greater need for harmonizing perceptions:

I do be thinking in the long nights it'd be a grand thing if we could see ourselves for one hour, or a minute itself, the way we'd know surely we were the finest man, and the finest woman, of the seven counties of the east ... [*bitterly*] and then the seeing rabble below might be destroying their souls telling bad lies, and we'd never heed a thing they'd say. (*CW* III 73)

Characteristically he dwells on the harmony he demands between sound and vision with thoughts of Molly Byrne: 'It should be a fine soft, rounded woman, I'm thinking, would have a voice the like of that.'

Here are the main theme and counter-theme, both of which will work their way through the first two acts, growing ever more strident and forceful as other voices are added, until the third act gives us first a false harmonization in the new hopes brought about by the promise of fresh blindness, only to be chased off by a growing dissenting chorus behind them. No wonder George Moore suggested that *The Well of the Saints* could easily be transposed into opera, 'the blind man, basso; his wife, mezzo; Timmy the Smith, tenor; his girl, of course, soprano; the Friar, baritone; and then the peasant chorus'. Charmed by 'the inevitableness of the words and the ease with which phrase is lined into phrase', on its first performance Moore wrote an enthusiastic letter to the editor of the *Irish Times*, praising 'the abundance and the beauty of the dialogue ... one listens to it as one listens to music'.[11]

Synge incorporated very little actual performed music – either sound effects or songs – in his plays. When he did, he turned to folk music which, as quoted above, he thought truest to its source. In addition to the *caoineadh* of *Riders to the Sea*, there are three folk ballads (and a reprise of one at the end of Act I) in *The Tinker's Wedding* – all sung by Mary Byrne, who is most attuned to nature and her place within it – and Michael James's offstage singing of another ballad in *The Playboy of the Western World*. But as Katharine Worth has observed with reference to *Deirdre of the Sorrows*, many of the great speeches throughout his plays 'function like arias; the movement of plot is suspended to allow a lyrical outpouring of feeling'.[12] And so we have the famous love duet between Christy and Pegeen and Christy's monologues both earlier and later; the lyrical wooing of the Tramp in *The Shadow of the Glen* – punctuated by Nora Burke's counterpoint of realism; and even the sonorous Latin malediction with which the Priest routs his attackers to conclude *The Tinker's Wedding*.

It is not only foolhardy but downright dangerous to add to Synge's soundscape in production. He tightly controls action, speed, sound effects and language. His punctuation is, like that of Shaw (another musician), more for the ear than the eye. And his dialogue, like the carefully interwoven action, is designed to sound like English being spoken with a familiar accent and line without actually copying natural pattern or intonation. It is a complete re-creation, an artifice to give the impression of 'real' rhythm and phrasing. Even the first Abbey theatre actors could not attack it naturally, and had to be trained to speak by Synge himself, phrase by phrase and sentence by sentence, observing each silence, pause and breath. Here is Máire Nic Shiubhlaigh on learning to speak the lines of Nora Burke:

At first I found Synge's lines almost impossible to learn and deliver. Like the wandering ballad-singing I had to 'humour' them into a strange tune, changing the metre several times each minute. It was neither verse nor prose. The speeches had a musical lilt, absolutely different to anything I had heard before. Every passage brought some new difficulty and we would all stumble through the speeches until the tempo in which they were written was finally discovered. I found I had to break the sentences – which were uncommonly long – into sections, chanting them, slowly at first, then quickly as I became more familiar with the words.[13]

Although he abandoned those early attempts to annotate his work like a musical score, Synge invariably used musical terms when he worked out the scenarios for his plays – crescendo, diminuendo, currents for tone colour or signature of each scene. His urgent defence of the construction of *The Playboy* would make perfect sense to a musicologist: 'the romantic note and a Rabelaisian note are working to a climax through a great part of the play, and ... the Rabelaisian note, the "gross" note, if you will, must have its climax no matter who may be shocked' (*CL* II 47). He marked the margins of his drafts with brief instructions approaching musical annotation. Did he know of Maurice Maeterlinck's notations – 'dots for pauses, careful distinctions between "silence" and "new silence" '?[14] He would certainly have been aware of 'the vast silence brooding around the characters', for he wrote approvingly in his notebooks of how Maeterlinck's dramas captured 'the mystery which lies about us', and elsewhere of how they are 'directly related to the feeling of the folksong'. When in charge of the Abbey, he produced at least one of Maeterlinck's plays. He encouraged Yeats's experiments with verse plays, even though he did not always approve of the final result. But his primary love remained music and musical form. As late as 23 November 1907 he wrote to Molly Allgood, 'I am not going to John Bull['s Other Island] or the Abbey today ... I do not feel the slightest inclination to go and see Shaw – I'd rather keep my money for Esposito's concert tomorrow and hear something that is really stirring and fine and beautiful ...' (*CL* II 84). And throughout his life, he maintained the supremacy, in both theory and practice, of the example of music: 'The World is an orchestra where every living thing plays one entry and then gives his place to another. We must be careful to play all the notes; it is for that we are created' (*CW* II 24).

Synge

His choice would be
the blue chasm of the waves
the clean sea.

He'd roll through the waste
forever
finding the taste

of weeds on his tongue
while in a small
white house among

the rocks, men and women
kept glancing
at the door open to admit him

and his fiddle perfectly tuned.
A shadow strayed along dark roads.
They went on dancing.

Appendix: Synge Summer School Programmes 1991–2000

1991

Opening guest speaker	Cyril Cusack
Lectures	Nicholas Grene, 'Synge and Wicklow'
	John Kelly, 'The Irish theatre movement and its contexts'
	Declan Kiberd, 'The Playboy of the third world'
	John McCormick, 'Dion Boucicault'
	Frank McGuinness, 'Synge and Ibsen'
	Anthony Roche, 'Contemporary Irish drama'
	Ann Saddlemyer, 'Synge's soundscape'
	G.J. Watson, 'Synge's tragedies'
	Katharine Worth, 'Beckett's voices'
Reading	Seamus Heaney
Panel discussion	'The Contemporary Irish Theatre'
	Alan Gilsenan
	Tom Hickey
	Lynne Parker
	Stephen Rea
Performance	J.M. Synge, *The Shadow of the Glen*, *The Tinker's Wedding*
	Harlequin Players

1992

Opening guest speaker	H.E. Dr Imre Pataki, Ambassador of the Republic of Hungary
Opening dinner guest of honour	Cyril Cusack
Lectures	Angela Bourke, 'Keening as theatre'
	Roy Foster, 'Yeats and Synge'

Nicholas Grene, 'Men and women in Synge'
Colbert Kearney, 'Synge, O'Casey, Behan'
Brendan Kennelly, 'Synge song'
W.J. Mc Cormack, '*When the Moon Has Set*'
Anthony Roche, 'Tom Murphy's *The Gigli Concert*'
Robert Tracy, '"Words alone are certain good" –
    Boucicault, Synge, Friel'
Katharine Worth, 'Playing a part to be yourself: individualism
    in the comedies of Goldsmith and Sheridan'
Steven Wilmer, 'Women in Irish theatre'

Reading	Brendan Kennelly
Panel discussion	'Irish Theatre Today'
	Olwen Fouere
	Judy Friel
Performance	*Sunshine and the Moon's Delight: An Evening With J.M.Synge*, Harlequin Players

1993

Opening guest speaker	Thomas Kilroy
Lectures	Bruce Arnold, 'Men of the Glens: John Synge and Jack Yeats'
	Terence Brown, '"Easter 1916": revolution as theatre'
	Nicholas Grene, 'The drama of *The Playboy*'
	Philip Edwards, 'The Abbey after Synge'
	Gerald Fitzgibbon, 'The theatre of Brian Friel'
	Declan Kiberd, 'Wilde and the theatre of subversion'
	Christopher Murray, 'O'Casey versus Synge'
	Riana O'Dwyer, 'Synge and Tom Murphy'
	Tom Paulin, '*Riders to the Sea*: a revisionist tragedy?'
Readings	Jennifer Johnston
	Tom Murphy
Talks	Barry McGovern
	Fiona Shaw
Performance	*Sunshine and the Moon's Delight: An Evening With J.M.Synge*, Harlequin Players

1994
Theme: Irish Theatre and Cinema

Opening guest speaker	Frank McGuinness
Lectures	Angela Bourke, 'Oral narratives and drama'
	Brian Cosgrove, 'Myths of redemption in the drama of Seamus Heaney and Frank McGuinness'

Elizabeth Butler Cullingford, 'Seamus and Sinéad from "Limbo" to *Saturday Night Live*'

Jean-Michel Déprats, 'Translating drama'

Gerald Dawe, 'Synge's poems'

Luke Gibbons, 'The maternal in recent Irish cinema'

Nicholas Grene, 'From Synge to Roddy Doyle'

Fintan O'Toole, 'Contemporary Irish theatre'

Lucy McDiarmid, 'Lady Gregory between two cultures'

Anthony Roche, 'Synge: *The Well of the Saints*'

Reading	John McGahern
Panel discussion	'Contemporary Irish Cinema'
	Barry Devlin
	Katie McGuinness
Performances	*A Certain Wildness*: a reading from the works of Synge, selected by Christopher Fitz-Simon, with members of the Abbey Theatre Company
	These our Actors: A Celebration of Irish Acting and Story-telling, Harlequin Players

1995
Theme: Staging Ireland

Opening guest speaker	Brendan Kennelly
Lectures	Patrick Crotty, 'Synge in Wales and Scotland: Caradoc Evans and Hugh MacDiarmid'
	Nicholas Grene, 'Shaw and the impossibility of staging Ireland'
	Declan Kiberd, 'Beckett's texts of laughter and forgetting'
	Thomas Kilroy, 'Theatre and ideas in Ireland'
	Fiona McIntosh, 'Staging Ireland through ancient Greece: Synge and the Greek classics'
	Derek Mahon, 'Writing for the Irish stage'
	Christopher Morash, 'Staging the famine at the century's end'
	Antoinette Quinn, 'Women and nationalist drama at the turn of the century'
	Ann Saddlemyer, 'The new stage Irishman in Lady Gregory and Synge's plays'
	Robert Tracy, 'Brian Friel and the matter of Ireland'
Reading	Seamus Heaney
Panel discussion:	'Contemporary Irish Theatre'
	Karen Ardiff
	Richard Cooke

Gavin Kostick

Lynne Parker

Performance   '*I must be talking to someone*': *An Anthology of Irish Writers*,
Harlequin Players

1996
Theme: Irish Theatre – National and International

Opening guest speaker Declan Kiberd
Lectures   Sebastian Barry, 'Following *The Steward of Christendom*'
Gerry Dukes, 'Synge and Beckett'
Isabelle Famchon, 'Modern Irish drama in France'
Roy Foster, 'Yeats's revolutionary theatre'
Adrian Frazier, 'George Moore and the Irish national theatre'
Nicholas Grene, 'Place and perspective in Synge'
Lyn Innes, 'Gender and national identity in the plays of
Synge, Soyinka and Walcott'
Richard Kearney, 'Brian Friel and Tom Murphy'
Anna McMullan, 'Beckett the Irish European'
Christina Hunt Mahony, 'Contemporary Irish drama:
fatherland or no man's land?'
Readings   Barry McGovern
Nuala Ní Dhomhnaill
Performance   *That Enquiring Man*, Harlequin Players

1997
Theme: The Imagination of Reality

Opening guest speaker Patrick Mason
Lectures   Angela Bourke, 'The vernacular imagination in Synge's
Ireland'
Terence Brown, 'Yeats and magic'
Nicholas Grene, 'Imagining the other: Frank McGuinness
and Sebastian Barry'
Martin Hilský, 'Re-imagining Synge's language: the Czech
experience'
W.J. Mc Cormack, 'Cherrie Matheson: a Synge biographer's
reassessment'
George O'Brien, 'Making it up: self, memory, imagination'
Riana O'Dwyer, 'The imagination of women's reality:
Christina Reid and Marina Carr'
Anthony Roche, 'Synge: the woman and the tramp'

Readings	Jennifer Johnston
	Brendan Kennelly
Panel discussion	'Irish Theatre Today'
	Jocelyn Clarke
	Anne Enright
	Conall Morrison
	Michael West
Performance	*A Last Evening in the Hills with J.M. Synge*, Harlequin Players

1998
Theme: Theatre and History

Opening guest speaker	Dame Veronica Sutherland
Lectures	Kevin Barry, 'Brian Friel's plays as a history of ideas'
	John Devitt, 'The wilderness years: the Abbey in the Queen's'
	Terry Eagleton, 'Oscar Wilde: divided self'
	Nicholas Grene, 'Synge and the politics of Irish drama'
	Lucy McDiarmid, 'The Irish art of controversy'
	Frank McGuinness, 'On writing history plays'
	Christopher Murray, 'The drums of Sean O'Casey: history into drama'
	Lynne Parker, 'Directing *Northern Star*'
	Tom Paulin, 'Ghosts walking: Synge, Hazlitt and 1798'
Reading	Seamus Heaney
Reading/performance	*Catalpa*, Donal O'Kelly
Performance	*Celtic Dawn: 1798, a Theatrical Revolution*, Harlequin Players

1999
Theme: 1899–1999, a Century of Irish Theatre

Opening guest speaker	Brian Farrell
Lectures	Terence Brown, 'Violence and Irish theatre'
	Philip Edwards, 'An imperfect combustion: the Irish Literary Theatre 1899–1901'
	Nicholas Grene, 'Black pastoral, or how to murder your mother'
	Nicholas Grene, 'The legacy of Synge'
	Conor McPherson, 'An Irish playwright in London'
	Christopher Morash, 'All playboys now: the audience and the riot'
	Anthony Roche, 'What's new in the Irish theatre'
	Ann Saddlemyer, 'Designing ladies: women artists and the Abbey stage'

Panel discussion	'Directors and directions in contemporary Irish theatre'
	Brian Brady
	Annie Ryan
Readings	John McGahern
	Barry McGovern
Performance	J.M. Synge, *The Tinker's Wedding*, Harlequin Players

2000

Theme: The Voices of Irish Drama

Opening guest speaker	Seamus Heaney
Lectures	Roy Foster, '*The Dreaming of the Bones* and Yeats's redis-covery of Fenianism'
	Nicholas Grene, 'Synge and the ventriloquism of Irish drama'
	Jennifer Johnston, 'Living with the theatre'
	Declan Kiberd, 'Dramatising poetry: Synge and the Gaelic tradition'
	Cathy Leeny, 'Performance: re-mixing revolution in Irish theatre'
	Ronan McDonald, 'Synge and tragedy'
	Christina Hunt Mahony, 'Harkening to the past: the voice of radio on the contemporary Irish stage'
	Martine Pelletier, 'The voices of Field Day'
Readings	Brendan Kennelly
	Tom Murphy
Performance	J.M. Synge, *The Playboy of the Western World*, Harlequin Players

Notes

INTRODUCTION

1. *The Letters of W.B. Yeats*, ed. Allan Wade (London, 1954), pp. 447–8.

2. 'The Passing of Anglo-Irish Drama', *An Claideamh Soluis*, 9 February 1907.

3. Pádraic H. Pearse, *Political Writings and Speeches* (Dublin, 1922), p. 145.

4. The last was Mary C. King, *The Drama of J.M. Synge* (London, 1985).

5. There appears to have been nothing since Maurice Harmon's edited collection *J.M. Synge: Centenary Papers 1971* (Dublin, 1972) and Paul Levitt's reference work *J.M. Synge: A Bibliography of Published Criticism* (Dublin, 1974); before that one has to go back to Daniel Corkery's polemic *Synge and Anglo-Irish Literature* (Cork, 1931) to find an Irish-published book devoted to Synge's work.

6. Apart from *The Shadow of the Glen*, *The Well of the Saints* and *The Tinker's Wedding*, all set in the valley of the Avonbeg, the unfinished *When the Moon Has Set* is placed within sight of Tonelagee, a mountain not far from Glendalough.

NICHOLAS GRENE, 'ON THE MARGINS: SYNGE AND WICKLOW'

1. Samuel Lewis, *A Topographical Dictionary of Ireland* (London, 1837), ii, p. 144.

2. The fortunes of the Synges seem to correspond almost exactly to the pattern of rise and decline of the landed gentry traced by L.M. Cullen in *The Emergence of Modern Ireland 1600–1900* (London, 1981), who posits a high point in landlord incomes in 1815, and associates the increasing troubles of the landlord class in the years following to an increased concern with education on their estates, provoking resistance from tenants.

3. Much of the biographical material here, as throughout this essay, is derived from the account of Synge's nephew, Edward Millington Stephens. His enormous manuscript Life of his uncle (now in Trinity College Library MS 6189–6197) has

been used in two published works: David H. Greene and Edward M. Stephens, *J.M. Synge 1871–1909* (New York, 1959, rev. ed. 1989), and *My Uncle John,* ed. Andrew Carpenter (Oxford, 1974). There remains, however, much that is valuable in the (still largely unpublished) manuscript. For readers' convenience I have given references in the text to the published works where possible (Greene and Stephens; *My Uncle John*); manuscript references are given as (Stephens MS).

4. Recorded in Mrs Synge's diary 28 February 1893, quoted by Samuel Synge, *Letters to my Daughter* (Dublin and Cork, 1931), p. 193.

5. 'Le premier resultat de l'application de Home-Rule en Irlande serait une guerre, ou du moins un grand conflit social entre Catholique et Protestant.' Letter to unidentified correspondent of mid-July 1895. See *CL* I 29.

6.   In the days of rack-renting
                 And land-grabbing so vile
                 A proud, heartless landlord
                 Lived here a great while.
                 When the League it was started,
                 And the land-grabbing cry,
                 To the cold North of Ireland
                 He had for to fly. (*CW* II 212)

The 'proud, heartless landlord', at the time of the Synges' residence in Castle Kevin, was Rev. Charles W. Frizell, who lived in Belfast as secretary to the Bishop of Down and Connor.

7. Stephens MS f. 1974. Florence Massey, who was already with the Synges in 1901 at the time of the Census returns of 1901, is listed as born in Dublin.

8. The incident took place on 27 August 1897. See Stephens MS f. 1262.

9. See *The Synge Manuscripts in the Library of Trinity College Dublin* (Dublin, 1971), p. 25.

10. The notebook TCD MS 4396 contains a plan for a projected 'Wicklow book' (ff. 4v–5). In the catalogue of the manuscripts (for which I was partly responsible) this notebook is said to date 'from the spring and summer of 1907' (*The Synge Manuscripts*, p. 46). Though it was used at this later date, the Wicklow material in it may well be from 1902, as E.M. Stephens maintains.

11. E.H. Mikhail, *J.M. Synge: Interviews and Recollections* (London, 1972), p. 34.

12. *Wicklow News-Letter,* 17 August 1901.

13. This description is taken from a draft which Synge never used in one of his published essays but which appears in 'People and Places', the editor's compilation, in *CW* II 197–8.

14. Lady Gregory, *Our Irish Theatre,* 3rd ed. (Gerrards Cross, 1972), p. 77.

15. This is a passage from a TS draft of 'The Oppression of the Hills', which Synge omitted from the published text (TCD MS 4335, f. 24).

16. See TCD MS 4421, Synge's diary entry for 12 January 1902.

17. The brief fragmentary draft, apparently entitled *Dead Man's Deputy* at this stage, is to be found in a notebook which also contains dialogue for *Riders to the Sea,* and *The Tinker's Wedding,* TCD MS 4348, ff 14–17.

18. See *Memoirs of Miles Byrne,* ed. Stephen Gwynn (Dublin, 1906), i, p. 221, and Charles Dickson, *The Life of Michael Dwyer* (Dublin, 1944), p. 119.

19. I am grateful to Joan Kavanagh of Wicklow County Heritage for the dates of birth, taken from the Baptismal Register of Rathdrum parish; the extent of the Harneys' land-holding is derived from the Valuation Office records, and the size of their house from the 1901 Census return. The ages of the Harneys on the Census return are given incorrectly as 50 (Michael), 42 (Esther), and 40 (James).

20. E.M. Stephens remarks that the unmarried Harney brothers and sister were 'without the company of any young people except when one of their nieces or nephews came to stay' (Stephens MS f. 1250).

21. The inquest was held under the coroner Thomas B. Doyle on 24 August 1901. There were full reports in *The Wicklow News-Letter* and *The Wicklow People* on 31 August 1901.

22. In the Census return of 1901 his age is given as 36, his wife Charlotte's as 35, and the three children as 5 (Sarah), 4 (John), and 3 (Richard).

23. This was a detail remembered by Thomas O'Neill of Ballinanty, Ballinaclash, who first suggested to me that the original of Patch Darcy was John Winterbottom. See my *Synge: A Critical Study of the Plays* (London, 1975), p. 190.

24. For this information I am indebted to Jimmy Winterbotham of Avoca, who was told by his father, a younger half-brother of John Winterbottom.

25. In the TS draft of the play, Synge had originally written 'in the spring of the year' and then altered it (TCD MS 4339, f. 33).

26. TCD MS 4339 f. 33.

27. See TCD MS 4339, ff. 9, 19, 63.

28. In *The Tinker's Wedding* again the fictitious 'Rathvanna' replaced the real 'Rathdangan'. See TCD MS 4336, f. 63.

29. Only two sons, George, a postman, and William, an apprentice, were living at home at the time of the 1901 Census, but there were several other children, including James (1874–1964), who was at this time in Glasgow and was to return home and set up a forge in another part of the village in 1909. I am grateful to the late Canon James Hartin, Rector of Ballinatone, and the late Jim Smith of Ballinaclash, for help with information on the Smith family.

30. The story was told me by Tom Cullen of Bahana Whaley, who said that his father could remember some of the tinkers with their wounds coming to the Cullens' farm after the fight.

R.F. FOSTER, 'GOOD BEHAVIOUR: YEATS, SYNGE AND ANGLO-IRISH ETIQUETTE'

1. See Nicholas Grene, 'Yeats and the Remaking of Synge', in *Tradition and Influence in Anglo-Irish Poetry*, ed. Terence Brown and Nicholas Grene (Basingstoke, 1989), pp. 47–62; T.R. Henn, *The Lonely Tower*, 2nd ed. (London, 1965), chapter 5; Ann Saddlemyer, 'Synge and Some Companions, with a Note

Concerning a Walk through Connemara with Jack Yeats', *Yeats Studies No. 2* (Shannon, 1972), p. 18; and 'Stars of the Abbey's Ascendancy', in *Theatre and Nationalism in Twentieth-century Ireland*, ed. Robert O'Driscoll (London, 1971). Chapter 1 of Weldon Thornton, *J.M. Synge and the Western Mind* (Gerrards Cross, 1979) is also relevant.

2. W.B. Yeats, *Essays and Introductions* (London, 1961), p. 32.

3. See *The Letters of W.B. Yeats*, ed. Allan Wade (London, 1954), p. 18; also Joseph M. Hassett, *Yeats and the Poetics of Hate* (Dublin, 1986), p. 151.

4. See Saddlemyer, 'Synge and Some Companions', p. 18; the quote comes from Yeats's preface to Synge's *Poems and Translations* (Dundrum, 1909).

5. See Declan Kiberd, *Synge and the Irish Language* (Totowa, N.J., 1979), pp. 36-7.

6. *Theatre Business: The Correspondence of the First Abbey Theatre Directors: W.B. Yeats, Lady Gregory and J.M. Synge*, ed. Ann Saddlemyer (Gerrards Cross, 1982), p. 27.

7. See Katharine Worth, *The Irish Drama of Europe from Yeats to Beckett* (London, 1978), chapters 5 and 6.

8. See *My Uncle John: Edward Stephens's Life of J.M. Synge*, ed. Andrew Carpenter (London, 1974), p. 30, for the Synge sense of being in a minority.

9. W.B. Yeats, *Memoirs*, ed. Denis Donoghue (London, 1972), p. 206.

10. Wade, p. 278.

11. See Wade, p. 68, for Synge's mystic interests.

12. See my 'Protestant Magic: W.B. Yeats and the Spell of Irish History', in *Paddy and Mr. Punch: Connections in Irish and English History* (London, 1993), pp. 212-32 for more detailed consideration of this.

13. George Mills Harper, *The Making of Yeats's 'A Vision': A Study of the Automatic Script* (London, 1987), vol. 2, p. 94.

14. Ibid., p. 108.

15. Ibid., p. 144.

16. See E.H. Mikhail, *Lady Gregory: Interviews and Recollections* (London, 1977), p. 107.

17. Robert Hogan and James Kilroy, *The Abbey Theatre: The Years of Synge 1905-1909* (Dublin, 1978).

18. See *CL* I 148ff., 161, 169.

19. *CL* I 149-50. See also Synge to Gregory, 9 June 1906, *CL* I 169: 'I am not writing much to Yeats while he is with Miss Horniman, he is so careless about his letters.'

20. See Adrian Frazier, *Behind the Scenes: Yeats, Horniman and the Struggle for the Abbey Theatre* (London, 1990).

21. Hogan and Kilroy, pp. 33, 36.

22. See *United Ireland*, as quoted in Hogan and Kilroy, pp. 63-4.

23. Kiberd, p. 238.

24. Hogan and Kilroy, pp. 33, 36.

25. Saddlemyer, *Theatre Business*, p. 205.

26. Hogan and Kilroy, p. 91.

27. For her resentment of Synge on tour, see Hogan and Kilroy, pp. 73–5.

28. Hogan and Kilroy, pp. 81–8.

29. Hogan and Kilroy, p. 99.

30. *Joseph Holloway's Abbey Theatre*, ed. Robert Hogan and M.J. O'Neill (Carbondale, Ill., 1967), p. 172.

31. See my 'Protestant Magic', op. cit.

32. Carpenter (ed.), *My Uncle John*, p. 53.

33. Lily Yeats to John Butler Yeats, 24 October 1909, Yeats Papers. I am indebted to William Michael Murphy for sharing with me his transcriptions of these and other Yeats letters.

34. 'There are sides of all that western life, the groggy-patriot-publican-general-shop-man who is married to the priest's half-sister and is second cousin once-removed of the dispensary doctor, that are horrible and awful ...' (13 July 1905, *CL* I 116–17).

35. Yeats to Gregory, 24 March 1909, quoted in *CL* II 55.

36. See Michael Steinman, *Yeats's Heroic Figures: Wilde, Parnell, Swift, Casement* (London, 1983); and note the Synge reference in Yeats's 'In Memory of Major Robert Gregory'.

37. In conversation: Hogan and O'Neill, p. 58 (26 April 1905).

38. 'Introduction' to *Selections from the Writings of Lord Dunsany* (Dundrum, 1912).

39. See Steinman, p. 71.

40. *Irish Independent*, 24 August 1909, quoted in Hogan and Kilroy, p. 295.

41. Preface to Oliver St. John Gogarty, *Wild Apples* (Dublin, 1930).

42. See Jonathan Swift, 'Good Manners and Good Breeding'; it is conveniently printed in *The Oxford Book of Essays*, ed. John Gross (Oxford, 1991).

43. See *Always Your Friend: The Gonne-Yeats Letters 1893–1938*, ed. Anna MacBride White and A. Norman Jeffares (London, 1992), p. 165.

44. John Morley, *Recollections* (London, 1917), vol. I, p. 238; see Steinman, p. 79, for a discussion of what this description meant to Yeats.

45. Cf. Grene, 'Yeats and the Remaking of Synge', p. 50.

46. Hogan and Kilroy, p. 183.

47. Carpenter (ed.), *My Uncle John*, pp. 132–3.

48. Denis Donoghue, *Warrenpoint* (London, 1990), pp. 49–50.

49. 'The Three Beggars', *The Variorum Edition of the Poems of W.B. Yeats*, ed. Peter Allt and Russell K. Alspach (London, 1957), p. 297.

50. Originally dated 4 June 1914, and first published in 1916.

51. 'The Fisherman', in Allt and Alspach, p. 348.

52. *Explorations* (London, 1962), p. 337.

ANGELA BOURKE, 'KEENING AS THEATRE: J.M. SYNGE AND THE IRISH LAMENT TRADITION'

1. Henry Sayre, 'Performance', in Frank Lentricchia and Thomas McLaughlin, eds, *Critical Terms for Literary Study* (Chicago and London, 1990), p. 103. Compare Johan Huizinga, *Homo Ludens: A Study of the Play Elements in Culture* (1949; rpt. London, 1970), p. 29: 'Play-grounds [are] forbidden spots, isolated, hedged round, within which special rules obtain. All are temporary moulds within the ordinary world, dedicated to the performance of an act apart.'

2. Declan Kiberd, *Synge and the Irish Language*, 2nd edn (London, 1993).

3. See Diarmuid Breathnach agus Máire Ní Mhurchú, *1882–1982: Beathaisnéis a Dó* (Dublin, 1990), pp. 41–3. Writing in *The Academy and Literature*, 6 September 1902, Synge was less than flattering about Goodman's knowledge of Irish literature, but Risteárd Ó Glaisne maintains (*Galvia* 10 [1964–5]) that this was unfair.

4. Mrs Morgan John O'Connell, *The Last Colonel of the Irish Brigade* (1892; rpt. Cork, 1977).

5. The lament for Sir James Cotter was made by his old nurse, and that for Diarmaid McCarthy by his mother. The text of *Caoineadh Airt Uí Laoghaire* was taken down from the recital of Norrie Singleton, herself a well-known *bean chaointe* in the area around Millstreet. For descriptions of other lamenters, see Thomas Crofton Croker, *Researches in the South of Ireland* (1824; rpt. Shannon, 1969), pp. 173–4.

6. See *The Oxford Companion to Irish Literature*, ed. Robert Welch (Oxford, 1996), p. 133.

7. This account of the publishing history of *Caoineadh Airt Uí Laoghaire* is heavily indebted to *Caoineadh Airt Uí Laoghaire*, ed. Seán Ó Tuama (Dublin, 1961), p. 48.

8. *Irisleabhar na Gaedhilge / The Gaelic Journal* VII (June 1896): 2, pp. 18–23. Bergin wrote: 'A rather mutilated edition of this poem has been printed in the appendix to Mrs M.J. O'Connell's "Last Colonel of the Irish Brigade." In its form as now published the poem is yet far from perfect. It is still widely known by oral tradition in Munster – what equivalent does "education" offer for the loss of such treasures to the people robbed of their native tongue? – and its publication should stimulate readers of the Journal to collect as many versions of it as possible, or even scraps of it. Those who succeed in doing so should commit what they can get of it to writing, and send it to Mr Osborn Bergin, Gaelic League, Cork. It will then, most probably, be possible to make out a fairly complete text of the poem.'

9. See Anne O'Dowd, 'Resources and Life: Aspects of Working and Fishing on the Aran Islands', Chapter 10 in *The Book of Aran: The Aran Islands, Co. Galway*, ed. John Waddell, J.W. O'Connell and Anne Korff (Kinvara, 1994), pp. 194–220. The photograph referred to appears on p. 199.

10. Albert B. Lord, *The Singer of Tales* (Cambridge, Mass., 1960).

11. *Songs of Aran: Gaelic Singing from the West of Ireland*, Ethnic Folkways Library Album No. FE4002 (1957). Reissued on cassette tape (Cork, 1989) OSS-16.

12. See Angela Bourke, 'More in Anger than in Sorrow: Irish Women's Lament Poetry', in *Feminist Messages: Coding in Women's Folk Culture*, ed. Joan N. Radner (Chicago, 1993), pp. 160–82.

13. Diarmaid Ó Muirithe, 'Tuairiscí na dTaistealaithe', in *Gnéithe den Chaointeoireacht*, ed. Breandán Ó Madagáin (Dublin, 1978), pp. 20–9.

14. See David Cairns and Shaun Richards, *Writing Ireland: Colonialism, Nationalism and Culture* (Manchester, 1988).

15. *The Poems of Blathmac, Son of Cú Brettan*, ed. James Carney (Dublin, 1964), p. 43.

16. Seán Ó Súilleabháin, *Irish Wake Amusements* (Cork, 1967), p. 135.

17. Mr and Mrs S.C. Hall, *Ireland, its Scenery, Character, etc.*, 3 vols (London, 1841); rpt. in condensed edn, 2 vols (London, 1984), pp. 85–7, 220–1.

18. Ó Tuama, p. 22n.

19. Ibid., p. 2.

20. See Alan Gailey, *Irish Folk Drama* (Cork, 1969), and Henry Glassie, *All Silver and No Brass: An Irish Christmas Mumming* (Dingle, 1983 [1975]).

21. Compare Huizinga, *op. cit.*, and see Bourke, 'More in Anger than in Sorrow: Irish Women's Lament Poetry', *Feminist Messages*, pp. 160-82, and Angela Bourke, 'Performing, not Writing: The Reception of an Irish Woman's Lament,' Chapter 9 in *Dwelling in Possibility: Women Poets and Critics on Poetry*, ed. Yopie Prins and Maeera Shreiber (Ithaca and London, 1997), pp. 132–46.

22. O'Dowd, p. 199.

DECLAN KIBERD, 'SYNGE'S TRISTES TROPIQUES: *THE ARAN ISLANDS*'

1. David H. Greene and Edward M. Stephens, *J.M. Synge: 1871–1909* (New York, 1966), pp. 83–4.

2. Martin Haverty, 'The Aran Isles: or a Report of the Excursion of the Ethnological Section of the British Association from Dublin to the Western Island of Aran in September 1852' (Dublin, 1859); rpt. in *An Aran Reader*, ed. Breandán Ó hEithir and Ruairi Ó hEithir (Dublin, 1991), pp. 43–6.

3. Douglas Hyde, 'The Necessity for deAnglicising Ireland', *The Revival of Irish Literature* (London, 1894), pp. 138–59.

4. An interesting sidelight on the affinities between the work of Synge and Roddy Doyle was offered by Nicholas Grene in his 1994 Synge Summer School lecture.

5. William Empson, *Some Versions of Pastoral* (London, 1935), passim.

6. Edward Said, *Orientalism* (New York, 1978); and see Declan Kiberd, *Inventing Ireland: The Literature of the Modern Nation* (London, 1995), pp. 287ff. for an earlier ventilation of the theme.

7. Susan Sontag, *On Photography* (Harmondsworth, 1979), p. 57.

8. Quoted by Marshall McLuhan, *War and Peace in the Global Village* (Harmondsworth, 1969), p. 53.

9. Quoted in Sontag, *On Photography*, p. 107.

10. John Berger, *About Looking* (London, 1980), p. 54.

11. Quoted in Sontag, *On Photography*, p. 69.

12. Berger, p. 55.

13. Sontag, *On Photography*, p. 167.

14. Walter Benjamin, *One Way Street and Other Writings*, trs. Edmund Jephcott and Kingsley Shorter (London, 1979), pp. 240–58; see also Berger, p. 60; and Roland Barthes, *Camera Lucida: Reflections on Photography*, trans. by Richard Howard (New York, 1981), passim.

15. Berger, p. 58.

16. The first study of anthropological elements in Synge's writings was Herbert J. Frenzel, *J.M. Synge's Work as a Contribution to Irish Folklore and to the Psychology of Primitive Tribes* (Duren-Rhld, 1932). Despite the unpromising title and its somewhat dated references, it is still a useful work, on which I have drawn in the preceding paragraphs.

17. Maurice Bourgeois, *John Millington Synge and the Irish Theatre* (London, 1913), p. 82.

18. For some thoughts on the problem of multiculturalism, see Declan Kiberd, 'Rushdie's Midnight's Children: Ireland and India'. University College Cork, Department of Sociology Occasional papers 2, No. 12 (Cork, 1992).

19. Mark Tully, *No Full Stops in India* (London, 1991); see especially pp. 1–14 and pp. 268–98.

20. Bob Quinn, *Atlantean* (Dublin, 1988). This is a study of cultural connections made by sea between North Africa and the West of Ireland.

21. Said, pp. 160–3.

22. Ibid., p. 173.

23. Ibid., pp. 185ff.

24. Ibid., p. 177.

25. W.B. Yeats, 'Preface to the First Edition of *The Well of the Saints*', *Essays and Introductions* (London, 1961), p. 299. For Yeats's many versions of the meeting, see Anthony Roche, 'Yeats, Synge and Emerging Irish Drama', *Yeats: An Annual of Critical and Textual Studies*, X (1992), pp. 32–9.

26. Karl Marx, 'The Eighteenth Brumaire of Louis Bonaparte', in *Surveys From Exile: Political Writings*, Vol. 2 (Harmondsworth, 1973), p. 239.

27. W.B. Yeats, *Autobiographies* (London, 1955), p. 345.

28. Arthur Symons, 'The Isles of Aran', *The Savoy*, No. 8, 1896, p. 75. For an earlier, extended analysis of Synge's debts to the Symons essay, see Declan Kiberd, 'Synge, Symons and the Isles of Aran', *Notes on Modern Irish Literature* (Fenelton, Penn.), 1 (1989), pp. 32–9.

29. Symons, p. 75.

30. Symons, p. 85; *CW* II 53.

31. Symons, p. 85.

32. Ibid., p. 77.

33. Ibid., p. 81.

34. Oscar Wilde, *The Artist as Critic*, ed. Richard Ellmann (London, 1970), p. 167. Synge was reading Wilde's essays as he began *The Aran Islands* in 1898–9: notebook MS 4378 in the Trinity College collection contains extracts from 'The Artist as Critic' and from Frazer's *The Golden Bough*.

35. Wilde, p. 267.

36. Ibid., p. 284.

37. Ibid., p.. 261.

38. Ibid., p. 261.

39. Ibid., pp. 262, 271.

40. Ibid., p. 263.

41. Yeats, 'J.M. Synge and the Ireland of his Time', *Essays and Introductions*, p. 339.

42. Mary C. King in *The Drama of J.M. Synge* (London, 1985), pp. 18–47, was the first critic to offer a sustained exploration of the traumatic impact on Synge of both the eviction and export scenes.

43. Alastair Horne, *The Fall of Paris: The Siege and the Commune* (Harmondsworth, 1981), p. 360.

44. Quoted in Greene and Stephens, p. 153.

45. *CW* III 80. Synge's notebooks contain the following entry:
'Frazer Golden Bough Ch 11
Iron ... disliked by the spirits, a superstition dating perhaps from the
time when iron was a novelty'. TCD MS 4378, f. 71.v.

46. J.G. Frazer, *The Golden Bough* (London, 1890; rpt. London, 1922), p. 49.

47. David Richards, *Masks of Difference: Cultural Representation in Literature, Anthropology and Art* (Cambridge, 1994), p. 169.

48. See Weldon Thornton, *J.M. Synge and the Western Mind* (Gerrards Cross, 1979), pp. 98ff.

49. Richards, p. 173.

50. Cited in Richards, p. 193.

51. Susan Sontag, *Against Interpretation* (New York, 1964), p. 70.

52. Ibid., p. 74

53. Richards, p. 233.

54. Ibid., p. 207.

55. T.S. Eliot, *Notes Towards the Definition of Culture* (London, 1962), p. 41.

56. See *Inventing Ireland*, pp. 166–88.

57. Cited in Sontag, *Against Interpretation*, p. 69.

58. Sontag, *Against Interpretation*, p. 75.

59. Herman Melville, *Moby-Dick*, ed. Harold Beaver (Harmondsworth, 1972), p. 150.

TOM PAULIN, '"RIDERS TO THE SEA": A REVISIONIST TRAGEDY?'

1. I say 'Yeats's' but really, as scholars now agree, it is a joint work of Yeats and Lady Gregory. It is published in Lady Gregory, *Selected Writings*, ed. Lucy McDiarmid and Maureen Waters (Harmondsworth, 1995).

2. Declan Kiberd points to this allusion in *Synge and the Irish Language* (London, 1979).

ANTOINETTE QUINN, 'STAGING THE IRISH PEASANT WOMAN: MAUD GONNE VERSUS SYNGE'

1. Synge's play was thus titled for the first perfomances; I use also the original spelling of the Yeats–Gregory play, *Kathleen ni Houlihan*. I am presuming that readers will be familiar with both these plays, but not with *Dawn*. *Dawn* was first published in the *United Irishman* on 29 October 1904; it was reprinted in *Lost Plays of the Irish Renaissance*, ed. Robert Hogan and James Kilroy (Dixon, Calif., 1970).

2. Throughout this essay I am using the term 'peasants' for the small-farming class who lived in cottages because it was the term commonly used by both Literary and Gaelic Revival writers at the time.

3. In order to focus exclusively on Gonne's involvement in nationalist theatre, I have avoided elaborating on biographical information which is readily available in Margaret Ward's biography, *Maud Gonne, Ireland's Joan of Arc* (London, 1990).

4. The inaugural meeting took place in Dublin in October 1900. Many of this talented group were already well known or were soon to become known as writers, actresses, editors, intellectuals: Jenny Wyse-Power, Anna Johnston and Alice Furlong were joint vice-presidents, and members included Alice Milligan, Ella Young, Máire Quinn, Máire Nic Shiubhlaigh, and Sara Allgood. They adopted the names of famous Irish women from history and myth; Maud Gonne was Maeve. For a full account of Inghinidhe na hEireann, see Margaret Ward, *Unmanageable Revolutionaries* (London, 1983).

5. Máire Nic Shiubhlaigh, *The Splendid Years* (Dublin, 1955), p. 17.

6. Ella Young, *Flowering Dusk* (London, 1945), p. 102.

7. *The United Irishman*, 24 October 1904.

8. See David H. Greene and Edward M. Stephens, *J.M. Synge 1871–1909* (New York, 1959), pp. 61–3.

9. The Gaelic League, which did recruit women, was still in 1900 a cultural rather than a political organization.

10. Two such well-known refrains from *The Spirit of the Nation*, a collection of nationalist ballads which ran to fifty-five editions between 1843 and 1896, were 'Steady, boys, and step together' and 'But a true man, like you, man / Will fill your glass with us.' Pearse also drew on such fraternal imagery, e.g., 'The Nation is a great household a brotherhood of adoption as well as of blood...'. *An Claidheamh*

Soluis, 5 October 1907. Throughout the present essay quotations from *An Claidheamh Soluis*, the organ of the Gaelic League, were supplied by Elaine Sisson.

11. The first two quotations are from Mary E. L. Butler, *Irishwomen and the Home Language*, Gaelic League Pamphlets no. 6 (Dublin, 1901); the third and fourth are from Patrick Pearse's editorials in *An Claidheamh Soluis*, 11 April and 28 November 1903 respectively.

12. Butler, *Irishwomen and the Home Language*.

13. One of the most persuasive critics of the feminizing of the nation is Eavan Boland in *A Kind of Scar* (Dublin, 1989).

14. *Bean na hEireann*, no. 16, 1910.

15. See Benedict Anderson, *Imagined Communities* (London, 1991).

16. Arthur Griffith, editor of the nationalist weekly the *United Irishman*, was paid an editorial subvention of twenty-five shillings a week by Maud Gonne. In return the journal publicized the activities of the Inghinidhe. Samuel Levenson, *Maud Gonne* (London, 1970), p. 150.

17. *United Irishman*, 10, 17 October 1903.

18. Ward, *Maud Gonne*, p. 65. The importance of theatre to the Inghinidhe may be gauged from the perception of one of the first members, Máire Nic Shiubhlaigh, that it was primarily a dramatic society. She writes: 'its object was to encourage young Dubliners to write for the stage and to establish the nucleus of a national dramatic company …' (*The Splendid Years*, p. 3).

19. Joseph Holloway was critical of the performance he attended in 1901, noting that, apart from the 'the excellence of the occasional solo and the novelty of the Irish ceilidh', the show was amateurish and ill-managed and the music dirge-like. Robert Hogan and James Kilroy, *The Irish Literary Theatre 1899–1901* (Dublin, 1975), p. 90. This would have been among the Inghinidhe's earliest productions.

20. The role of Alice Milligan in the Irish theatre movement has not yet been fully assessed. I hope to consider this on a future occasion. Though she was far more involved in theatre than Maud Gonne, Milligan's contribution is not as relevant for my present purposes.

21. Maud Gonne and Máire Quinn each wrote to Milligan at the end of December 1900, requesting her assistance with St. Patrick's Day *tableaux* for 1901. Letters to Alice Milligan, ms. 5048, the National Library of Ireland.

22. Hogan and Kilroy, *The Irish Literary Theatre*, pp. 85, 135.

23. 'I have a beautiful untidy grey wig, a torn grey <flannil> flannel dress *exactly* like the old women wear in the west, bare feet and a big hooded cloak.' *The Gonne–Yeats Letters 1893–1938*, ed. with introduction by Anna MacBride White and A. Norman Jeffares (London, 1992), p. 151.

24. The *Daily Express* review makes it clear that the rejuvenated Kathleen was not seen by the audience.

25. Delia's and Bridget's final embrace was suggested by the Inghinidhe and the Fays during rehearsals (MacBride White and Jeffares, p. 150).

26. See James Pethica, ' "Our Kathleen": Yeats's Collaboration with Lady Gregory in the writing of *Cathleen ni Houlihan*', *Yeats Annual*, no. 6, 1988.

27. Lady Gregory, *Selected Writings*, ed Lucy McDiarmid and Maureen Waters (Harmondsworth, 1995), p. 436.

28. Pethica, p. 14.

29. Robert Hogan and James Kilroy, *Laying the Foundations, 1902–1904* (Dublin, 1976), p. 15.

30. Ibid., pp. 17–18.

31. Nic Shiubhlaigh, p. 19.

32. Levenson, p. 195.

33. George L. Mosse, 'Nationalism and Sexuality', in *Nationalisms and Sexualities*, ed. Andrew Parker et al. (London, 1992), p. 12.

34. 'Her beauty was *startling* ...' (Nic Shiubhlaigh, p. 19). For Mary Colum too 'her beauty was startling in its greatness, its dignity, its strangeness ...' (*Life and the Dream* [Dublin, 1966], p. 124). Her late arrival is from Nic Shiubhlaigh, p. 17.

35. Yeats quoted in Hogan and Kilroy, *Laying the Foundations*, p. 15; Nic Shiubhlaigh, p. 17; Holloway in Levenson, p. 195.

36. Anna Johnston died on 2 April 1902, the date of the première. Jenny Wyse-Power wrote to Alice Milligan: 'it pained me more than I can tell to think they went on with the plays the night of the day she passed away – out of respect for her memory they should have been postponed that evening ...' She continued, 'Mr Russel [*sic*] and Mr Yates [*sic*] each made speeches ... and never once referred to the Society that had financed the whole affair.' Letters to Alice Milligan, ms. 5048, the National Library of Ireland.

37. In her letter of resignation from the recently formed National Theatre Society, to which she had been elected vice-president following her success as Kathleen ni Houlihan, Gonne reveals that she had joined because she thought it shared the same theatrical aims as the Inghinidhe (MacBride White and Jeffares, p. 178).

38. Greene and Stephens, p. 68.

39. Nora Burke was played by Máire Nic Shiubhlaigh, a member of Inghinidhe na hEireann but not an officer in the society.

40. Hogan and Kilroy, *Laying the Foundations*, p. 65.

41. Butler, *Irishwomen and the Home Language*.

42. *United Irishman*, 17 October 1903.

43. James Connolly, *Selected Writings*, ed. Beresford Ellis (Harmondsworth, 1975), pp. 190–1.

44. *United Irishman*, 24 October 1903.

45. Ibid.

46. Ibid., 17 October 1903.

47. Ibid., 24 October 1903.

48. The play was signed with the pseudonym Conn. I attribute the authorship to Griffith because in his first attack on Synge's play he had misnamed it *In a Wicklow Glen*.

49. *United Irishman*, 31 October 1903.

50. Levenson, pp. 230–1.

51. MacBride White and Jeffares, pp. 183–5.

52. MacBride White and Jeffares, p. 30.

53. Maud Gonne MacBride, *A Servant of the Queen*, new revised edition by A. Norman Jeffares and Anna MacBride White (Gerrards Cross, 1994), p. 113. All page numbers are from the revised edition.

54. First printed in her Paris-based paper, *l'Irlande Libre*, as 'Reine de la Disette' and reprinted in the *United Irishman*, 7 April 1900, it is included in *In Their Own Voice, Women and Irish Nationalism*, ed. Margaret Ward (Dublin, 1995), pp. 10–13.

55. Gonne MacBride, pp. 241–58.

56. *Freeman's Journal*, 9 March 1898.

57. *Freeman's Journal*, 9 March 1898, and *Irish Daily Independent*, 10 March 1898.

58. *Irish Daily Independent*, 10 March 1898.

59. See Gonne MacBride, pp. 255–6: 'starving people are not the best material for a fight'.

60. C.L. Innes, *Woman and Nation in Irish Literature and Society, 1880–1935* (London, 1993), p. 50.

61. In Mayo, Maud was told that Brian Ruadh had prophesied the coming of a 'woman who is to bring war and victory' (Gonne MacBride, pp. 252–3).

62. Colum, p. 124.

63. *Dawn* is to be reprinted in the fourth volume of the *Field Day Anthology of Irish Writing*.

CHRISTOPHER MORASH, 'ALL PLAYBOYS NOW: THE AUDIENCE AND THE RIOT'

1. *Theatre Business: The Correspondence of the First Abbey Theatre Directors: William Butler Yeats, Lady Gregory and J.M. Synge*, ed. Ann Saddlemyer (Gerrards Cross, 1982), p. 205. In the account of the production of the *Playboy* I have drawn upon the following principal sources: *The Abbey Row* (Dublin, 1907); Robert Hogan and James Kilroy, *The Abbey Theatre: The Years of Synge 1905–1909* (Dublin, 1978); *Joseph Holloway's Abbey Theatre*, ed. Robert Hogan and Michael O'Neill (Carbondale, 1967); James Kilroy, *The 'Playboy' Riots* (Dublin, 1971).

2. Hogan and Kilroy, p. 123.

3. Saddlemyer (ed.), *Theatre Business*, p. 205.

4. *The Arrow*, I:2, 24 November 1906, 1.

5. J.W. Whitbread, *Wolfe Tone*, in *For the Land They Loved: Irish Political Melodramas 1890–1925*, ed. Cheryl Herr (Syracuse, N.Y., 1991), p. 173.

6. *The Letters of Sean O'Casey: 1910–1941*, Vol. I., ed. David Krause (London, 1975), p. 148.

7. Willie Fay fluffed the line; as written by Synge it was 'a drift of chosen females, standing in their shifts itself'.

8. Hogan and O'Neill (eds), *Joseph Holloway's Abbey Theatre*, p. 82.

9. Roy Foster, *W.B. Yeats: A Life: Volume 1, The Apprentice Mage 1865–1914* (Oxford, 1997), p. 360.

10. W.B. Yeats, *The Collected Letters of W.B. Yeats*, Vol. III, ed. John Kelly and Ronald Schuchard (Oxford, 1994), p. 642.

11. Kilroy, pp. 32–3.

12. Augusta Gregory, *Our Irish Theatre: A Chapter of Autobiography* (Gerrards Cross, 1972), p. 68.

13. Saddlemyer (ed.), *Theatre Business*, p. 214.

14. Kilroy, p. 86.

15. Foster, p. 365.

16. Kilroy, pp. 82–3.

17. Saddlemyer (ed.), *Theatre Business*, p. 213.

18. Hogan and Kilroy, p. 136.

19. Foster, p. 363.

20. Frank Fay, 'Irish Drama at the Queen's Theatre', *United Irishman* II:44 (30 December 1899), p. 7.

21. Kilroy, pp. 64, 363.

22. In what follows I have relied on two main sources for the account of the 'Bottle Riot': *Williamite Scrap Book; or Chronicle of the Times.* No. 1 (Dublin, 1823), and *The Only Accurate and Impartial Report of the Trials of James Forbes, Henry Handwich, William Graham, Mathew Handwich, George Graham, and William Brownlow, in the Court of King's Bench, Monday, February 3, 1823, and following days, for a Conspiracy, Riot and an attempt to Assault the Most Noble Marquis Wellesley, Lord Lieutenant of Ireland, &c., &c., on his Visit to the Theatre, 14th December, 1822 on an Ex-officio Information filed by the Right Hon. W. C. Plunkett, His Majesty's Attorney General,* 2nd edn. (Dublin, 1823).

23. *Williamite Scrap Book*, pp. 28–9.

24. *The Only Accurate and Impartial Report*, p. 90.

25. Hogan and Kilroy, p. 140.

26. *The Abbey Row*, p. 10.

MARTIN HILSKY, 'RE-IMAGINING SYNGE'S LANGUAGE: THE CZECH EXPERIENCE'

1. Quoted in Declan Kiberd, *Synge and the Irish Language* (London, 1979), p. 204.

2. Quoted in Donna Gerstenberger, *John Millington Synge* (New York, 1964).

3. Kiberd, p. 214.

4. Ibid.

5. I am indebted to many Irish scholars for the comments that helped me solve some of the textual cruxes of the play. Particularly helpful was Nicholas Grene's commentary in 'Approaches to *The Playboy*', in *Synge: A Critical Study of the Plays*, (London, 1975), and his 'Mental Mapping in *The Playboy of the Western World*', in *Traduire le Théâtre aujourd'hui?*, ed. Nicole Vigouroux-Frey (Rennes, 1993).

6. *Hrdina Západu*, trs. by Karel Mušek (V staré Říši na Moravě, 1914), p. x–xi.

7. P.L. Henry, 'The Playboy of the Western World', *Philologica Pragensia*, 8 (1965), pp. 189–201.

ANTHONY ROCHE, 'J.M. SYNGE AND MOLLY ALLGOOD: THE WOMAN AND THE TRAMP'

1. All subsequent biographical details are drawn from Ann Saddlemyer's annotations to the two-volume *Collected Letters*, unless otherwise indicated. This edition preserves Synge's erratic spelling, including 'changling' as his pet name for Molly Allgood.

2. Vivian Mercier, *Modern Irish Literature: Sources and Founders*, ed. Eilís Dillon (Oxford, 1994), p. 203.

3. Angela Bourke, *The Burning of Bridget Cleary: A True Story* (London, 1999), p. 107.

4. Ibid., p. 177.

5. Mercier, p. 209.

6. Ibid., p. 211.

7. Cited in Robert Hogan and James Kilroy, *Laying the Foundations 1902–1904* (Dublin, 1976), p. 79.

8. 'In Memory of Major Robert Gregory', *W.B. Yeats: The Poems*, ed. Daniel Albright (London, 1994), p. 182.

ANN SADDLEMYER, 'SYNGE'S SOUNDSCAPE'

1. James Joyce, *Ulysses* (New York, 1934), p. 197.

2. TCD MS 4386. I am indebted to Dr Bernard Meehan and to the Board of Trinity College Dublin, for permission to quote from Synge's notebooks.

3. Reproduced as frontispieces in the original Oxford University Press edition of *CW* III and *CW* IV.

4. TCD MS 4382.

5. I am indebted to John Beckett, who kindly provided me with his manuscript 'Synge the Musician', a radio broadcast in 1971, for a summary of Synge's extant compositions.

6. David H. Greene and E.M. Stephens, *J.M. Synge 1871–1909*, rev. ed. (New York, 1989), p. 23.

7. TCD MS 4384 and 4349.

8. Quoted in Ann Saddlemyer, ' "A Share in the Dignity of the World": J.M. Synge's Aesthetic Theory', in *The World of W.B. Yeats*, ed. Robin Skelton and Ann Saddlemyer (Dublin, 1965), p. 244.

9. Samuel Beckett to Cyril Cusack, quoted in *Samuel Beckett: An Exhibition held at Reading University Library May to July 1971* (London, 1971), p. 23.

10. *Essays and Introductions* (London, 1961), pp. 527–8.

11. *Irish Times*, 13 February 1905, and Lennox Robinson, *I Sometimes Think* (Dublin, 1956), pp. 48–9.

12. *The Irish Drama of Europe from Yeats to Beckett* (London, 1978), p. 125.

13. Máire Nic Shiubhlaigh and Edward Kenny, *The Splendid Years* (Dublin, 1955), pp. 42–3.

14. Worth, pp. 75–6.

Notes on Contributors

Angela Bourke is Senior Lecturer in Irish at University College Dublin. Her published work includes *Caoineadh na dTrí Muire*, a study of religious oral poetry in Irish published as Angela Partridge (1983), *By Salt Water*, a short-story collection (1996), and *The Burning of Bridget Cleary: A True Story* (1999).

Gerald Dawe is Lecturer in English and Director of the Oscar Wilde Centre for Irish Writing at Trinity College Dublin. He has published several books of poetry including *The Lundys Letter*, *Sunday School*, *Heart of Hearts* and *The Morning Train*; among his collections of essays are *Against Piety* and *The Rest is History*.

R.F. Foster is Carroll Professor of Irish History at the University of Oxford. His many books include *Charles Stewart Parnell: The Man and his Family*, *Modern Ireland 1600–1972*, *Paddy and Mr Punch: Connections in Irish and English History* and *W.B. Yeats, A Life, vol. I: The Apprentice Mage*.

Nicholas Grene is Professor of English Literature at Trinity College Dublin, and has directed the Synge Summer School since its establishment in 1991. His books include *Synge: A Critical Study of the Plays*, *Bernard Shaw: A Critical View*, *Shakespeare's Tragic Imagination* and, most recently, *The Politics of Irish Drama*.

Seamus Heaney won the Nobel Prize for Literature in 1995. His most recent publications are *Opened Ground: Poems, 1966–96* and *Beowulf: A New Translation*.

Martin Hilsky is Professor of English and Director of English Literary Studies at Charles University, Prague. A distinguished translator of Shakespeare, his version of *The Playboy of the Western World* was produced by the Czech National Theatre in 1996 and published as *Hrdina Západu* in 1996.

Brendan Kennelly is Professor of Modern Literature at Trinity College Dublin, and one of Ireland's best-known poets. His many books include *My Dark Fathers*, *Cromwell*, *The Book of Judas* and, most recently, *Begin*.

Declan Kiberd is Professor of Anglo-Irish Literature and Drama at University College Dublin. Among his books are *Synge and the Irish Language*, *Men and Feminism in Modern Literature*, *Idir Dhá Chultúr* and the award-winning *Inventing Ireland: The Literature of the Modern Nation*.

Frank McGuinness is an award-winning playwright whose plays include *Observe the Sons of Ulster Marching Towards the Somme*, *Carthaginians*, *Someone Who'll Watch Over Me* and *Dolly West's Kitchen*. He is Writer-in-Residence at University College Dublin.

Christopher Morash is Senior Lecturer in English at the National University of Ireland, Maynooth. He is the editor of *The Hungry Voice* and the author of *Writing the Famine*. At present he is completing *A History of the Irish Theatre 1600 to 2000*.

Nuala Ní Dhomhnaill is one of Ireland's most accomplished Irish-language poets. She has published several collections of her poetry in Irish, including *Feis*, and a number of selections with accompanying versions in English, among them *Pharaoh's Daughter*, *The Astrakhan Coat* and *The Water Horse*.

Tom Paulin, poet and critic, is G.M. Young Lecturer in English Literature at Hertford College, Oxford. He has published six books of poetry, most recently *The Wind Dog*, and a number of critical works including *Minotaur: Poetry and the Nation State* and *The Day-Star of Liberty: William Hazlitt's Radical Style*.

Antoinette Quinn is Senior Lecturer in English and Fellow of Trinity College Dublin, where she was one of the founding members of the Centre for Women's Studies. She has published *Patrick Kavanagh, Born-Again Romantic*, has edited Kavanagh's *Selected Poems* and is currently completing a biography of the poet.

Anthony Roche is Senior Lecturer in Anglo-Irish Literature and Drama at University College Dublin. He is the author of *Contemporary Irish Drama: From Beckett to McGuinness* and the editor of *Irish University Review*.

Ann Saddlemyer is Professor Emeritus of English and Drama at the University of Toronto, where she was formerly Master of Massey College. The editor of the definitive edition of Synge's plays, she has also edited the two-volume *Collected Letters of John Millington Synge* and the four volumes of Lady Gregory's *Collected Plays*.

Index